BORN IN THE U.S.A.

Born down in a dead man's town
The first kick I took was when I hit the
    ground
You end up like a dog that's been beat too
    much
Till you spend half your life just covering
    up

    Born in the U.S.A.
    I was born in the U.S.A.
    I was born in the U.S.A.
    Born in the U.S.A.

Got in a little hometown jam so they put a
    rifle in my hand
Sent me off to a foreign land to go and kill
    the yellow man

    Born in the U.S.A.
    I was born in the U.S.A.
    I was born in the U.S.A.
    I was born in the U.S.A.
    Born in the U.S.A.

Come back home to the refinery
Hiring man says "son if it was up to me"
Went down to see my V.A. man
He said "son don't you understand now"

Had a brother at Khe Sahn fighting off
        the Viet Cong
They're still there he's all gone
He had a woman he loved in Saigon
I got a picture of him in her arms now

Down in the shadow of the penitentiary
Out by the gas fires of the refinery
I'm ten years burning down the road
Nowhere to run ain't got nowhere to go

Born in the U.S.A.
I was born in the U.S.A.
Born in the U.S.A.
I'm a long gone Daddy in the U.S.A.
Born in the U.S.A.
Born in the U.S.A.
Born in the U.S.A.
I'm a cool rocking Daddy in the U.S.A.

* *

Only in recent years have Viet Vets begun to learn how severe and widespread their problems are. Still, no comprehensive, easily read, and widely distributed book has existed to assist them. For these reasons, **THE VIET VET SURVIVAL GUIDE** fills a large and immediate need.

THE VIET VET SURVIVAL GUIDE

describes in depth the problems of the vet, the benefits and services available, and the veterans' issues that will be decided in the next several years. Most important, it helps vets understand how various agencies and processes work, not just in theory but in practice, and how vets can cut through the bureaucracy and confusion and get that to which they're entitled. This book, therefore, is a *consumer guide to veterans' affairs.*

It is written in a clear, simple manner to explain what to do from Step One forward.

"Use this book to find out what you can do for yourself and whom you might want to go to for assistance. Remember, you've *earned* your entitlements. If you let frustration defeat your getting your due, you'll be the only loser. Good luck!"

**Robert Muller, President
Vietnam Veterans of America**

* *

For the nine million Vietnam Era Vets and their families

★★★★ THE ★★★★
VIET
VET
SURVIVAL
GUIDE

HOW TO CUT THROUGH THE BUREAUCRACY AND GET WHAT YOU NEED— AND ARE ENTITLED TO

BY CRAIG KUBEY · DAVID F. ADDLESTONE
RICHARD E. O'DELL · KEITH D. SNYDER
BARTON F. STICHMAN · AND
VIETNAM VETERANS OF AMERICA

BALLANTINE BOOKS ● NEW YORK

Library of Congress Catalog Card Number: 85–90753

ISBN 0–345–32127–8

Manufactured in the United States of America

First Edition: November 1985

To those who, in mind or body, have not yet returned to "the World." And also to Dean K. Phillips, June 7, 1943–August 22, 1985, a gentle warrior and staunch advocate for Vietnam Veterans rights and a just society.

CONTENTS

ACKNOWLEDGMENTS

Publishing a book on the complicated area of veterans affairs is no simple matter. And the task is made harder when one of the coauthors works in California and the others have their offices in Washington, D.C. and Virginia. So we needed help, and we have many people to thank.

First, we thank the clients of the Vietnam Veterans of America (VVA) Legal Services, from whose lives we have learned most of what we—through this book—pass on to others.

We also offer special thanks to our agent, Joe Spieler. It was Joe's idea that this book should be produced by one coauthor who is primarily a writer and by others who are primarily experts on veterans issues. Without Joe's idea, this book would not exist.

Also making a critical early contribution were Ray Bonner and Gloria Emerson. These two authors of prominent books on Vietnam Veterans put the coauthors in touch with each other.

Bob Wyatt, Richard McCoy, and many others in the editorial, production, publicity, and sales departments at Ballantine Books undertook many unusual burdens to publish this book.

We also thank the following people:

Jenny Schnaier, of the VVA national staff, who wrote the chapter on women veterans.

Dennis Rhoades, Executive Director of VVA, who wrote

the chapter on the Veterans Administration and commented on the chapters on employment and education.

Ken Berez, of the VVA national staff, who wrote the history of VVA.

Richard Borrego, of the VA Readjustment Counseling Service (the Vet Centers), who wrote the section (in the psychological readjustment chapter) on Hispanic veterans.

Frank Montour, of the Readjustment Counseling Service National Working Group on American Indian Vietnam Veterans, who wrote the section on Native American veterans.

Steve Tice, of the Eugene, Oregon, Vet Center and the Readjustment Counseling Service National Working Group on Physically Disabled Vietnam Veterans, who wrote the section on disabled veterans.

M.G. Diamond, of the VVA Legal Services staff, who wrote a draft of the case history in the discharge upgrading chapter and assisted with that chapter and the one on claims and appeals.

Eric Gerdeman, of the Silver Spring, Maryland, Vet Center, who wrote a draft of the section (in the psychological readjustment chapter) on Vet Centers.

Rick Weidman, of the VVA national staff, who commented on the chapters on employment and education.

Mary Stout, of the VVA national staff, who commented on the women veterans chapter.

John Terzano, Vice President of VVA, who commented on the Agent Orange chapter and reviewed the entire manuscript.

Georgyne Johnson, of the VVA national staff, who typed, photocopied, and otherwise helped make possible coast-to-coast collaboration.

Michael Ettlinger, of the VVA Legal Services staff, who assisted with the chapters on discharge upgrading and claims and appeals.

Rose Sandecki, of the Concord, California, Vet Center, who commented on the chapters on women veterans and psychological readjustment.

Mark Kaufman, of Delaware County Legal Assistance, and Mike Leaveck, of the VVA national staff, who commented on the housing chapter.

Joe Berry, of the Virginia Division of War Veterans' Claims, who commented on the chapters on compensation, pensions, and medical services.

Mona DeMasi, of Arnold Real Estate in Davis, California, who raised issues for the housing chapter.

Katherine Lane, of Rosenfeld, Meyer & Susman in Beverly Hills, who raised issues for the chapter on psychological re-adjustment.

Ray Scurfield, of the Readjustment Counseling Service, and Jack Smith, of the Center for Stress Recovery (in Cleveland), who commented on the psychological readjustment chapter.

Bob Muller, VVA's President, who wrote the foreword, commented on the shape the book should take, commented on the medical services chapter, and provided important support for the project.

Craig Kubey would also like to thank Symeta Kuper, John Sproul, and Bob Thau for their assistance, which helped make it possible for him to work on this book.

FOREWORD

By Robert Muller
President
Vietnam Veterans of America

"It ain't worth it," "The hell with it" are comments heard all too often from Vietnam Veterans who walk away from benefits and services they are entitled to because they can't deal with all the B.S. that's involved in trying to get them. The way the system works in running you around in circles, putting unnecessary obstacles in your path—demanding copies of documents you don't have, "Fill out these forms," "Come back at 3:00," etc.—would frustrate the most patient person. We as vets tend not to be patient—quite the contrary. Many of us have short fuses, particularly when dealing with VA bureaucrats who may not be all that sympathetic to our situation.

This book is designed to help you figure out what you are entitled to and how to go about getting it. It is a no-nonsense guide to how the system really works and how to advance your just claim most effectively.

The first thing to understand is that there is often a tremendous gap between what the government says it will do for you and what it really provides. A lot of laws are written with not much real intent behind them to help you. For one thing, it costs money to provide benefits and services. Sometimes government bureaucrats seem to consider themselves guardians at the gate to the U.S. Treasury. Promotions are given for cost savings, not for giving funds away. Suffice it to say that in a bureaucracy, budget sensitivity is extreme.

More important, perhaps, is the fact that the VA in particular is an old agency that has operated the same way for decades.

It became dominated after the Second World War by what is commonly referred to as the "Class of '46," which was responsible for the agency's thinking and sensitivity for the next 30 years. An institutional mind-set developed, not only at the VA but in Congress and among traditional veterans organizations, which too often failed to recognize that while ours wasn't the "Big One," it was a war nonetheless and our needs are as legitimate as those of any other group of American veterans.

The facts that the war was unpopular and that Vietnam Vets themselves failed at first to organize on their own behalf only compounded the problem.

Progress has been realized in the past couple of years. Vietnam Vets are increasingly being elected to Congress. We are also taking over more important positions within federal agencies. Most importantly, Vietnam Vets are truly beginning to organize into groups like VVA, which is finally making them a political constituency which has to be dealt with.

Despite the progress the best general principle to remember is that you've got to take care of yourself and fight for yourself. Use this book to find out what you can do for yourself and whom you might want to go to for assistance. Remember, you've *earned* your entitlements. If you let frustration defeat your getting your due, you'll be the only loser. Good luck!

INTRODUCTION

For 220 million Americans, the Vietnam War ended in April 1975. For nine million others, it continues to this day.

These are the nine million men and women classified by the federal government as "Vietnam Era Veterans." Of these, three million served in Vietnam.

All nine million have been affected by having served in the military during a war that provoked unprecedented opposition in their home country. The three million who were stationed in Vietnam have special problems. As Vietnam Veterans of America noted in a recent court brief, Viet Vets

- Fought in jungles against a native revolutionary army. Success was measured not by territorial conquest but by body count.

- Unlike in other wars, went to the war zone individually and came home individually. Most Viet Vets were therefore forced to deal with stress by themselves.

- Felt to a greater degree than other Vietnam Era Vets the impact of serving during a war opposed by most of their fellow citizens: those who served in Vietnam were seen as bearing a special responsibility for the war.

- Served in a war that by many measures the United States *lost*. The returning Viet Vet was met not by victory parades but by condemnation or apathy.

The three million also suffered the often-catastrophic symptoms of Post-Traumatic Stress Disorder, the physical and psychological ravages of Agent Orange, and the disabling and disfiguring injuries of combat.

The United States took the nine million into military service and sent the three million to war. In so doing it took upon itself moral and legal obligations of the most serious nature. But the United States has not fulfilled its duties. It has breached its contract with the men and women who risked—and sometimes ruined—their lives in service to their country.

The federal government has responded to the needs of veterans primarily through the Veterans Administration. Although in recent years the VA has provided vast amounts of assistance to Viet Vets and has even taken some innovative steps to deal with their distinctive problems, it has not done enough. Many vets say VA assistance has been too little and too late. Though the VA boasts of hiring more Vietnam Era Vets than other government agencies, too many VA staff members are insensitive to the special needs of Viet Vets. The VA has become known for inaction, extreme delay, and regulations that even lawyers sometimes cannot understand.

Agent Orange presents just one example of the bizarre horrors many vets have experienced in dealing with the VA. Agent Orange contains dioxin. Dioxin, which has been responsible for mass evacuations from several U.S. cities, has been demonstrated to cause cancer, birth defects, liver damage, chloracne (a severe skin disease), numbness of the extremities, loss of sex drive, and personality change. From 1962 to 1971, the U.S. dropped more than 10.6 million gallons of Agent Orange and other herbicides (some more dangerous than Agent Orange) on Vietnam. Some 2.4 million Americans were in Vietnam during the use of these defoliants. Hundreds of thousands of Viet Vets believe they have been damaged by Agent Orange. Yet to this day, the VA has refused to pay even a single disability compensation claim based on exposure to the herbicide.

In addition to the federal Veterans Administration, there is a veterans department in almost every state. These agencies vary in size, facilities, and quality.

Opposed by the North Vietnamese and Viet Cong during the war and by their own countrymen upon returning to America, and inadequately aided by the VA and state agencies once they sought assistance, Vietnam Era Vets are urgently in need of help.

There are dozens of nongovernment veterans organizations, many existing solely for Viet Vets. With few exceptions, however, they are small and weak, and work with little contact and cooperation with each other. The relatively powerful groups—the American Legion, AMVETS, the Disabled American Veterans, and the Veterans of Foreign Wars—were founded to deal with a broad spectrum of veterans issues spanning all eras. None of the four organizations just mentioned is made up exclusively of Viet Vets. These organizations therefore spend much of their time on matters important mostly to veterans of middle age and beyond, including in particular matters of concern to the veterans of World War II. The only large, national organization on the cutting edge of Viet Vet advocacy is Vietnam Veterans of America. Headquartered in Washington, D.C., it in 1985 had 170 chapters.

Only in recent years have Viet Vets begun to learn how severe and widespread their problems are. Still, no comprehensive, easily read, and widely distributed book has existed to assist them. For these reasons, THE VIET VET SURVIVAL GUIDE fills a large and immediate need.

THE VIET VET SURVIVAL GUIDE describes in depth the problems of the vet, the benefits and services available to him, and the veterans issues that will be decided in the next several years. Most important, it helps the vet understand how various agencies and processes work not just in theory but in practice and how the vet can cut through the bureaucracy and confusion and get that to which he's entitled. The book therefore is a *consumer guide to veterans affairs*.

And it is a consumer guide aimed precisely at the veteran. The book is written in a clear, simple manner and explains what to do from Step One forward.

1. BASIC SURVIVAL INFORMATION

How to Use this Book, Notes from the Authors

Life is unfair.
—John F. Kennedy

This book will help you survive in the world of the veteran. This world, like the world at large, is not a fair world. Your country asked you to take years out of your life and to risk life itself. But when you came back, it gave you little praise and little comfort. Instead, it gave you the Veterans Administration.

Though there are other federal agencies that benefit the veteran, and though there are many state programs for veterans, the VA is more important to most vets than all the rest combined. But the VA isn't what it should be. It's a bureaucracy. Full of programs that cover enough vets and programs that don't, full of people who care and people who don't, full of prompt responses and endless delays, and full of rules, rules, rules.

This book focuses on programs run by the VA. It also deals with programs administered by other federal agencies and the states. These programs—especially those of the VA—can save your life. VA medical care can repair your body. VA educational benefits can put you through school. VA disability compensation and pensions can pay many of your bills. VA loans can make it possible for you to buy a home.

But to get the most out of the VA, or the Small Business Administration, or the veterans department in your home state, you have to know what you're doing. You have to know the benefits to which you're entitled, the problems you may face and how to solve them, and where to go for help.

This book contains all of that. But we—the authors of this book—want you to know how to get the most out of it. We do not suggest that all veterans read every page of this book. For most veterans, that is not a good use of time. We suggest that you look through the table of contents and then carefully read each chapter that you know applies to you or that you think *may* apply to you. We further suggest that you *skim* every page of all the other chapters. For one thing, you may very well come across a benefit program or other information that—surprise—can help you. For another thing, you may find something that you will want to pass along to a friend who is a veteran.

Now *we* want to pass along some information, most of it very important, that applies to most or all the chapters in this book. That way, we won't have to bore you by repeating the same points chapter after chapter.

QUALIFYING FOR BENEFITS

To get benefits from the VA or any other agency, you (or your dependents) must be both *eligible* and *entitled*. To be *eligible* for benefits, you must meet certain general requirements. These may have to do with how long you served, what kind of discharge you received, and whether any disability you have is connected to your military service. To be *entitled* to benefits, you personally must be approved to receive them.

Most of the time, but not always, if you are eligible, all you have to do to become entitled is to submit a form and wait for approval. But there are exceptions. For instance, *you* may know the facts of your case prove you should be approved, but the VA may disagree. So you may have to appeal or at least provide more information. Another example is that you may be eligible for care at a VA hospital, but the nearest hospital may say it doesn't have room for you, at least right now.

Specific chapters in this book explain how to qualify for specific benefits. But here are some general guidelines:

Type of Discharge

There are important exceptions, but the great majority of programs of the VA, other federal agencies, and state veterans departments require that the veteran was separated under "conditions other than dishonorable." You and your dependents are therefore eligible for benefits if you received an honorable discharge, a general discharge, or a lower discharge that has been upgraded to honorable or general. You are in almost all cases not eligible if you have a dishonorable discharge or a bad conduct discharge issued by a general court-martial. If you have a bad conduct discharge not issued by a general court-martial or if you have a discharge called "under other than honorable conditions" or "undesirable," the VA (or other agency) *may* find you eligible (this is especially likely if you were discharged for homosexuality or for minor offenses). The VA (or other agency) will make a determination of "character of discharge," based on the facts of your case: it will decide if you were separated under "dishonorable conditions" or "other than dishonorable conditions."

See Chapter 15, "Upgrading Your Discharge," for a discussion of discharges and how to get a bad discharge upgraded as well as for a chart showing the type of discharge required for specific programs of the VA and other federal agencies.

Type of Service

To be eligible for federal and state veterans programs, you must in almost all cases have had "active service." Active service includes, but is not limited to

"*Active duty*"—This includes full-time service in the Army, Navy, Marine Corps, Air Force, or Coast Guard and certain other kinds of service.

"*Active duty for training*"—during which the individual was disabled or died from a disease or injury that occurred or was made worse in the line of duty. "Active duty for training" includes certain members of the reserve, ROTC, and national guard on full-time duty, for training purposes, in the armed forces and also includes those traveling to and from duty.

Service in Wartime

The VA pension program requires the veteran to have served during wartime. This does not mean the veteran must have engaged in combat or served in a combat zone (such as Vietnam). The vet must only have served during a period officially designated as wartime. The Vietnam Era has been designated as wartime and was proclaimed by President Ford as being from August 5, 1964, through May 7, 1975. So if you served anywhere—in Vietnam, in West Germany, or in Kansas— anytime during the Vietnam Era, you qualify as having served during wartime.

Other Rules

The VA also has rules determining who qualifies as a spouse or child of a veteran. Check with a service representative (also called a "service officer") who works for a veterans organization such as Vietnam Veterans of America (VVA) or check with a VA Regional Office.

DEALING WITH THE VA AND OTHER AGENCIES

Throughout this book we tell you what you can get and how to get it. We tell you what forms to use and sometimes even tell you how to fill them out. But there are some general rules we should include here:

To get forms, call, write, or visit a VA Regional Office. Forms relating to medical care can also be obtained from a VA medical facility. Some veterans organizations and their service representatives also have forms. Return most forms to a VA Regional Office; return medical forms to the medical facility where you want to be examined or treated.

Although this book reprints some VA forms, don't tear out the ones printed in this book. Get the latest, full-size copy available from the VA and fill it out with information relating specifically to your case.

If possible, type your information onto the forms. Type any additional documents you send to the VA or to anybody else. If that isn't possible, print. Typing and printing are easier to read than handwriting and may make it easier for the VA to process your claim.

Before you submit your forms and documents, make photocopies. Photocopy machines may be found in most libraries and post offices as well as at photocopy shops. Staple the original forms to the copies of documents. Keep a copy of the forms and keep the original documents: never submit original documents.

You need not personally deliver your forms and documents to the VA. It's fine to mail them. But if you do mail them, send them by certified mail, "return receipt requested." This is simple to do; any post office will help you. Your return receipt will let you know the VA got what you sent. And if you ever need to prove the VA got it, your receipt will be your proof. Keep it with your copies.

If you don't know where the nearest VA Regional Office or medical facility is, use the phone book. The phone book is also helpful in finding other government agencies, veterans organizations, and most anybody else. For the VA and other federal agencies, look in the white pages in the "United States" listings. For state agencies, look in the listings for the name of your state. If you live in a rural area or even a small city, your phone book may not list many federal or state agencies other than the post office and the department of motor vehicles. If your phone book doesn't list the agency or organization whose number you need, look in a phone book for the nearest big city or call directory assistance for that city.

In dealing with people at the VA or elsewhere, be confident and assert yourself. Avoid the extremes: don't be timid, but don't scream at people, either, even if they deserve it. You should feel confident because—after reading this book—you will know your rights. You should feel assertive because you answered your country's call to military duty.

GETTING HELP

In many situations, you will do better if you get somebody to help you. This is often true if you're applying for benefits, and it's particularly true once you get involved in complicated matters, such as appealing a VA decision or applying for an upgrade of discharge.

Over and over in this book we will suggest that you get help from service representatives. Who are these people? They are people who work—sometimes as unpaid volunteers—for veterans organizations. Some are called "service representatives"; some are called "service officers." Veterans organizations include the Veterans of Foreign Wars (VFW), the Disabled American Veterans (DAV), AMVETs, and The American Legion. They also include the largest national organization of Vietnam Era Veterans, Vietnam Veterans of America (VVA). VVA, of course, has a special interest and special expertise relating to Vietnam Era Vets; it also is the major force behind this book. Find service representatives by contacting the organization for which they work. Again, use the phone book. If all else fails, you can find out if there is a VVA service representative in your area by calling the VVA national office at (202) 686-2599.

Some service representatives are terrific. They're bright, knowledgeable, caring, and reliable. Some are jerks. This is also true of every other kind of person from whom you may seek help: lawyers, doctors, employees at VA Regional Offices, and staff members at Vet Centers.

Don't trust service reps just because they're service reps. And don't trust doctors just because they're doctors. As Ann Landers says, "Fifty percent of the doctors now practicing medicine graduated in the bottom half of their class."

Evaluate the people with whom you deal. Do they have experience in the area that concerns you? Do they know what they're talking about? (We may have made a few mistakes someplace in this book, but if your service representative repeatedly tells you things that contradict this book, the service rep is a turkey.) Do they have time for you and time to work on your case (and not just at the last minute)? Do they show up when and where they're supposed to? Do they keep good records? Do they have the books and manuals necessary to do the best possible job? (A service representative is especially well prepared if he or she has the VVA *Service Representatives Manual*.) Are they courteous?

Shop around until you find somebody who seems well qualified and who seems like somebody with whom you can get along. If you later decide you don't like the person who is helping you, find somebody else.

Most of the time, a service representative is the best person with whom to start. Sometimes, however, the best person is someone who works at a Vet Center (see Chapter 8, "Psychological Readjustment"). Or it might be a doctor. Or someone in the district office of your Member of Congress (especially if you need a politician to apply pressure on your behalf—but be sure the Member's caseworker follows through rather than just making a routine inquiry). Or the best person might be a reporter for a newspaper or TV station. Or even—yes, it's true—a lawyer.

Lawyers present problems for everybody, and they present special problems for vets. This isn't all the fault of the lawyers. Ever since the Civil War there has been a law limiting the amount a lawyer can charge a veteran for work relating to veterans benefits. At the end of the Civil War, the limit was $5. Now it's $10. This, of course, makes no sense. But it's the law. It's being challenged, but for now you have to live with it.

This means that if you have a problem getting benefits from the VA, you probably can't use a lawyer in private practice. If you have little income, however, you may qualify for free representation by an attorney who works for a Legal Aid or Legal Services office. And remember, you *can* hire a lawyer (the $10 rule doesn't apply) in cases not directly relating to getting benefits: cases involving subjects such as VA efforts to get you to pay back alleged "overpayments," lawsuits for VA medical malpractice, and efforts to get military records corrected or to get a discharge upgraded.

But even if the $10 rule doesn't apply, watch out for lawyers. Lawyers have never been—we're talking generally of course, especially because most of the authors of this book are lawyers—a trustworthy lot. And things may be worse now, because there are too many lawyers for the number of clients able to pay fees. So you may very well run into a lawyer who tells you he or she can handle your case even if he or she has no idea how to do so, or a lawyer who says he or she has represented many veterans, even though this is not true.

Check into the attorney's reputation, background, and experience. If you like a particular lawyer, consult with him or her briefly about your case and then ask for an estimate (preferably in writing) of your chances of success, what you will gain if you win, how much the lawyer will charge you in fees and expenses, and when the lawyer expects to be paid. If you ask for a firm estimate, you risk making the lawyer angry. If this occurs, you may have to find another lawyer. Don't worry: there are more than 600,000 of them.

If you need a referral to a local lawyer with experience in veterans matters, the VVA Legal Services may be able to find one for you. Write to VVA Legal Services; 2001 S St., N.W., Suite 710; Washington, DC 20009.

LADIES AND GENTLEMEN

As we began this book, we authors had a dispute. Some of us wanted, every time we referred to the veteran, to say "he or she" or "(s)he" or something like that. Others, equally concerned about women's rights and equally aware of the equality of the sexes, thought that would clutter up the book. The anti-clutter forces won. To make this book as easy as possible to read, this book (except in the chapter on women vets) refers to the veteran as "he." In references to other people, such as service representatives, VA employees, and lawyers, we use "he or she."

YOU CAN'T HAVE EVERYTHING

This book is very complete. This book is very up-to-date. But it could be more complete: the VVA *Service Representatives Manual*, for instance, has more than *six hundred* pages, and those pages are letter size. We wanted to cover all the key points and none of the obscure ones and we wanted to publish a book that was not so long that veterans wouldn't want to read it. So there are many details and many exceptions to rules that we have left out. Some of these details and exceptions may apply to you. That's one reason why we say, over and over, to check with an expert.

We could also have made this book more up-to-date. But only by publishing it later than we did. And of course, that later book would start going out of date as soon as *it* was done. Veterans issues are constantly changing, especially these days, as veterans organizations and individual veterans are working to improve the treatment of vets in areas such as Agent Orange, medical care for women, and extension of the G.I. Bill. So some information in this book may become incomplete or incorrect by the time the book gets to the stores, or months or years later. Again, stay in touch with your service rep.

(VVA members can stay up-to-date by reading the *VVA Veteran*, which comes to all members. There is a membership application at the end of this book for those who may want to join VVA.)

SQUEAK

"The squeaky wheel gets the grease." This is true of wheels and it is true of veterans. Except that squeaky veterans don't get grease. They get increased disability compensation, special devices for the handicapped, discharge upgrades, better medical care, and so on and so on.

So squeak. After risking your life and maybe harming your life as a member of the American armed forces, you deserve benefits and other assistance from the VA and other agencies. Ask for what you need, even if it's not standard. Ask again. Ask more persuasively. Ask somebody higher up. Make phone calls, write letters, make personal visits. Do some research. Get help from your service representative, or maybe a Vet Center or a doctor or a lawyer or a reporter or a Member of Congress.

Be as tough as a Vietnam Veteran. Hang in there as long as a marathon runner. And be as prepared as someone who has read THE VIET VET SURVIVAL GUIDE.

2. THE VETERANS ADMINISTRATION

Two Agencies, Maybe Three

If any man shalbee sent forth as a souldier and shall return maimed, hee shalbee maintained competently by the collonie during his life.

> —Law enacted in 1636 by the Pilgrims of Plymouth colony

By Dennis Rhoades, Executive Director, VVA

If you plan to take advantage of your rights as a Vietnam Era Veteran, sooner or later you are going to have to deal with the Veterans Administration. Like any other large bureaucracy, the VA can be slow, frustrating, and confusing, and you are going to find that to be the case no matter how much you know about it. Using this book, and the advice of a veterans service organization such as VVA, however, can help you spot errors and unusual delays within the VA, as well as preventing you from going down a lot of blind alleys trying to get what you need. If you plan to take advantage of any of the rights this book describes, you should read this chapter.

WHAT THE VA DOES AND DOES NOT DO

Many veterans seem to think the VA can provide for their every need, and, while it is true that the VA's programs provide a broad spectrum of benefits, the VA is not all things to all veterans. The VA provides medical care for veterans with service-connected disabilities and—if they are unable to pay for it and there is space available at the VA medical center—for other vets. The VA provides educational benefits for veterans and, in some cases, their dependents. And it provides vocational rehabilitation, home loans, compensation for veterans with service-connected disabilities, pensions for vets with other disabilities, and burial benefits. Each of these services is provided with a lot of "ifs," which the VA calls "eligibility."

In a number of areas, the VA does *not* provide services to veterans. For instance, unless it has trained you in a vocational rehabilitation program, the VA will generally not help you find a job. Jobs are the responsibility of the Veterans Employment and Training Service in the Department of Labor. The VA will not provide you with assistance or loans if you want to start a small business—that's the job of the Small Business Administration. The VA will not lend you or give you money to help you out in an economic emergency, or during periods when you aren't working. That is the job of state and local agencies.

Understanding what the VA can and cannot do will save you a lot of time and frustration, and help you avoid useless confrontations with VA employees. Reading this book will help you further understand what your rights are and are not, and where you go to apply for those you do have.

THE TWO (POSSIBLY THREE) VA's

The VA is the third largest federal agency, with a quarter million employees and an annual budget of about 29 billion dollars. Any bureaucracy that large has a number of different departments or divisions. In the VA's case, there are basically two divisions of concern to Vietnam Era Vets. These divisions are so independent of one another, and their functions so different, that it is safe to say that there are actually two VAs. The first VA is a hospital. The second VA is a bank. And, just as you don't go to a bank to see a doctor, or to a hospital to get money, you don't go to one VA expecting the services provided by the other.

THE VA AS HOSPITAL

The VA operates the largest hospital system in the world. Fully 90 percent of the VA's quarter million employees are the doctors, nurses, orderlies, and other health care employees the veteran encounters when he visits the hospital. Most VA hospitals operate independently—that is, to apply for admission to a VA hospital, you must generally apply to a particular one. Generally, VA medical care for veterans with disabilities that are not service-connected is limited to hospital care on a space-available basis. Once you are actually admitted to the hospital, however, you become entitled to the entire range of VA medical services (including dental care), regardless of the illness for which you were originally admitted.

Do not attempt to apply for hospital admission through a VA Regional Office. The office will only end up sending you to the hospital to apply directly for admission, and you will have wasted a trip. Similarly, don't attempt to apply for educational benefits or disability compensation at a VA hospital (unless you are already a patient). VA Regional Offices maintain one or two employees at VA hospitals to initiate claims, but their services are generally restricted to patients.

THE VA AS BANK

Virtually all the programs that the VA runs involving payment of money (that is, education, home loans, compensation, pension, vocational rehabilitation) are administered by the VA through regional offices. Most states have one regional office, although some large states, such as Pennsylvania, New York, and Texas, have two regional offices, and California has three. If you don't live near a regional office, you may contact the VA through toll-free numbers. These are in the "United States" listings in the phone directory, under "Veterans Administration Regional Office."

The most important thing to realize about your benefits is that the VA Regional Office is essentially a bank. You, as a veteran, in most cases have a certain "entitlement" based upon eligibility. Your entitlement is the amount of money the VA will provide to you under specific VA programs. Once your entitlement is established, you may draw on it. To establish your entitlement, however, you need proof. Your most important proof is your Form DD 214 (your separation document). When you apply for VA benefits, you will need either your original DD 214 or a certified copy. (Otherwise the VA will have to order your records.) If you bring your original DD 214 to the VA, let them make a copy: keep the original yourself. If you still have your original DD 214, you should submit it to your county hall of records. That way, if you ever need a certified copy, you can get one.

When you call or visit a VA Regional Office, you will talk with a Veterans Benefits Counselor. This counselor works for the Veterans Services Division of the regional office. This division is responsible for most of the regional office's contact with the veteran. The counselor will provide you with information about how to apply for benefits. Keep in mind, though, that the counselor does *not* handle your case or make a decision about your entitlement. Such decisions are instead made by an *Adjudicator*. When a decision is made on your claim, the letter from the VA will be signed by the Adjudication Officer, who supervises all the VA Adjudicators. If you are applying for disability compensation or a pension, you will be rated by degree of disability—that is, 20 percent, 30 percent, etc. Ratings involve examinations by VA doctors, but these doctors do not make the decision on your rating. That decision is made by the Rating Board at the VA Regional Office.

Any questions or problems you may have concerning VA benefits should—if you are inquiring within the VA—first be discussed with a Veterans Benefits Counselor. Generally, you will not be permitted to discuss your claim with the VA Adjudicator. If you cannot get a clear explanation from the counselor, you should ask to see the Veterans Service Officer, who supervises all of the counselors. The Veterans Service Officer is the head of the Veterans Service Division.

THE THIRD VA: VET CENTERS

The beginning of this chapter said there are essentially two VAs, one a hospital, the other a bank. Actually, there is a third distinct part of the VA, which is mentioned last because it is technically part of the hospital system. This is the system of Vet Centers. The Vet Centers were created in 1979 to deal with the psychological readjustment problems of Vietnam Veterans (see Chapter 8, "Psychological Readjustment"). Unlike other VA offices, Vet Centers are normally operated in local communities, with small offices in storefronts and shopping centers. Although they are part of the VA health care system, the Vet Centers operate independently. This means that although Vet Center personnel may occasionally be able to assist you with other programs and services run by the VA, you still must contact a VA Regional Office for benefit assistance or a VA hospital for medical care.

DEALING WITH THE VA

To help you as you attempt to get the services you need, this chapter has briefly described how the VA works. For routine services, dealing with the VA directly should be fairly simple. If your problem is complicated, or if you find yourself frustrated in working with the VA, you should seek the help of a service representative (also called "service officer") who works for a veterans organization such as Vietnam Veterans of America (VVA).

Here's an inside tip that will help you deal effectively with the VA: get a phone book. Better, get two. If your dealings with the VA are confined to the regional office, ask that office for a copy of its phone book. If you are frequently in touch with the VA Central Office in Washington, ask it for *its* directory. The phone books will help you get around the VA employees who answer the phone and say they'll take a message and have someone send you a written reply. With the phone book you can find the numbers of VA officials and call them (or at least their offices) *directly*. This in many cases will get

you much quicker action than would otherwise be possible. To
find out whom you should call about a specific kind of problem,
check with your service representative. The one drawback to
all this advice is that if you ask for a phone book you may
very well be refused. But you don't have to quit there. Write
a letter to the office that refused you and say, "I am requesting
your phone directory under the Freedom of Information Act.
I request a fee waiver." These magic words will probably do
the trick.

One final thing to remember: Because the VA is large, and
the laws that it administers are often complex, do not expect
immediate results. It takes time to be admitted to a VA hospital,
it takes time to get rated for a disability, and it takes time to
receive educational benefits. If your need for money is immediate, you may want to seek the help of state and local
agencies.

3. Compensation

Payments for Disability and Death

VA money often determines whether a Vietnam Era Veteran can successfully adjust to life after military service. Money can pay for general living expenses. Money can pay for private doctors, nursing care, medical devices, and medicines. Money can give the vet a sense of having been justly compensated by his government for the injuries and illnesses he has suffered as a result of serving in the armed forces.

One of the chief sources of VA money is called "compensation." Compensation usually is for military-connected disability, though it can also be paid as a death benefit. Though this chapter will discuss death benefits, it will deal mostly with disability compensation.

Before getting into the specifics of compensation, it is essential to make one point: THIS IS A VERY COMPLICATED AREA AND YOU SHOULD GET ADVICE BEFORE ENTERING IT. In particular, some disabilities qualify you for compensation, while other disabilities (which often seem very similar in type and severity) do not. In addition, the *same disability* may qualify you for no compensation, a small amount of compensation, or a large amount. What happens in your case depends not just on the injury or illness you sustained, but also on when and how you sustained it. And it depends on how you present your case.

It is important that you present your case as strongly as possible the first time you present it. It is much easier to win fair compensation when you first present your case than it is to succeed later by asking for a new hearing of your case or by appealing a decision made against you.

And even though many vets are well educated and even though some vets are familiar with veterans laws and regulations, it takes a true expert to ensure that the vet has his best possible chance to receive compensation at all and to receive the amount due him.

Therefore this chapter is not intended to be so detailed that once the vet has read it he will be ready to represent himself in an application for compensation. Rather, it is intended to make the vet familiar with what is involved in getting compensation. And it is intended to give him enough information so that when he *does* consult with a representative the vet will understand what the representative is saying, will be able to provide the representative with useful information, will be able to ask the representative helpful questions, and—perhaps most important—will be able to get a good idea of whether the representative knows what he or she is doing.

Once you have read this chapter (and have read the other parts of this book that relate to your case), you should find an effective representative. At this writing, you cannot depend much on attorneys. This is because federal law prohibits lawyers from receiving more than $10 for assisting a veteran in benefit cases. In June 1984, Federal District Court Judge Marilyn Patel ordered the VA to stop enforcing this law, but in July 1985 the U.S. Supreme Court upheld it. Still, in some areas of the country, vets can receive free representation from attorneys in Legal Services or Legal Aid offices. To find such an office, check your phone directory under "Legal Aid" or "Legal Services" or ask your county bar association or a lawyer practicing in your area.

Your best bet for representation are the service representatives who work for veterans organizations such as Vietnam Veterans of America (VVA). While these representatives usually are not attorneys, they are familiar with the confusing complexities of veterans laws and regulations and can often guide you to a result better than the one you would have achieved by yourself.

Choose your representative carefully. Be sure he or she responds to your requests and is willing to spend enough time on your case. If at any point you are not satisfied with your representative, find another one. It's your case and you're the boss.

Here, then, is a general outline of veterans compensation for disability and death.

DISABILITY COMPENSATION

If you were discharged "under conditions other than dishonorable" and have a disability that occurred or was made worse during military service, you are entitled to VA disability compensation. (The term "under conditions other than dishonorable" is not the same as "with other than a dishonorable discharge." For an explanation, see Chapter 15, "Upgrading Your Discharge.")

Your disability qualifies for compensation if it occurred or was made worse during military service or even if it is a "secondary" disability: one resulting from *another* service-connected disability. And a disability is considered to have occurred during military service simply if it occurred while you were in the military: it need not have occurred during combat or other military activity; it could even have occurred while you were on leave. On the other hand, certain disabilities that are congenital or developmental, even if they get worse during military service, may not qualify for compensation.

If you are able to prove to the VA that your disability is service-connected, your task is only partly over. It remains for you to prove *how seriously disabled you are*.

A VA Rating Board may determine that you are anywhere from 0 percent to 100 percent disabled. It rounds its ratings off to the nearest 10 percent (so a 27 percent disability and a 34 percent disability are both rated as 30 percent). The higher your rating, the higher your monthly disability payment.

Among the 587,032 Vietnam Era Vets involved in active

compensation cases as of September 1983, 231,965, or 39.5 percent, were rated as having a 10 percent disability. 17.2 percent had a 20 percent disability, 12.9 percent had a 30 percent disability, and only 6.4 percent were rated as being 100 percent disabled.

Here are the monthly compensation rates, as of December 1984, for single veterans with disabilities rated from 10 percent to 100 percent:

Degree of Disability	Monthly Rate
10%	$66
20%	$122
30%	$185
40%	$266
50%	$376
60%	$474
70%	$598
80%	$692
90%	$779
100%	$1,295

Rates are higher for veterans who are rated 30 percent or more disabled and who have dependents, but not by as much as you might guess. For instance, while a 30 percent disabled veteran with no dependents receives $185 a month, a 30 percent disabled vet with a spouse and child receives only $40 more, or $225.

If your injuries are particularly severe, you may be entitled to "special monthly compensation." This is compensation *in addition to* the compensation paid on the basis of disability ratings.

Vets entitled to special monthly compensation include those who have lost one or more feet or hands (or have lost the use of one or more feet or hands), suffer blindness in one or both eyes, are permanently bedridden, and/or need regular attendance by a nurse. The complete list of disabilities qualifying for special compensation may be found in title 38 of the *United States Code*, in sections 314 (k) through (t). You do not need to be a lawyer to find and understand this list. The U.S. Code (a set of books containing all federal laws) can be found in most any city, county, or university law library, in most Legal

Aid offices, and at the offices of most veterans organizations, such as Vietnam Veterans of America (VVA). The maximum special compensation a severely disabled vet may receive is $2,255 per month.

All disability compensation is tax-free.

Even a rating of 0 percent disability can help the vet. This is because *any* disability rating establishes that a condition is service-connected. If you receive a rating of 0 percent disability but your condition later becomes worse—bad enough to deserve a rating greater than 0 percent—you will have a better chance of receiving compensation than will a vet who has never received a rating.

When you multiply a monthly amount of compensation by the many months contained in many years, the difference between various monthly rates can become huge. Even over a single year, the difference between the compensation for 30 percent disability, 60 percent disability, and 100 percent disability are dramatic: these levels total $2,220, $5,688, and $15,540 per year, respectively. Over a ten year period, the levels would amount to $22,200, $56,880, and $155,400, respectively. And remember that once you receive a certain disability rating it is difficult to change it. So if you don't do your best job of presenting your first case for a disability rating, you may lose (over the years) tens of thousands of dollars.

Understanding the Rules

As stated, a disability from an injury or illness or from the worsening of an injury or illness is generally covered by the compensation program if the injury or illness occurred while a vet was in the service. Also covered are "secondary" disabilities: disabilities stemming from *another* service-connected disability.

Here is an example of a secondary disability: Say the VA has determined you have a disability due to a shell fragment wound to the left knee. And say the knee injury has made you favor one leg over another, making you walk unevenly and eventually causing your pelvis to tilt. And say the pelvic tilt has given you chronic low-back pain. You can claim the back problem as secondary to the pelvic tilt, which itself was caused by the initial disability of the knee.

But not everything is covered. An injury or illness will not qualify for disability compensation if it occurred as the result of "willful misconduct." Depending on the circumstances, venereal disease, alcoholism, drug use, and suicide may or may not be determined to be willful misconduct. As the result of recent lawsuits, VA rules on alcoholism may soon change. Generally, occasional use of alcohol or drugs is *not* willful misconduct. But if drinking results in immediate disability it may be considered willful misconduct, and addiction to nonprescribed drugs may be considered in the same way.

You need not prove you were in good health before military service. Generally, the VA *presumes* you were in good health before you entered the military.

Also, an injury or illness diagnosed *after* your separation from service will be compensated if you can show that it *originated* while you were in the military.

In addition, Congress has determined that certain conditions, if they occur in veterans who have had at least ninety days of wartime service, will be presumed to be connected to their military service. Among those illnesses covered—provided they occur within a set period after service—are forty chronic diseases and sixteen tropical diseases. For certain conditions occurring in former POWs, there is no time limit. A service representative should have a list of the diseases and conditions just mentioned.

You are also due compensation for an injury or illness that occurred before service but got worse during service. This is true, however, only if the increase in disability was greater than would have occurred through just the natural progression of the condition. It is especially hard to prove that a pre-service psychiatric problem became worse during military service.

VA Rating Boards use a Schedule of Rating Disabilities. This schedule contains (1) a list of diagnoses (each diagnosis has a number, called a "diagnostic code"), (2) findings that are required in order to demonstrate the severity of a condition, and (3) a rating (a percentage) of the degree of impairment caused by each condition.

Here are two examples:

DC 5285: vertebra, fractures/residuals:
—with cord involvement, bedridden, or requiring long leg braces . . . 100%.
—without cord involvement; abnormal mobility requiring neck brace . . . 60%.

DC 9410: other and unspecified neurosis:
—ability to establish or maintain effective or favorable relationships with people is substantially impaired. By reason of psychoneurotic symptoms the reliability, flexibility and efficiency levels are so reduced as to result in severe industrial impairment . . . 50%.

The percentage ratings are designed to represent the degree to which certain disabilities reduce the typical veteran's ability to earn a living.

A VA Rating Board rates each disability of each veteran who applies for disability compensation. When a vet has two or more disabilities, the Rating Board will determine a *combined rating*, and compensation will be based on this figure.

To establish a combined rating for a vet with two disabilities, the Rating Board begins by subtracting the higher rating from 100 percent. Then the remainder is multiplied by the lower rating. The resulting figure is added to the higher rating. The sum of these two figures is the total disability.

If, for instance, a vet has two disabilities, one of 30 percent and the other of 20 percent, the 30 percent is subtracted from 100 percent, leaving 70 percent. Then the 20 percent is multiplied by the 70 percent, making 14 percent. 30 percent and 14 percent are then added, making 44 percent, which is rounded to 40 percent. The vet's total disability is therefore figured at 40 percent.

Another rating formula applies when both arms, both legs, or a pair of skeletal muscles are involved. Still other formulas apply to other special cases.

If physical and/or psychological impairment is so great that it would be impossible for the average person with such impairment to maintain substantial employment, the vet will be classified as *totally disabled* and therefore will receive a rating of 100 percent disability. If the total disability is reasonably certain to continue for the life of the veteran, he may be rated as having a *permanent* total disability. Permanent total disability includes the disability from the permanent loss of the use of both hands or both feet or one of each or from becoming permanently bedridden or helpless.

In some cases, a veteran whose physical condition would not ordinarily result in a 100 percent disability rating will receive such a rating by showing that he is unemployable. But the VA is very skeptical about veterans who claim a 100 percent disability on this basis. Such veterans may more easily qualify for compensation from the Social Security Disability program.

Special issues exist for the vet who claims he is disabled due to exposure to Agent Orange; due to exposure to radiation; or due to psychiatric symptoms, including in particular Post-Traumatic Stress Disorder (PTSD), also called Delayed Stress Syndrome. These issues are discussed in later chapters.

Special Benefits for the Severely Disabled

If a veteran is severely disabled and requires a car, truck or other vehicle specially adapted for use by the disabled, the VA may grant the vet money toward the purchase of the vehicle.

Blind veterans may be furnished with a trained guide dog. They may also be given travel and other expenses involved in traveling to and staying near a facility designed for blind persons learning to use a guide dog.

In the case of certain disabilities, the VA may provide the vet with braces, orthopedic shoes, a hearing aid, a wheelchair, other medical accessories and appliances, or artificial limbs. If a disabled vet uses a device that damages his clothing, the VA may authorize an annual clothing allowance.

If a vet is entitled to compensation for a permanent and total disability, he may be eligible for specially adapted housing.

Robert Muller is President of Vietnam Veterans of America. Due to a combat injury suffered in Vietnam, he uses a wheelchair. Muller has this advice for the severely disabled veteran:

> Particularly with severe disability, the VA has great latitude in what assistance it can provide. Almost anything can qualify as a therapeutic medical device—from central air conditioning to an electric typewriter. The key is to fight for what you want. In the words of a VA doctor, "The squeaky wheel gets the grease." Since the authority to provide services is so open-ended, the VA is reluctant to open its inventory of possible benefits. Just remember, you can get just about anything from

which you might reasonably benefit—including state-of-art medical devices—if you're willing to fight for it.

Alternative Programs

If you have a disability that was or should have been detected at the time of your separation from military service, you may be entitled to Armed Services Disability Retirement compensation. If you qualify for this program, you must decide between it and VA disability compensation. For most Viet Vets, more money is available through the VA program. Therefore, few Viet Vets should attempt to convert from VA compensation to the military disability retirement program, but most Viet Vets in the military program should attempt to qualify instead for VA disability compensation. For more information, see Chapter 14, "Correcting Your Records."

A vet who is denied VA disability compensation may be eligible for Social Security benefits. *Some vets qualify for both the VA program and a Social Security program.* Check with your service representative or the nearest Social Security office, listed in your phone book under "United States."

Remember that accepting VA, military, or Social Security disability benefits may reduce or eliminate the payments you might receive through a private disability insurance policy. If you have such a private insurance policy, check with your service representative or the insurance company before applying for VA, military, or Social Security benefits.

DEATH BENEFITS FOR DEPENDENTS

The VA pays two types of monthly benefits to the dependents of a veteran whose death has been determined to have been connected to his military service. One type, Death Compensation, applies only to deaths occurring before 1957. Deaths occurring in or after 1957 are covered by Dependency and Indemnity Compensation (DIC). DIC is paid to the surviving spouse, children, and dependent parents of a vet who has died as a result of a service-connected disability. DIC may also be awarded if the veteran's service-connected disability *hastened or contributed to* his death from other causes. If a vet has been rated as 100 percent disabled for at least ten continuous years immediately before his death, DIC may be awarded regardless of the cause of death.

The amount of DIC paid to a surviving spouse or child is based on the deceased vet's highest pay grade. DIC payments to dependent parents are based on their annual income.

PREPARING YOUR CASE

In many ways, applying for disability and death benefits (and appealing a decision you believe is unfair) is like applying for other kinds of VA benefits (and appealing other kinds of decisions). It is therefore important to read Chapter 16, "Claims and Appeals."

There are, however, certain kinds of preparation and certain procedures that are important especially to claims for disability.

First, remember it is important to act quickly. If you win your claim for disability, payments will be made for the period beginning on one of two "effective dates." If you file your claim within one year of separation from active duty, the effective date will be the day after the date of separation. If you file after the first year, the effective date will be the first day of the month following the month in which you filed your claim.

To file a claim for disability compensation:

STEP 1: Obtain your complete service medical records and personnel file. Even if the VA gets these files before you do, you are entitled to review them and copy them. Note, however, that medical records are often incomplete. Also, get any records of treatment in VA facilities. In addition, obtain *civilian* medical records relating to your disability. See Chapter 13, "Getting Your Records."

STEP 2: Assemble other documents. Among documents that may be useful are marriage and birth certificates (to establish who your dependents are), an employment history (you can type this or have it typed), and private doctors' medical reports to indicate the current degree of impairment you suffer due to a service-connected injury or illness. If your military medical records are incomplete, prepare your own typed summary of missing information. If your service records do not provide clear and complete information on injuries you suffered, it is useful to get "buddy statements" from people who saw you as you were injured or shortly after. Also helpful are statements from family, friends, and others describing your current health problems. If you need a copy of a VA medical exam, use VA Form 00–3288 (sometimes numbered 70–3288). This and other VA forms may be found at any VA Regional Office and at the offices of many veterans organizations. Submit the form to the VA Medical Center where your exam was conducted or to the VA Regional Office that will handle your compensation claim.

STEP 3: Obtain and prepare VA Form 21–526 (and, if you claim you are unemployable, Form 21–8940 as well) and attach to it documents that support your claim. You need complete the sections on pensions only if you are applying for a pension at the same time you apply for compensation. If possible, type the form or have someone else type it. In filling it out, write clearly and give specifics. It is not enough to describe your injury as "foot." It is better to say, for instance, "Fractured right foot during parachute jump. Ankle is always swollen and painful. See attached medical documents and supporting statements." Be sure your claim makes clear that your disability is service-connected (that it occurred or was made worse while you were in the service). The less obvious the service connection, the more documentation you will need (for instance, you will need more evidence for a psychiatric claim than for a shrapnel wound).

If you are disabled due to Agent Orange or if you suffer from Post-Traumatic Stress Disorder, it will help your claim if you attach to your claim form one of the printed attachments prepared by the Vietnam Veterans of America (VVA) Legal Services office. See Chapter 7, "Agent Orange," or Chapter 8, "Psychological Readjustment."

APPEALING A DENIAL OF A CLAIM; REOPENING A CLAIM

In the opinion of many veterans organizations, a large percentage of VA decisions give a disability rating that is unfairly low.

After you have received your rating decision, you may want to appeal it (if you have been denied *any* disability rating or if you believe you should receive a higher rating). Appeals must be filed within one year of a denial. To appeal, file a Notice of Disagreement on VA Form 21–4138, Statement in Support of Claim. If you are appealing because your claim for a disability rating has been denied, be sure to provide convincing arguments against each reason the VA has given for denying your claim. First, go over the VA's denial with your service representative. Do your best to include on the form *new evidence* in support of your claim: if you can tell the VA only what it has already heard, your chances for a better decision are small. If possible, attach information that supports your position and that argues against the reasons for the original denial.

If the one-year deadline for appeals has passed, you may want to *reopen* your claim. But remember there is a danger in doing so if all you are seeking is an increase in compensation: it is possible the VA will find your condition has gotten better rather than worse; if so, it may assign you a lower disability rating (with the result that you will receive less compensation). Of course, some disabilities do improve (for instance, PTSD, if treated, usually improves) and, when they do, the disability rating should be reduced.

Regarding filing, appealing, and reopening a claim, see Chapter 16, "Claims and Appeals."

CLAIMS FOR DEATH BENEFITS

For death benefit claims, one of two forms must be used. A widow, widower, or child making a claim must use VA Form 21–534. Dependent parents must file VA Form 21–535.

GET HELP

Always remember that compensation is a complicated area. And remember that it is an area whose laws and regulations are constantly subject to change. For these reasons, certain parts of this chapter may be out of date by the time you read them. Also for these reasons, *it is very important that before filing your claim you obtain the assistance of a service representative or other representative who deals with veterans compensation on a regular basis.*

4. OVERPAYMENTS

What to Do When the VA Says You Owe It Money

I want my money back!
—Anon.

VA money is not like a river. Rivers flow one way. VA money is like an ocean. An ocean can come in, but it can also go out.

In other words, the VA will often determine that it has paid a veteran whom it should not have paid or that it has paid a veteran too much. Any full or partial payment the VA should not have made is called an "overpayment."

Unfortunately for veterans, VA determinations of overpayment are no rare occurrence. If they were, this book would not be devoting a whole chapter to them. In fact, even though the VA has already recovered vast sums from veterans, there remains some $1.4 billion that the VA says it has overpaid some one million vets and family members but has not yet gotten back. And the VA has filed more than 127,000 lawsuits against vets who have not repaid alleged overpayments.

So it (a VA attempt to recover a supposed overpayment) *can* happen to you. If it does, this chapter will help.

Although this chapter follows the chapter on compensation for disability and death, those areas are *not* common areas of overpayment. The most common areas are pensions and educational benefits. Another important area is VA home loans (overpayment occurs when the property is sold to a nonvet who defaults on the mortgage).

An overpayment may be mostly the fault of the veteran (as when he receives educational benefits but drops out of school). It may be mostly the fault of the VA (as when it pays for school courses it has not approved). Sometimes there is almost no fault at all.

Regardless of fault, if there is no reason to excuse the veteran from repayment, he must repay the difference between the amount he received and the amount he *should have* received.

"Overpayment" is a technical term. Technically, no overpayment exists until the VA discovers it. The VA Regional Office (VARO) that has your claims folder determines whether the VA has made an overpayment to you. The most common reason for the VARO to determine the VA has made an overpayment is that the VARO has received a report showing your income has increased. Another common reason is that the VARO learns from a school that you are taking a reduced course load.

Once the VA discovers an overpayment, it will begin the process of collecting the debt.

Generally, the VA will either demand repayment or will "offset" the debt against benefits it continues paying you. If it offsets the debt, it will reduce your monthly benefits until the amount it has saved by not paying you equals the amount it has overpaid you in the past. (The VA will do this no matter how long ago the overpayment first occurred.)

Regardless of which way the VA chooses to collect the overpayment, its notice to you is the same. It will issue a "notice of indebtedness." This notice will state the amount of the debt and the reason for the debt. It will also tell you that you can request a "waiver" of the debt; that is, you can ask to be allowed not to repay the overpayment. In addition, the notice will say that you can ask for a hearing on your waiver request and that you can appeal any decision the VA makes in your case. The notice will also explain that the VA can charge administrative costs (68 cents a month in 1985) and interest on the debt (the same interest the federal government pays on money it borrows; in 1985 the rate is 15.5 percent). And the notice will state the VA can collect the debt by "offsetting" it against current or future benefits.

As with many other important problems you may have regarding the VA, the first thing you should do after receiving a notice of indebtedness is to find an effective representative who specializes in veterans issues. Due to recent changes in VA rules on overpayment, a vet attempting to represent himself may be at a serious disadvantage.

In looking for help, among your best bets are the service representatives who work for veterans organizations such as Vietnam Veterans of America (VVA). Although veterans *generally* cannot use attorneys because of the rule limiting attorney fees in VA benefits proceedings to $10, that rule does not apply here; you therefore may want to consider employing a lawyer. Of course, you must take into account that many lawyers, regardless of their statements to the contrary, know very little about veterans law. And you must consider that service representatives do not charge for their assistance.

If you think you want to hire a lawyer, first figure out how much money you stand to lose if the VA wins the case. Then ask any lawyer you are considering hiring how much you will have to pay—in both legal fees and expenses—for the lawyer to handle the case. Weigh the lawyer charges against the amount at stake.

If you want to use a lawyer but you have little income, you may qualify for free assistance from an attorney in a Legal Aid or Legal Services offices. If you cannot find a Legal Aid or Legal Services office listed in the phone book, call your county bar association or a local attorney and ask for the name of the nearest office.

If you believe the VA is unfair in determining that an overpayment has been made, or if you simply cannot repay all of the overpayment, you (or your representative) should request a waiver of collection of the overpayment. If you are currently receiving benefits, *you have only thirty days* to reply to the VA's notice of indebtedness. If you do not respond by the deadline, the VA will begin to reduce the benefits you are receiving. To get the VA to delay collecting any overpayment until it has heard your side of the story, you must within thirty days ask for a waiver. In asking for a waiver, you must also ask for a hearing on your waiver request. If you miss the thirty-day deadline, you may still have time to request a waiver. If a waiver is granted, you can get back the money the VA withheld.

If you are not currently receiving benefits and the notice of indebtedness is dated after March 31, 1983, you have six months to request a waiver. (Veterans receiving previous notices had two years.)

The VARO official who makes the determination that an overpayment has occurred is the Chief of the Fiscal Activity. He or she may suspend (delay) or terminate VA action on debts under $20,000. A debtor hoping for a suspension will be more likely to get one if one or more of the following is true:

1. The debtor needs more time to get money to repay the debt.
2. The debtor has requested a waiver of collection.
3. The debtor has appealed the denial of a waiver request.
4. The debtor cannot currently repay the debt.
5. The VA cannot currently force the debtor to repay the debt.

If one of the following is true, the collection activity will probably be terminated once and for all:

1. The VA does not expect to ever be able to collect a substantial part of the debt.
2. The VA cannot locate the debtor.
3. The debtor is dead.
4. The amount of the debt is not large enough to justify the amount it would cost to collect it.
5. There is no legal merit to the claim that there has been an overpayment.
6. The debtor has been determined by a court to be bankrupt.

Standards for a waiver of debt are in some ways similar to but in many ways different from the standards for suspending or terminating collection activities. These standards, according to VA regulations, involve these factors:

1. The fault of the debtor
2. Balancing the fault of the debtor against the fault of the VA
3. Undue hardship to the debtor

4. Detrimental reliance (a situation in which the debtor relied on a statement by the VA and because of his reliance
   was harmed)
5. Unjust enrichment (a situation in which the VA has unfairly gained or would unfairly gain money from the
   debtor)
6. Whether denying a waiver would defeat the purpose of
   the original payment to the debtor

Still, VA rules state that even if a waiver ordinarily would
be granted, it will *not* be granted if the veteran has engaged in
fraud or misrepresentation, if he is substantially at fault, or if
he has shown a lack of good faith.

The facts just stated about suspension, termination, and
waiver give you some guidance as to the kinds of argument
you can use to favorably influence the VA in your case. Not
only can you ask for a waiver of the debt; you can also protest
the way the VA plans to get its money back.

In planning your strategy with your representative, you should
follow the instructions on the notice of indebtedness. In addition, be sure to keep a copy of all notices, letters, and other
documents the VA has sent you and a copy of everything you
send the VA. It is best to send letters and other documents via
certified mail, "return receipt requested": this way, you will
get a receipt that proves the VA received what you sent.

If you receive a notice of indebtedness, here are some actions
you should consider taking:

1. Collecting facts (especially by collecting documents) to
   support your case
2. Asking for a waiver and asking for a hearing to argue
   your case
3. Preparing an explanation to support a waiver
4. Making a compromise offer
5. Other actions, including filing for bankruptcy

COLLECTING FACTS

Find out what information the VA used to decide how much
money you owe. To get this information, go to the VA Regional
Office (VARO) and look at your claims file. Ask for an ac-

counting (a "paid and due" statement) of the money the VA says it paid you. If your case involves educational benefits, ask for any letters or other documents your school(s) sent the VA. If you cannot visit the VARO or if the VARO refuses to furnish you all the information you need, file a Freedom of Information Act request and a Privacy Act request for the needed documents. (Your service representative can help you prepare such a request and may be willing to prepare it for you.) Check the accuracy of all the information you receive.

REQUESTING A WAIVER (AND EXPLAINING YOUR REQUEST)

Remember the deadline: thirty days from the date on the VA letter of indebtedness—if you are receiving benefits and want to keep them from being reduced until you have had a hearing. Otherwise, six months.

Here is a sample request for waiver:

SAMPLE REQUEST FOR WAIVER

Name:
Claim File No.:
Address:
Date:

I request waiver of collection of the overpayment with which I have been charged. I also request a personal hearing to determine whether waiver is appropriate in my case. Principles of equity and good conscience demand that a waiver be granted because of the following reasons:

1. I did not know nor could I reasonably have known at the time I cashed my checks that I was not entitled to the full amount of the checks.

2. My age and ill health prevent me from being able to repay the debt.

3. My monthly expenses exceed my monthly income.

4. I have a family to support and cannot afford to repay the debt.

5. I thought a decrease in my overall income supported the increase in my VA benefits.

6. My large medical expenses prevent me from being able to repay the debt.

7. I did not know when I cashed my educational benefits check that I would later withdraw from school and it was not my fault I had to withdraw.

8. I thought my course of study had VA approval.

9. I did not know I was not making satisfactory progress in school.

10. I was not at "material fault" in the creation of the debt.

11. The overpayment was not caused through any fault on my part.

12. All of my dealings with the VA were conducted in good faith.

Of course you should use only those statements from the sample request that apply to your case. And you should add other arguments that apply to your case but do not appear in the sample. In your request, be sure to use the word "waiver." (If you just tell the VA that you think it is wrong, the VA will not consider your communication to be a waiver request.)

If possible, *type* the request. At the bottom, type your name, and sign above it. If you have documents you believe will help persuade the VA that you should receive a waiver, staple one copy of each document to your request. Keep a copy for yourself of everything you send the VA.

MAKING A COMPROMISE OFFER

The VA generally will not accept compromise offers of less than 50 percent of the debt.

The factors that determine whether the VA will accept a compromise offer include the factors mentioned earlier that apply in determining whether the VA will grant a waiver. In addition, the VA will consider the age and health of the debtor; his present and potential income, assets, and prospects for inheritance; VA benefits against which the debt may be "offset"; and the VA's prospects for recovering the debt by suing the debtor.

Even if you make a compromise offer and it is rejected, you may get the VA to reconsider compromise if you make a higher offer or if you submit new information that makes a stronger case for compromise. (Such information, for example, might show more clearly than before that you are unable to pay the whole amount of the debt.)

MORTGAGE DEFAULTS

The process for requesting a waiver or compromise regarding home loan (mortgage) overpayments is very similar to the process regarding other overpayments. But it is not only the veteran receiving the initial loan who can request a waiver. Also eligible are a veteran-transferee, a veteran-purchaser on a vendee account, a veteran's spouse or former spouse, and a veteran's widow or widower. Your service representative can explain the technical terms in the list just given and can help you determine whether a particular person is eligible.

It may surprise many vets to learn how a mortgage overpayment is created. It is easy to see that when a vet defaults on a mortgage and loses his home, he has some responsibility regarding the debt. What can also happen, however, is that a vet sells his house to a nonvet but fails to get a "release of liability" from the VA. If the nonvet defaults and the mortgage company forecloses on the home, the VA will come after the *vet* to recover the costs it had in reimbursing the mortgage company for the loan to the nonvet. (Vietnam Veterans of America [VVA] is very interested in mortgage overpayments and encourages vets notified of a mortgage overpayment to contact it. Write to VVA Legal Services; 2001 S St., N.W., Suite 710; Washington, DC 20009.)

For more information on VA home loans, see Chapter 11, "Housing."

SCHOOLS

If the overpayment to you has resulted from a school's failure to report excessive absences or withdrawal from school, *the school itself*, not you, may have to repay the overpayment. Generally, if the school was negligent (careless) in its failure to report, or if it intentionally failed to report, it will be required to make the repayment.

For more information on VA educational benefits, see Chapter 10, "Education and Rehabilitation."

BANKRUPTCY

Bankruptcy is a technical area. Remember, however, that not all court determinations that a vet is bankrupt will terminate the vet's debt to the VA. If you intend to declare bankruptcy, first get advice from an attorney. In your bankruptcy petition, be sure to itemize your VA debt. (And, if you have a VA home loan, also make certain your list of creditors includes not only the mortgage company handling the loan but also the VA itself.)

LAWSUITS

If the VA wants you to repay the overpayment (as opposed to wanting to offset the overpayment against benefits it is paying you) and you do not repay the VA, it will send you a "demand letter." If after the demand letter you still do not repay—and if the alleged overpayment is $200 or more—the VA will almost certainly file a lawsuit against you. If this occurs, forget any ideas you may have about representing yourself and get an attorney. Remember that the general rule against being able to pay a lawyer more than $10 does *not* apply in overpayment cases. You can therefore hire anybody you want. If you are considering hiring an attorney in private practice, ask the attorney how much the case will cost you in fees and expenses. Compare this to the amount you stand to lose if the VA wins the case. If you can't afford to hire a private attorney, contact the nearest Legal Aid or Legal Services office and ask if an attorney there can represent you (at no charge).

Statute of Limitations: A statute of limitations is a law that states that after a certain period of time a lawsuit can no longer be used regarding a certain kind of claim. The statute of limitations that applies here says that after six years following the VA's discovery of an overpayment, the VA generally cannot sue a vet to force repayment. (Still, some VA offices ignore the statute and, more than six years after discovery, ask and sue for repayment. Apparently the offices hope vets are unaware of the statute.) Whether the statute of limitations has "run" (whether the period specified in the statute has run out) in a given case is a technical question. Ask your service representative or your lawyer.

Packet: If you decide to defend against a VA lawsuit for overpayment, you or your attorney should send for the Overpayments Packet available from Vietnam Veterans of America (VVA). The packet includes extensive information on the laws, regulations, and court cases that pertain to overpayment lawsuits. Write to VVA Legal Services; 2001 S St., N.W., Suite 710; Washington, DC 20009.

5. PENSIONS

Getting What's Coming to You

It will surprise some readers to learn that pensions are a subject that may become important to any veteran.

Some veterans incorrectly believe that to receive a veterans pension they must have served in combat and must be at least sixty-five years old. In fact, however, *neither* of these factors is required for a pension. So read on: particularly if you are disabled, *you may be eligible now.*

Different veterans react in different ways to the VA pension system. Veterans pensions have been around since the Revolutionary War to reward those who have served in their country's armed forces. Still, many vets believe the pension system is just another humiliating welfare program. Some also criticize it as a system that large veterans organizations support in order to impress vets and recruit them as members. And others object to the large sums paid by the pension system: they believe this money is drained from programs for vets with service-connected disabilities. Regardless of how you feel about the pension system, it is a potential source of income for Vietnam Vets and other vets.

With very rare exceptions, three VA pensions apply to Vietnam Era Veterans: the Improved Pension, the Improved Death Pension, and the Medal of Honor Pension.

IMPROVED PENSION

The maximum Improved Pension for a single veteran is more than $5,700 per year. The exact amount of the pension for which you may qualify depends on many factors, including how many dependents you have.

For you to qualify for the Improved Pension, *all* of the following must be true:

1. *You must have served during wartime*. This does not mean you must have served in a war zone. See the explanation later in this chapter.
2. *You must be "permanently disabled."*
3. *You must be "totally disabled."* This does not mean what it says. More later.
4. *You must meet certain income guidelines*.
5. As with most benefits, *you must have been discharged under "other than dishonorable conditions"* and have served for a certain length of time.

Service During Wartime

You need not have served in a war zone or in combat. You need only have served on active duty during a war, including the Vietnam War. In the case of the Vietnam War, you must have served during the period President Ford proclaimed as the Vietnam Era, namely August 5, 1964, through May 7, 1975.

You must also have served for any of the following:

1. At least ninety days during the Vietnam Era.
2. At least ninety days that began or ended during that era.
3. A combination of at least ninety days in two or more wartime periods (for instance, the Vietnam Era and the Korean War Era)

4. *Any* period (even a day) during wartime *if* you were discharged due to a disability that occurred in the line of duty.

Permanent Disability

A disability is "permanent" when it is reasonably certain to continue throughout the veteran's life. (Remember that although disability is important in qualifying for a pension, pensions are separate from disability compensation. You may qualify for *both*. But if you do, you will be paid not by both programs but under the one that provides more money.)

Total Disability

Here, there is a big difference between what you might think the phrase means and what it actually does mean. A veteran need not be 100 percent disabled (under the VA disability rating schedule) to qualify as having a total disability.

If you are younger than 55: You must have either a single disability that can be rated at 60 percent or more or a combined disability that can be rated at 70 percent or more. If you have a combined disability, one of your individual disabilities must be ratable at 40 percent or more.

If you are 55–59: You must have a disability ratable at 60 percent or more.

If you are 60–64: You must have a disability ratable at 50 percent or more.

If you are 65 or older: The VA *presumes* you are totally disabled.

If you are younger than sixty-five, you must provide medical documentation to prove your total disability. This documentation must demonstrate that you are unemployable. If you are sixty-five or over, no documentation is needed.

EXCEPTIONS TO THE RULES:

(1) Even if your disability or disabilities are not ratable at a level high enough to fulfill the normal requirements, you may

qualify for a pension if your disability or disabilities have made you unable to be employed in a normal job.

(2) If your disability or disabilities have been caused by what the VA considers "willful misconduct" or "vicious habits," your disablity or disabilities may not qualify you for a pension. The VA considers drug or alcohol abuse to be a "vicious habit" (unless it resulted from a service-connected illness).

Remember: To qualify for the Improved Pension, it is not enough to be permanently disabled *or* totally disabled. You must be *both*.

For more information on disability ratings, see Chapter 3, "Compensation."

Income Restrictions

Each year the VA mails to those receiving VA pensions— veterans, survivors, and parents—an income questionnaire. This questionnaire must be filled out and returned. Once the VA has received the questionnaire, it will take the maximum annual Improved Pension to which the veteran (or other recipient) is entitled and will reduce it, dollar for dollar, for income received by the veteran (or other recipient), his spouse, and his dependents.

In other words, if a veteran is entitled to a maximum Improved Pension of $8,000 per year but he, his wife, and his dependent children have an income of $3,500, his pension will be reduced to $4,500.

Almost any money that comes to you and your immediate family counts as income. Included are salaries (of dependents), business and farm income, interest income, Social Security income, certain insurance proceeds, and death benefits. Among the exceptions are welfare; Supplemental Security payments; Medicaid; maintenance furnished by a relative, friend, or charity in a private home or rest home; and VA pension benefits. Certain health care expenses can be used to *reduce* income. (In other words, if your family income is $10,000 but you have qualifying health care expenses of $8,000, The VA will count your income as being only $2,000.) Sometimes it is unclear whether a particular amount of money counts as income or whether a particular expense can be deducted from income. If you disagree with the VA's determination, get advice from your service representative.

Additional Benefits

Additional Improved Pension benefits are available for the veteran who is "housebound" or "in need of regular aid and attendance."

A veteran is considered "housebound" if he has a 100 percent rating for a single permanent disability *and* has one or more additional disabilities rated at 60 percent or more; or if he has a 100 percent rating for a single permanent disability *and* is "permanently housebound." Being "permanently housebound" means that the veteran, due to his disability, is substantially confined to his house or clinical ward and that his confinement is reasonably certain to continue for the rest of his life.

A veteran is "in need of regular aid and attendance" if he is a patient in a nursing home or is so helpless or has such poor eyesight that he requires the regular aid and attendance of another person.

How to Apply

To apply for an Improved Pension, file VA Form 21–526, Veteran's Application for Compensation or Pension.

The pension is effective on the earlier of two dates:

1. The first of the month following the month in which your claim is received by the VA. (So, if your claim is approved, payments will be made *retroactive* to the first of the month following the month in which your claim was received.)
2. The first of the month following the month in which the veteran became "permanently and totally disabled." This date applies if the vet files the claim within one year of the date of disability.

If you are under sixty-five, it is best to file medical documentation with your application.

To qualify for benefits for being "housebound" or "in need of regular aid and attendance," you must first be awarded pension benefits (or at least have a decision made on your eligibility). To qualify for "housebound" or "aid and attendance" benefits, it is critical to file detailed medical documentation.

A person qualifying for "aid and attendance" is automatically considered to also be "housebound." But a person who is "housebound" does not necessarily qualify for "aid and attendance." As a result, a person qualifying for "aid and attendance" receives larger payments than a person qualifying only as "housebound." If you apply for "aid and attendance" and are rejected, you will automatically be considered for possible classification as "housebound."

Following are two forms that indicate the information it would be helpful for a physician to provide and for you to send with your application. If you want to use one of these forms, do not tear it from this book or photocopy it. Instead, type (or ask the doctor's office to type) the form on regular letter-size paper (perhaps the doctor's stationery). Ask your doctor to fill in the form. It's fine if he or she prefers to write a letter or other statement instead of completing the form. It is important, however, that his or her statement include all information requested in the form. And be sure to explain to your doctor that for you to receive a pension, the doctor must state (for instance, in item 8 of the first form) that you are *permanently and totally disabled* and that you are *unemployable*.

With pensions, as with most other veterans programs and issues, it is best to get help from a service representative who works for a veterans organization such as Vietnam Veterans of America (VVA).

Following is a copy of Form 21–526. (Don't use this one: submit your own, full-size form.)

FORM APPROVED
OMB NO. 2900-0001

VA Veterans Administration | VETERAN'S APPLICATION FOR COMPENSATION OR PENSION

IMPORTANT: Read attached General and Specific Instructions before completing this form. Type, print or write plainly.

| 1A. FIRST NAME - MIDDLE NAME - LAST NAME OF VETERAN | 1B. TELEPHONE NO. (Incl. Area Code) | (DO NOT WRITE IN THIS SPACE) VA DATE STAMP |

2. MAILING ADDRESS OF VETERAN (Number and street or rural route, city or P.O., State and ZIP Code)

3A. VETERAN'S SOC. SECURITY NO.

3B. SPOUSE'S SOC. SECURITY NO.

| 4. DATE OF BIRTH | 5. PLACE OF BIRTH | 6. SEX | 7. RAILROAD RETIREMENT NO. |

8. HAVE YOU EVER FILED A CLAIM FOR COMPENSATION FROM THE OFFICE OF WORKERS' COMPENSATION PROGRAMS?
(Formerly the U.S. Bureau of Employees' Compensation)

☐ YES ☐ NO

9A. VA FILE NUMBER

C—

9B. HAVE YOU PREVIOUSLY FILED A CLAIM FOR ANY BENEFIT WITH THE VETERANS ADMINISTRATION?

☐ NONE
☐ HOSPITALIZATION OR MEDICAL CARE
☐ WAIVER OF NSLI PREMIUMS
☐ DISABILITY COMPENSATION OR PENSION
☐ VOCATIONAL REHABILITATION (Chapter 31)
☐ VETERANS EDUCATIONAL ASSISTANCE (Chapter 34 or 34)
☐ WAR ORPHANS OR DEPENDENTS EDUCATIONAL ASSIST. (Chap. 35)
☐ DENTAL OR OUTPATIENT TREATMENT
☐ OTHER (Specify)

9C. VA OFFICE HAVING YOUR RECORDS (If known)

SERVICE INFORMATION

NOTE: Enter complete information for each period of active duty including Reservist or National Guard Status. Attach Form DD 214 or other separation papers for all periods of active duty to expedite processing of your claim. If you do NOT have your DD 214 or other separation papers check (√) here ☐

10A. ENTERED ACTIVE SERVICE		10B. SERVICE NO.	10C. SEPARATED FROM ACTIVE SERVICE		10D. GRADE, RANK OR RATING, ORGANIZATION OR BRANCH OF SERVICE
DATE	PLACE		DATE	PLACE	

10E. HAVE YOU EVER BEEN A PRISONER OF WAR?

☐ YES   ☐ NO   *(If "Yes," complete Items 10F and 10G)*

10F. NAME OF COUNTRY

10G. DATES OF CONFINEMENT

11. IF YOU SERVED UNDER ANOTHER NAME, GIVE NAME AND PERIOD DURING WHICH YOU SERVED AND SERVICE NO.

12. IF RESERVIST OR NATIONAL GUARDSMAN, GIVE BRANCH OF SERVICE AND PERIOD OF ACTIVE OR INACTIVE TRAINING DUTY DURING WHICH DISABILITY OCCURRED

13A. IF YOU ARE NOW A MEMBER OF THE RESERVE FORCES OR NATIONAL GUARD GIVE THE BRANCH OF SERVICE

13B. RESERVE STATUS

☐ ACTIVE   ☐ INACTIVE   ☐ RESERVE OBLIGATION

13C. RESERVE OR NATIONAL GUARD UNIT ADDRESS

14A. ARE YOU NOW RECEIVING OR WILL YOU RECEIVE RETIREMENT OR RETAINER PAY FROM THE ARMED FORCES?

☐ YES   ☐ NO   *(If "Yes," complete Item 14B, 14C, and 14D)*

14B. BRANCH OF SERVICE

14C. MONTHLY AMOUNT

$

14D. RETIRED STATUS

☐ PERMANENT   ☐ TEMPORARY DISABILITY RETIRED LIST

15A. HAVE YOU EVER APPLIED FOR OR RECEIVED DISABILITY SEVERANCE PAY FROM THE ARMED FORCES?

☐ YES   ☐ NO   *(If "Yes," complete Item 15B)*

15B. AMOUNT

$

16A. HAVE YOU RECEIVED LUMP SUM READJUSTMENT PAY FROM THE ARMED FORCES?

☐ YES   ☐ NO   *(If "Yes," complete Item 16B)*

16B. AMOUNT

$

MARITAL AND DEPENDENCY INFORMATION

17A. MARITAL STATUS *(Check one)*

☐ MARRIED   ☐ WIDOWED   ☐ DIVORCED   ☐ NEVER MARRIED *(If to do not complete Items 17B through 21D)*

17B. SPOUSE'S BIRTHDATE

17C. NUMBER OF TIMES YOU HAVE BEEN MARRIED

17D. NUMBER OF TIMES YOUR PRESENT SPOUSE HAS BEEN MARRIED

17E. IS YOUR SPOUSE ALSO A VETERAN?

☐ YES   ☐ NO *(If "Yes," complete Item 17F.) (If known)*

17F. SPOUSE'S VA FILE NO

C–

18A. DO YOU LIVE TOGETHER?

☐ YES   ☐ NO   *(If "No," complete Items 18B through 18D)*

18B. REASON FOR SEPARATION

18C. PRESENT ADDRESS OF SPOUSE

18D. AMOUNT YOU CONTRIBUTE TO YOUR SPOUSE'S SUPPORT MONTHLY

$

19. CHECK (x) WHETHER YOUR CURRENT MARRIAGE WAS PERFORMED BY

☐ CLERGYMAN OR AUTHORIZED PUBLIC OFFICIAL   ☐ OTHER *(Explain)*

VA FORM 21-526
SEP 1984

SUPERSEDES VA FORM 21-526, JUL. 1982.
WHICH WILL NOT BE USED

NOTE: Furnish the following information about each of your marriages. A certified copy of the public or church record of your CURRENT marriage is required.

20A. DATE AND PLACE OF MARRIAGE	20B. TO WHOM MARRIED	20C. TERMINATED (Death, Divorce)	20D. DATE AND PLACE TERMINATED

FURNISH THE FOLLOWING INFORMATION ABOUT EACH PREVIOUS MARRIAGE OF YOUR PRESENT SPOUSE

21A. DATE AND PLACE OF MARRIAGE	21B. TO WHOM MARRIED	21C. TERMINATED (Death, Divorce)	21D. DATE AND PLACE TERMINATED

IDENTIFICATION OF CHILDREN AND INFORMATION RELATIVE TO CUSTODY

NOTE: Furnish the following information for each of your unmarried children. A certified copy of the public or church record of birth or court record of adoption is required.

22A. NAME OF CHILD (First, middle initial, last)	22B. DATE OF BIRTH (Month, day, year)	22C. SOCIAL SECURITY NUMBER OF CHILD	22D. CHECK EACH APPLICABLE CATEGORY				
			MARRIED PREVIOUSLY	STEPCHILD OR ADOPTED	ILLEGI-TIMATE	OVER 18 ATTENDING SCHOOL	SERIOUSLY DISABLED

22E. NAME(S) OF ANY CHILD(REN) NOT IN YOUR CUSTODY	22F. NAME AND ADDRESS OF PERSON HAVING CUSTODY	22G. MONTHLY AMOUNT YOU CONTRIBUTE TO CHILD'S SUPPORT
		$

23A. IS YOUR FATHER DEPENDENT UPON YOU FOR SUPPORT?

☐ YES ☐ NO (If "Yes," complete 23B)

23B. NAME AND ADDRESS OF DEPENDENT FATHER

23C. IS YOUR MOTHER DEPENDENT UPON YOU FOR SUPPORT?

☐ YES ☐ NO (If "Yes," complete 23D)

23D. NAME AND ADDRESS OF DEPENDENT MOTHER

23E. NAME AND ADDRESS OF NEAREST RELATIVE

23F. RELATIONSHIP OF NEAREST RELATIVE

NATURE AND HISTORY OF DISABILITIES

24. NATURE OF SICKNESS, DISEASE OR INJURIES FOR WHICH THIS CLAIM IS MADE AND DATE EACH BEGAN

25A. ARE YOU NOW OR HAVE YOU BEEN HOSPITALIZED OR FURNISHED DOMICILIARY CARE WITHIN THE PAST 3 MONTHS?

☐ YES ☐ NO (If "Yes," complete 25B and 25C)

25B. DATES OF HOSPITALIZATION OR DOMICILIARY CARE

25C. NAME AND ADDRESS OF INSTITUTION

NOTE Items 26, 27, and 28 need NOT be completed unless you are now claiming compensation for a disability incurred in service.

IF YOU RECEIVED ANY TREATMENT WHILE IN SERVICE, COMPLETE THE FOLLOWING INFORMATION

26A. NATURE OF SICKNESS, DISEASE OR INJURY	26B. DATES OF TREATMENT	26C. NAME, NUMBER OR LOCATION OF HOSPITAL, FIRST AID STATION, DRESSING STATION OR INFIRMARY	26D. ORGANIZATION AT TIME SICKNESS, DISEASE OR INJURY WAS INCURRED

LIST CIVILIAN PHYSICIANS AND HOSPITALS WHERE YOU WERE TREATED FOR ANY SICKNESS, INJURY OR DISEASE SHOWN IN ITEM 26A, BEFORE, DURING OR SINCE YOUR SERVICE, AND ANY MILITARY HOSPITALS SINCE YOUR LAST DISCHARGE

27A. NAME	27B. PRESENT ADDRESS	27C. DISABILITY	27D. DATE

LIST PERSONS OTHER THAN PHYSICIANS WHO KNOW ANY FACTS ABOUT ANY SICKNESS, DISEASE OR INJURY SHOWN IN ITEM 26A, WHICH YOU HAD BEFORE, DURING OR SINCE YOUR SERVICE

28A. NAME	28B. PRESENT ADDRESS	28C. DISABILITY	28D. DATE

IF YOU CLAIM TO BE TOTALLY DISABLED (Complete Items 29A through 32E)

29A. ARE YOU NOW EMPLOYED?	29B. IF YOU WERE SELF-EMPLOYED BEFORE BECOMING TOTALLY DISABLED, WHAT PART OF THE WORK DID YOU DO?

29C. DATE YOU LAST WORKED	29D. IF YOU ARE STILL SELF-EMPLOYED WHAT PART OF THE WORK DO YOU DO NOW?

30A. EDUCATION (Circle highest year completed)

1   2   3   4   5   6   7   8 | 1   2   3   4 | 1   2   3   4
(GRADE SCHOOL)   (HIGH SCHOOL)   (COLLEGE)

30B. NATURE OF AND TIME SPENT IN OTHER EDUCATION AND TRAINING

LIST ALL YOUR EMPLOYMENT, INCLUDING SELF-EMPLOYMENT, FOR ONE YEAR BEFORE YOU BECAME TOTALLY DISABLED

31A. NAME AND ADDRESS OF EMPLOYER	31B. KIND OF WORK	31C. MONTHS WORKED	31D. TIME LOST FROM ILLNESS	31E. TOTAL EARNINGS

LIST ALL YOUR EMPLOYMENT, INCLUDING SELF-EMPLOYMENT, SINCE YOU BECAME TOTALLY DISABLED

32A. NAME AND ADDRESS OF EMPLOYER	32B. KIND OF WORK	32C. MONTHS WORKED	32D. TIME LOST FROM ILLNESS	32E. TOTAL EARNINGS

NET WORTH OF VETERANS AND DEPENDENTS *(See attached Instructions for Items 33A to 33E inclusive)*

NOTE: Items 33A through 33E should be completed ONLY if you are applying for non-service connected pension.

ITEM NO.	SOURCE	AMOUNTS		
		VETERAN	SPOUSE	NAME OF CHILD(REN)
33A.	STOCKS, BONDS, BANK DEPOSITS	$	$	$
33B.	REAL ESTATE *(Do not include residence)*			
33C.	OTHER PROPERTY			
33D.	TOTAL DEBTS			
33E.	NET WORTH	$	$	$

INCOME RECEIVED AND EXPECTED FROM ALL SOURCES

NOTE: Items 34A through 39B should be completed ONLY if you are applying for non-service-connected pension.

34A. HAVE YOU OR YOUR SPOUSE APPLIED FOR OR ARE YOU RECEIVING OR ENTITLED TO RECEIVE ANY BENEFITS FROM THE SOCIAL SECURITY ADMINISTRATION (OTHER THAN SSI) OR RAILROAD RETIREMENT BOARD?	34B. MONTHLY AMOUNT (Include Medicare Deduction)	34C. BEGINNING DATE	34D. DATE YOU EXPECT BENEFITS TO BEGIN
☐ YES ☐ NO (If "Yes," complete Items 34B through 34F as applicable)	VETERAN $		
	SPOUSE $		
	34E. WILL YOU OR YOUR SPOUSE APPLY FOR EITHER BENEFIT DURING THE NEXT 12 MONTHS?	34F. DATE OF INTENTION TO APPLY	
	VETERAN ☐ YES ☐ NO	VETERAN	SPOUSE

35A. HAVE YOU OR YOUR SPOUSE APPLIED FOR OR ARE YOU RECEIVING OR ENTITLED TO RECEIVE ANNUITY OR RETIREMENT BENEFITS OR ENDOWMENT INSURANCE FROM ANY OTHER SOURCE?

☐ YES ☐ NO   (If "Yes," complete Items 35B through 35E, as applicable)

35B. MONTHLY AMOUNT	35C. BEGINNING DATE	35D. DATE OF INTENTION TO APPLY	35E. SOURCE OF BENEFIT
VETERAN $			
SPOUSE $			

SOURCE OF VETERAN AND DEPENDENTS INCOME		AMOUNT OF INCOME		
		VETERAN	SPOUSE	NAME OF CHILD/REN
36. AMOUNT RECEIVED FROM JAN. 1 TO THE DATE YOU SIGN THIS STATEMENT	A. EARNINGS	$	$	$
	B. SOCIAL SECURITY (GREEN CHECK)			
	C. OTHER ANNUITIES AND RETIREMENTS			
	D. DIVIDENDS AND INTEREST, ETC.			
	E. SUPPLEMENTAL SECURITY INCOME (GOLD CHECK)			
	F. ALL OTHER INCOME			
37. AMOUNT EXPECTED FROM DATE YOU SIGN THIS	A. EARNINGS	$	$	$
	B. SOCIAL SECURITY (GREEN CHECK)			
	C. OTHER ANNUITIES AND RETIREMENTS			

(Specify source for Items 36F, 37F and 38F "ALL OTHER INCOME" in Item 40, "REMARKS")

STATEMENT TO END OF THIS CALENDAR YEAR	D. DIVIDENDS AND INTEREST, ETC.		
	E. SUPPLEMENTAL SECURITY INCOME (GOLD CHECK)		
	F. ALL OTHER INCOME		
38. AMOUNT EXPECTED FOR THE NEXT CALENDAR YEAR	A. EARNINGS		
	B. SOCIAL SECURITY (GREEN CHECK)		
	C. OTHER ANNUITIES AND RETIREMENTS		
	D. DIVIDENDS AND INTEREST, ETC.		
	E. SUPPLEMENTAL SECURITY INCOME (GOLD CHECK)		
	F. ALL OTHER INCOME		

39A. GROSS AMOUNT OF FINAL PAY RECEIVED

$

39B. DATE FINAL PAY WAS RECEIVED

40. REMARKS *(Identify your statements by their applicable item number. If additional space is required, attach separate sheet and identify your statements by their item numbers)*

NOTE: Filing of this application constitutes a waiver of military retired pay in the amount of any VA compensation to which you may be entitled. See instructions for Items 14A and 14 D inclusive, Retired Pay.

CERTIFICATION AND AUTHORIZATION FOR RELEASE OF INFORMATION - I certify that the foregoing statements are true and complete to the best of my knowledge and belief. I CONSENT that any physician, surgeon, dentist or hospital that has treated or examined me for any purpose; or that I have consulted professionally, may furnish to the VETERANS ADMINISTRATION any information about myself, and I waive any privilege which renders such information confidential

41. DATE SIGNED	42. SIGNATURE OF CLAIMANT SIGN HERE

WITNESSES TO SIGNATURES OF CLAIMANT IF MADE BY "X" MARK

NOTE: Signature made by mark must be witnessed by two persons to whom the person making the statement is personally known, and the signatures and addresses of such witnesses must be shown.

43A. SIGNATURE OF WITNESS	44A. SIGNATURE OF WITNESS
43B. ADDRESS OF WITNESS	44B. ADDRESS OF WITNESS

PENALTY - The law provides severe penalties which include fine or imprisonment, or both, for the willful submission of any statement or evidence of a material fact, knowing it to be false, or for the fraudulent acceptance of any payment to which you are not entitled.

**MEDICAL STATEMENT
IN SUPPORT OF PENSION**

DATE OF EXAMINATION: _____
VA FILE NUMBER: _____
SOCIAL SECURITY NUMBER: _____

1. VETERAN'S NAME: _____
                    Last   First   Middle

2. ADDRESS: _____
   _____

3. COMPLETE DIAGNOSIS: _____
   _____
   _____

4. SYMPTOMS (Include brief history): _____
   _____

5. PHYSICAL AND MENTAL FINDINGS: _____
   _____

6. WEIGHT _____ HEIGHT: _____ BLOOD PRESSURE: _____
   AGE: _____

7. EYES (Corrected Visual Acuity): R _____ L _____

   HEARING: R _____ L _____

8. REMARKS (Employability): _____
   _____

9. IF POSSIBLE, PLEASE ATTACH COPIES OF OFFICE OR
   HOSPITAL RECORDS CONCERNING THE VETERAN'S
   RECENT MEDICAL HISTORY.

   I CERTIFY THAT THE ABOVE IS TRUE AND CORRECT.

   PHYSICIAN'S NAME &
       ADDRESS
   (Please Type or Print)

   _____   _____
   _____   Examining Physician's Signature
   _____

MEDICAL STATEMENT FOR CONSIDERATION FOR AID AND ATTENDANCE (OR HOUSEBOUND BENEFITS) FOR CLAIMANT

(Please circle the appropriate answer and objectively explain each answer.)

DATE OF EXAMINATION: _____

VA FILE NUMBER: _____

SOCIAL SECURITY NUMBER: _____

VETERAN'S NAME: _____

              Last   First   Middle

CLAIMANT'S NAME _____

              Last   First   Middle

1. COMPLETE DIAGNOSIS: _____
_____
_____

2. IS THE CLAIMANT ABLE TO WALK UNAIDED?   YES NO
   EXPLANATION: _____
   _____

3. IS THE CLAIMANT ABLE TO FEED HIMSELF OR   YES NO
   HERSELF?
   EXPLANATION: _____
   _____

4. IS THE CLAIMANT ABLE TO BATHE AND KEEP   YES NO
   HIMSELF OR HERSELF CLEAN IN OTHER WAYS?
   EXPLANATION: _____
   _____

5. IS THE CLAIMANT ABLE TO CARE FOR THE   YES NO
   NEEDS OF NATURE?
   EXPLANATION: _____
   _____

6. IS THE CLAIMANT CONFINED TO BED?   YES NO
   EXPLANATION: _____
   _____

7. IS THE CLAIMANT ABLE TO SIT UP?   YES NO
   EXPLANATION: _____
   _____

8. IS THE CLAIMANT BLIND? CORRECTED VISION: YES NO
   L ___ R ___
   EXPLANATION: _____
   _____

9. IS THE CLAIMANT ABLE TO TRAVEL?   YES NO
    EXPLANATION: _____
    _____

10. CAN THE CLAIMANT LEAVE HOME WITHOUT   YES NO
    ASSISTANCE? (If yes, how far can he/she go [1 block,
    ½ mile, etc.])?
    EXPLANATION: _____
    _____

11. DOES THE CLAIMANT REQUIRE NURSING HOME YES NO
    CARE?
    EXPLANATION: _____
    _____

12. IN YOUR OPINION, ARE THERE OTHER PERTINENT
    FACTS WHICH WOULD SHOW THE CLAIMANT'S NEED
    FOR AID AND ATTENDANCE?
    EXPLANATION: _____
    _____

13. IF POSSIBLE, PLEASE ATTACH COPIES OF OFFICE OR
    HOSPITAL RECORDS CONCERNING THE CLAIMANT'S
    RECENT MEDICAL HISTORY.

    I CERTIFY THAT THE ABOVE IS TRUE AND CORRECT.

    PHYSICIAN'S NAME &
        ADDRESS
     (Please Type or Print)

    _____   _____
    _____   Examining Physician's Signature
    _____

IMPROVED DEATH PENSION

This pension is for the surviving spouses and dependent children of veterans who served during wartime but whose death was *not* related to their military service. If the death *was* related to military service, the survivors are entitled not to a death pension but to death benefits for dependents. For a discussion of these benefits, see Chapter 3, "Compensation."

A survivor is eligible for a death pension if the deceased veteran served long enough during wartime and had an appropriate discharge (see earlier in this chapter). A survivor must also meet certain income guidelines.

A "surviving spouse" must have been the lawful spouse of the veteran at the time of his death and must have lived with him continuously from the date of marriage to the date of death. (There are certain exceptions to this rule, such as where a separation was the fault of the veteran.) Once a surviving spouse remarries, she loses her pension eligibility. (She regains this eligibility if her later marriage is ended by death, divorce, or annulment.)

To be eligible for a pension as a "child of a veteran," a person must be dependent on the veteran *and* must be one of the following:

1. An unmarried person who is a legitimate child of a veteran
2. A person legally adopted before age 18 by a veteran
3. A person who before 18 became the stepchild of a veteran and who is a member of the veteran's household or was a member of that household when the veteran died
4. A person under 18 who is the illegitimate child of a veteran
5. A legitimate or illegitimate child or stepchild of a veteran, if the child before becoming 18 became permanently unable to support himself or herself
6. A legitimate or illegitimate child or stepchild of a veteran, if the child is between 18 and 23 and is pursuing a course of instruction at a college or school approved by the VA

If the surviving spouse or child is disabled, she or he may be eligible for benefits for the "housebound" and for those "in need of regular aid and attendance." To qualify, the survivor must fulfill the same requirements the veteran would have had to fulfill (see earlier in this chapter).

As with the Improved Pension for veterans themselves, the Improved Death Pension for survivors will be reduced dollar-for-dollar by family income (see earlier in this chapter).

To receive a death pension, a survivor must file VA Form 21–534, Application for Dependency and Indemnity Compensation or Death Pension by a Surviving Spouse or Child. (Generally, one survivor may file a form for all survivors.)

MEDAL OF HONOR PENSION

Veterans who have received a Medal of Honor are entitled to a special pension of $200 per month. This pension is available in addition to any other pension to which the veteran may be entitled and is not counted as income for the purposes of determining the amount of the VA pension for which the veteran may be eligible.

To obtain a Medal of Honor pension, write a letter to the Secretary of the service of which you were a member, asking that your name be entered on the Medal of Honor Roll and that you be awarded a Medal of Honor pension.

Army veterans should write to the Secretary of the Army, The Pentagon, Washington, DC 20310.

Navy and Marine vets should write to the Secretary of the Navy, The Pentagon, Washington, DC 20350.

If you are an Air Force veteran, write to the Secretary of the Air Force, Washington, DC 20330.

PENSION RATES

Following is a chart of VA pension rates in effect in early 1985. By the time you read this, rates may be slightly higher. The chart gives the *annual* amount to which each veteran or survivor is entitled. Pension payments, however, are made *monthly*.

IMPROVED PENSION

Dependent Codes	Veteran P/T	Veteran P/T & H/B	Veteran P/T & A/A	TWO VETERANS MARRIED TO ONE ANOTHER					
				Both P/T	Both P/T One H/B	Both H/B	Both P/T One A/A	One A/A Other H/B	Both A/A
00 Veteran	$5,709	$6,977	$9,132						
10/81 V-W or V-1C	$7,478	$8,747	$10,902	$7,478	$8,747	$10,017	$10,902	$12,170	$14,324
11/82 V-W-1C or V-2C	$8,446	$9,715	$11,876	$8,446	$9,715	$10,985	$11,870	$13,138	$15,292
12/83 V-W-2C or V-3C	$9,414	$10,683	$12,838	$9,414	$10,683	$11,953	$12,838	$14,106	$16,260
for each additional child—Add	$968	$968	$968	$968	$968	$968	$968	$968	$968

IMPROVED DEATH PENSION

Dependent Codes	Surviving Spouse	Surviving Spouse & H/B	Surviving Spouse & A/A
10 Widow/er	$3,825	$4,677	$6,119
11 W-1C	$5,011	$5,860	$7,303
12 W-2C	$5,979	$6,828	$8,271
13 W-3C	$6,947	$7,796	$9,239
For each additional child add	$968	$968	$968

ABBREVIATIONS:

V = veteran
W = wife
C = child

P/T = permanent and total
H/B = housebound
A/A = aid and attendance

6. MEDICAL SERVICES

What's Available and How to Qualify

If you need VA medical care, you should watch TV.

TV won't cure your problems, but it will teach you a lot about the system in which you are about to become involved. Not just any TV show will teach you this. Only one will. It's called *AfterMASH*.

AfterMASH—now seen only in reruns or on private video-tapes—takes place in a VA hospital just after the Korean War (or, as the government likes to call it, the Korean Conflict). Though the characters and stories are fictional, the general portrayal of VA hospital care—in the 1980s as well as the 1950s—is stunningly accurate. The message you learn from *AfterMASH* and the message this book wants to communicate is that most anything can and will happen in a VA hospital. You might be admitted promptly, diagnosed accurately, and treated effectively. Then again, you might not. You might be assisted by physicians and staff of great ability, compassion, and integrity. Then again, you might not.

The official name of a VA hospital is "VA Medical Center." This is often abbreviated to "VAMC," which has come to be pronounced "VEE-mac" (or, in the South, "VAM-see"). The

VAMCs make up the largest hospital system in the world. Each VAMC has great latitude to operate as it thinks best.

Veterans groups and studies by medical groups often harshly criticize the quality, speed, and availability of care in VA hospitals. Critics often focus on the facts that VAMCs use a medical census to establish budgets and that they heavily rely on medical schools. Using the medical census—a count of inpatients and outpatients—encourages hospital stays that are longer than those in private hospitals. Arrangements with medical schools give great authority to medical school committees.

Committee power means much of the medical work in VAMCs is done not by doctors but by medical students. Veterans cannot refuse to be treated by students. Also, many veterans feel like guinea pigs because students often seem to be using their patients for learning purposes. (On the other hand, the students' supervisors—their professors—are often experts in their fields.)

Veterans have other complaints about care in VAMCs. One is that generally when they ask for a second opinion—an examination and diagnosis by a doctor other than the original one—they are refused.

Vietnam Veterans of America (VVA) believes that vets eligible for VA medical care should be able to select a "provider of choice." Under the VVA proposal, each veteran could use a "payment voucher"—a federal government promise of payment—to shop around and select the doctor and hospital he prefers. Under this "freedom of choice" system, VAMCs would compete with private physicians and private facilities for funds allocated for veterans. The result of the system would be that veterans would get better care and VA hospitals would be forced to improve.

But the "freedom of choice" system does not yet exist. So this book must deal with the VA medical system as it stands.

In every area covered by this book, the veteran must be vigilant: he must be careful to get everything that's coming to him and must be careful to avoid harm at the hands of people who may act unfairly or incompetently. Nowhere else is vigilance as important as it is in the area of VA medical services. In an area such as pensions or disability compensation, if something goes wrong you might lose some money. In medical care, however, if something goes wrong you might lose your health—or your life.

Many kinds of care are available to veterans. First, this chapter will explain the types of care and the factors that determine whether you are eligible for each. Then, the chapter will give you some advice on what to do if something goes wrong.

Watch an episode of *AfterMASH*, then read on.

GENERAL

The VA medical system is huge. In the fall of 1982, there were 172 full-scale VA hospitals, 99 VA nursing homes, 16 VA domiciliary (resident) care facilities, 150 VA "mental hygiene" clinics, 60 VA day treatment centers, and 40 VA day hospitals.

In the VA fiscal year ending September 30, 1982, the VA treated 1,401,018 inpatients and 18,509,552 outpatients; the cost of care of these patients totalled $7.2 billion.

Because the system is so large and because many veterans believe they should be entitled to VA medical care (which is free), many veterans believe the VA is required to treat any veteran for any medical problem. This is by no means true.

A veteran will be treated by the VA only if the VA has determined he is eligible for care, entitled to care, and in need of care and—if his condition is not service-connected—the VA has room for him in an appropriate facility.

There are so many rules that may stand in the way of the veteran getting the kind of care he needs that medical services, like so many other subjects, is an area in which most veterans will benefit if they get advice from a service representative who works for a veterans organization such as Vietnam Veterans of America (VVA).

This chapter, however, will explain the general rules. Before doing so, it will first point out that veterans generally cannot, within the VA, appeal medical decisions on issues such as which treatment or facility is appropriate in a given case. See Chapter 16, "Claims and Appeals."

HOSPITALIZATION

Qualifying for Care

If VA facilities have room for you, you can generally get admitted for hospital care if one or more of the following is true:

1. You have a service-connected disability.
2. You have a disability not connected to military service but you cannot pay for hospital care.
3. You were discharged for a disability that occurred or was made worse in the line of duty (even if the VA has not yet determined you have a service-connected disability).
4. You are receiving VA disability compensation (or you are entitled to it but aren't getting it because you are getting military retirement pay instead).
5. You are a former POW.
6. You were exposed to herbicides or defoliants (such as Agent Orange) in Vietnam or were exposed to radiation from the explosion of an atomic bomb *and* your illness is clearly not due to a cause other than exposure.
7. You have a disability not connected to military service but you are 65 or older. (Veterans fitting this description, regardless of their ability to pay, will be admitted, provided space is available.)

Because facilities are limited, the VA has come up with a list of twelve categories of patients. The higher you rank on this list, the more likely you will be to be admitted to a VAMC. Here are the five highest categories:

1. Emergency cases: cases where delay could result in death or serious damage.
2. Patients already on a VA hospital's rolls (patients who have been treated by the hospital for a condition from which they still suffer) who are not now occupying a bed but who need to be readmitted to the hospital.
3. Priority Group I:
   a. Veterans who need treatment for service-connected

disabilities or "adjunct" disabilities ("adjunct" disabilities are disabilities caused or made worse by a
service-connected disability and disabilities that have
made a service-connected disability worse).
  b. Active duty personnel who are retiring from the service.
  c. Veterans who need vocational rehabilitation or are
involved in vocational rehabilitation, but who need
treatment in order to begin or continue rehabilitation.
(Subcategory "a" is of higher priority than "b," which is
higher than "c.")
4. Priority Group II:
  a. People for whom authorized VA officials have requested observation and/or examination.
  b. Veterans who are receiving VA benefits but are patients
at a hospital not operated by the VA or another federal
agency.
5. Priority Group III:
  a. Certain veterans who are receiving outpatient care at
a VA hospital, nursing home, or domiciliary facility
and who request a transfer to a VAMC for medical
reasons.
  b. Veterans who are in a VAMC but not the one nearest
the one to which they originally applied for admission.
  c. Veterans who request a transfer from one VAMC to
another at their own expense.

The other seven categories include other veterans (especially
those 65 or older who do not fit the higher categories) and the
survivors and dependents of certain veterans.
Even with all twelve categories, there are *further* classifi-
cations: within each category, patients whose cases doctors have
decided are "urgent" get a bed before patients whose cases have
been labeled "routine."

Services Available

The bad news is that VA care is often second-rate and is available only to vets who qualify for it, and then only if space is
available. The good news is that the VA offers very extensive
services. It provides not just free medical services but also

payment for travel and incidental expenses. Its offerings include medical exams, treatment, rehabilitation, surgery, dentistry, optometry, podiatry, wheelchairs, artificial limbs, trusses and similar appliances, special clothing needed due to prosthetic devices, and other services and supplies the VA determines to be reasonable and necessary.

The veteran may, under certain circumstances, even be admitted (at VA expense) to a hospital other than a VA facility. He may be admitted to a hospital operated by the Department of Defense or the Public Health Service, or to most any public or private hospital.

Admission to a hospital other than a VA or other federal hospital, however, is very much the exception rather than the rule. The VA will approve admission to a private or public hospital only if a VA or other federal facility is not "feasibly" available. Unless your case is an emergency, you must have prior VA authorization before being admitted at VA expense to a private or public hospital. And, generally speaking, if you live in a state with a VA hospital that provides the kind of care you need and your case is not an emergency, the VA will refuse to have you admitted to a private or public facility.

Special Compensation

If you have a service-connected disability that requires hospital treatment for more than twenty-one days, you will receive a total disability rating (a rating of 100 percent disability). This is true even if your normal disability rating is lower. And even if you were not originally hospitalized for a service-connected disability, you will receive the 100 percent rating if during your hospitalization you receive treatment for a service-connected disability and your treatment continues for more than twenty-one days. You will keep the increased rating only temporarily.

Even if you have never received a 100 percent rating before getting one under the "Twenty-One-Day Rule," you may, after hospitalization, qualify for such a rating.

Even if the Twenty-One-Day Rule does not apply to you, you may be granted a temporary 100 percent rating after you have been discharged from the hospital. This is most likely if your hospital treatment for a service-connected disability involved surgery with serious aftereffects that require you to undergo a period of convalescence.

For more information on disability compensation in connection with hospitalization, check with your service representative. For more information on disability compensation in general, check with your service rep and see Chapter 3, "Compensation."

OUTPATIENT CARE

VA medical care is by no means limited to care to patients admitted to VA or other hospitals. You may also be entitled to *outpatient care*. This is care you receive at a hospital or other facility without being *admitted* to that facility.

In most cases, you will be able to obtain free outpatient care *only if it is rendered at a VA facility*. But if you can get the VA to authorize it, you can be treated most anywhere and have the VA pay for it: a local hospital, a doctor's office, or another medical facility. The VA authorization must come *before* you receive treatment outside the VA system.

If you are eligible for, or are receiving, an allowance (an additional pension allowance) for "aid and attendance" or because you are "housebound," the VA can provide medicines prescribed by a doctor. The prescribing physician need not be a VA physician. Take your prescription to the nearest VA facility that has a pharmacy. If you are in the "aid and attendance" or "housebound" category, you also may be examined by a private optometrist, but if you receive a prescription for glasses, it must be filled at a VA facility.

As with hospitalization, there are rules that determine who is eligible for outpatient care and who has the greatest priority for treatment.

According to these rules, outpatient medical services may be provided for

1. A service-connected disability
2. A disability for which a veteran was separated from service

3. Veterans entitled to vocational rehabilitation who need medical services to allow them to enter or continue in a vocational rehabilitation program

4. Care before hospital admission for veterans eligible for hospitalization, if the pre-hospital care is to prepare them for admission or is used to avoid the use of a bed

5. Care after hospitalization for veterans eligible for hospital care, if the post-hospital care is to complete treatment begun during hospitalization or in connection with hospitalization

6. For adjunct (related additional) treatment for a condition that, if untreated, would worsen a service-connected disability

7. Veterans with a service-connected disability rated at 50 percent or more

8. Veterans who are "housebound" or "in need of aid and attendance"

9. Home health services necessary for "effective and economical treatment"

The priority given to patients for outpatient care follows. Unless there are compelling medical reasons not to follow this list, veterans higher on the list will be provided with outpatient care before those who are lower.

1. A veteran with a service-connected disability. Also, a veteran being examined to determine whether he has a service-connected disability or to determine the rating of a disability

2. A former POW. Also, a veteran being treated for a condition that may have resulted from exposure to Agent Orange, a toxic substance, or radiation from an atomic bomb

3. A veteran who is "housebound" or "in need of aid and attendance"

DENTAL CARE

Rules, rules, rules. Here are some more. The VA has one set
of rules for veterans needing a dental *exam* and a separate set
of rules for those who need dental *treatment*. If you need to
see a dentist—if you have cavities or need a tooth pulled or a
bridge made or have problems with your bite or your jaw—
here are some rules you must understand.

You can get dental services at the VA facility nearest your
home. If, however, the nearest VA hospital is far away or does
not offer the services you need, you may be able to see a
private dentist and have the VA pay for it.

Dental Exams

The VA may authorize a dental exam for certain veterans. These
include those with a service-connected dental disability and
those with a *medical* disability that is being made worse by a
dental condition. For other categories that qualify, check with
your service representative.

Outpatient Dental Treatment

The VA may approve dental treatment for vets who have service-
connected disabilities, who hold disability discharges, or who
are entitled to vocational rehabilitation.

Remember, regardless of how serious your dental problem
is, the VA requires that you get an exam before you get treatment.

There are, believe it or not, *eleven* categories of veterans
who may be eligible for dental treatment. Most of these categories deal with dental or medical disabilities. For details, ask
your service rep.

If you have facial or head injuries, your related dental problems may justify a disability rating and compensation for your
disability. Regarding compensation in general, see Chapter 3,
"Compensation."

HOW TO APPLY FOR HOSPITAL OR DENTAL CARE

To apply for hospital inpatient or outpatient care or to apply for a dental examination or dental treatment, the same form must be filled out and submitted to the nearest VAMC. This is VA Form 10–10, Application for Medical Benefits. It is best to also file a veteran's DD Form 214, Report of Separation (your separation papers) or the equivalent.

If the military has determined that your injury occurred or was made worse in the "line of duty" and is therefore service-connected, the VA must accept the military's decision—even if the VA has not already determined that your injury is service-connected. And even if the military says your injury did not occur in the line of duty, the VA is free to make its own decision that the injury *is* service-connected.

Even if you did not receive a disability discharge, you can be approved for VA care if your records show that at the time of discharge you were being treated for a disability.

If you have applied for hospital care and it is urgent that you receive it, the VA can tentatively approve you for care. This is true even if a determination has not yet been made on an issue such as whether your problem is service-connected. Tentative eligibility (eligibility that is subject to change) can also be approved for vets separated during the past six months. VA rules require that tentative eligibility be approved if "eligibility for care probably will be established."

Certain vets seeking care for disabilities that are *not* service-connected will be required to swear or demonstrate they are unable to pay for hospital care.

It is important to keep your appointments, to cancel them at least twenty-four hours ahead of time, or to provide a good excuse for missing them. If you miss two appointments without canceling early enough and without a reasonable excuse, the VA may determine you are "not entitled to treatment."

NURSING HOME CARE

Veterans are also eligible for care in nursing homes. Nursing home care is provided to veterans who are not acutely ill and who do not need hospitalization but who do need skilled nursing care and related medical services. (Acute illnesses are relatively short-term illnesses; they differ from chronic illnesses, which may go on for years.) Nursing homes are located in VAMCs. In addition, the veteran may be eligible for placement in a public or private nursing home with which the VA has a contract, or in a state nursing home. Because most nursing home residents are over sixty-five, few Vietnam Era Veterans fit the characteristics of the typical nursing home patient. For this reason, this book will not provide much information about nursing homes. (Your service representative can give you more.) It should be stated, however, that rules about eligibility and priority are very similar to those for hospitalization. Again, Form 10–10 is used.

DOMICILIARY CARE

The VA operates sixteen domiciliary facilities, which accommodate about seven thousand veterans. Like nursing homes, these facilities mostly house veterans older than those who served in Vietnam. They provide shelter, food, clothing, and other necessities of life, including medical care.

Generally, those eligible for VA domiciliary facilities are veterans who have a service-connected disability or are eligible for VA pensions. Eligible veterans must be able to feed and dress themselves and perform other basic functions without assistance.

Thirty-three states operate veterans homes. They vary from state to state but are in many ways similar to VA domiciliary facilities. If you or a veteran you know is interested in the possibility of moving to a VA or state facility, check carefully to determine whether the best available alternative is a VA domiciliary facility or a veterans home operated by your state.

OTHER MEDICAL SERVICES

Other kinds of care and assistance are available from the VA. Your service representative can tell you about many of these. They include hospital-based home care, day and residential care for the elderly, and devices such as braces, orthopedic shoes, corset belts, glasses, hearing aids, and aids for the blind. As noted in Chapter 3, "Compensation," almost anything is available, and it's the squeaky wheel who gets the grease (it's the aggressive vet who gets the hearing aid).

CARE FOR DEPENDENTS AND SURVIVORS

The VA has a program that provides medical care for spouses and dependents of living veterans and for survivors of veterans who are deceased. This is the Civilian Health and Medical Program of the VA, abbreviated as CHAMPVA. Generally, CHAMPVA care is *not* provided at VA facilities, although the VA may soon begin to provide more care at its facilities.

Medical care may be available to

1. The spouse or child of a veteran who has a total, permanent, service-connected disability
2. The surviving spouse or child of a veteran who died due to a service-connected disability or who, when he died, had a total, permanent disability that resulted from a service-connected disability. Such a spouse or child is eligible for CHAMPVA only if *not* eligible for the Armed Forces "CHAMPUS" program
3. The surviving spouse or child of a member of the armed services who died in the line of duty and not due to his own misconduct

To apply for care at a VA facility, the dependent or survivor must file VA Form 10–10d, Application for Medical Benefits for Dependents or Survivors.

To apply for reimbursement for care at a non-VA facility or

by a non-VA doctor or other professional, the dependent or survivor must get VA Form 10–583, Claim for Payment of Cost of Unauthorized Medical Services. Most medical facilities that provide non-VA care have copies of the form.

Dental benefits for dependents and survivors are extremely limited.

TRAVEL AND INCIDENTAL EXPENSES

Travel and incidental expenses can sometimes be critical to the veteran's ability to receive care. In addition to travel, expenses to which a vet may be entitled include meals, lodging, sleeping car accommodations on a train, and the services of an attendant.

Travel may be authorized for

1. Admissions of eligible persons to hospitals, nursing homes, and domiciliary facilities (Eligible persons include dependents and survivors of some veterans)
2. Readmissions
3. Care in preparation for hospitalization. Also, post-hospital care
4. Authorized absences from health care facilities (such as in emergencies)
5. Transfers between facilities
6. Discharges (to go home)
7. Outpatient services for:
   a. Physical examinations
   b. Treating service-connected or related disabilities
   c. Treating conditions that are not service-connected, when treatment is needed to avoid interrupting vocational rehabilitation training
   d. Certain veterans and family members for consultation, professional counseling, training, and mental health services

Those eligible for reimbursement of travel and incidental expenses are

1. Veterans and others receiving benefits relating to a service-connected disability

2. Some veterans receiving a pension for a disability that is not service-connected
3. Certain other veterans receiving pensions

Exceptions to the general eligibility rules may be made in an emergency or if a special mode of transportation is needed.

Generally, to get VA reimbursement for travel and incidental expenses, veterans and others must get authorization from the VA *before* they pay these expenses. Different forms apply to different types of travel. Check with the nearest VA medical facility or with your service representative. Persons who must qualify on the basis of limited income must complete VA Form 60–2323 (also numbered 00–2323), Certification of Inability to Pay Transportation Costs.

Travel and incidental expenses can be very costly. As a result, the VA in some cases will issue a "fee basis card" that the veteran can use to get treatment from a local, private physician or other professional for service-connected disabilities. The VA doctor handling the veteran's case generally is the one who decides whether a fee basis card will be issued. Only vets with disabilities rated at more than 50 percent have much chance to get such a card. You will be most likely to receive a fee basis card if you prepare persuasive arguments to present to your VA doctor. These arguments might cover subjects such as the cost and difficulty of travel to VA facilities and the harmful effect travel may have on your condition.

SPECIAL AREAS

There are many important special medical areas that concern veterans. Most of these will be described in detail later in this book. They include

1. Agent Orange. See Chapter 7, "Agent Orange."
2. Post-Traumatic Stress Disorder (PTSD), also called Delayed Stress. See Chapter 8, "Psychological Readjustment."
3. Drug and Alcohol Dependence. See Chapter 8, "Psychological Readjustment."

4. Readjustment counseling. See Chapter 8, "Psychological Readjustment."
5. Health services for women. See Chapter 17, Women Veterans."

No veteran who needs medical services in any of these five areas should rely on this chapter alone; it is very important that he—or, in the case of women vets, she—also read the later chapter that applies to his or her case.

Radiation

Because there is no separate chapter on this issue, radiation is briefly covered here.

Radiation is a complicated and controversial area. Experts differ in their opinions about whether many veterans have been seriously affected by exposure to "ionizing radiation" (radiation from the bombings of Hiroshima and Nagasaki near the end of World War II and from nuclear weapons tests). The VA has revised its rules regarding the medical services that will be provided to veterans suffering symptoms that may be due to exposure to radiation. Because of the complexity of the area and because, apparently, few Vietnam Era Veterans have been exposed to ionizing radiation, this book cannot devote much space to the issue.

It is important to note, however, that in April 1983, the VA issued a new rule regarding veterans exposed to ionizing radiation. Under this rule:

1. Health care services are limited to hospital and nursing home care in VA facilities and to outpatient care in VA facilities in connection with hospitalization or to avoid hospitalization.
2. Care will be provided without regard to the veteran's age, to whether his problems are service-connected, or to his ability to pay.
3. Each veteran who participated in the testing of a nuclear device or in the occupation of Hiroshima or Nagasaki between September 11, 1945, and July 1, 1946, and who

requests VA care will receive a physical examination and "appropriate diagnostic studies."

4. Treatment *may* be authorized.

After completing a study required by Congress, the VA will issue more rules in late 1985.

Veterans who believe they may now or in the future suffer symptoms due to exposure to ionizing radiation should request information from the National Association of Atomic Veterans; P.O. Box 707; Eldon, MO 65026.

Those who may want to file a claim for VA benefits— including disability compensation—should get a copy of the sixteen-page *Self-Help Guide on Radiation* published by the Veterans Education Project. Write to Veterans Education Project; P.O. Box 42130; Washington, DC 20015.

PATIENT RIGHTS

Under VA rules, all patients who are voluntarily admitted to VA facilities have the following rights:

1. To be treated with dignity
2. To receive prompt and appropriate treatment
3. To have the least restrictive conditions necessary to achieve the purposes of treatment
4. To hold property, execute legal documents, enter into contracts, vote, and to get married or divorced
5. To communicate freely and privately with persons outside the facility
6. To wear their own clothing
7. To keep personal possessions
8. To keep and spend money
9. To spend time with others, to exercise, and to worship

If a valid reason exists to do so, some of these rights may be restricted. Patients also have certain rights regarding restraint, seclusion, medication, confidentiality, and patient grievances.

As noted, the rights just listed apply to persons who are *voluntarily* admitted to VA facilities. Some people—because of a psychiatric condition believed to have made them dangerous—are *involuntarily committed* to a VA facility. These patients have rights provided under the law of the state in which they are committed.

If you believe your rights as a patient have been violated, see, later in this chapter, the section titled "Complaints about Medical Care."

CHARGES AND REIMBURSEMENT FOR CERTAIN SERVICES

If the VA provides hospital or medical services to a veteran it has tentatively determined to be eligible but the veteran is later found to be ineligible, the VA will charge the veteran for the services.

The VA will also charge for treating a disability that is not service-connected and that is due to an on-the-job injury covered by workers' compensation; due to a car accident in a state that requires auto insurance; or due to a crime that occurred in a state that provides free health care to victims of crime. The VA may charge the veteran himself or (more likely) may charge an insurance company or a state.

Your service representative can provide details.

COMPLAINTS ABOUT MEDICAL CARE

While the VA is full of complex official rules about the kinds of care for which a veteran is or is not eligible, about which form to file, which deadlines to meet, and so on and so on, it has no official rules about how to file a complaint about the quality of medical care.

Because the VA has no system-wide program for handling complaints and because it may have a conflict of interest in investigating any complaints made against its own facilities and personnel, it is probably best for the veteran who has a complaint to first contact someone *outside* the VA. The best person to contact first may be the veteran's service representative. If, however, you would prefer to handle a complaint yourself, you should type a letter and, after making a copy for yourself, address it to the director of the facility where you received care (phone the facility to find out his or her name). You can also make a complaint by phone to the office of the VA Inspector General in Washington, DC. The toll-free number there is (800) 368-5899.

Vietnam Veterans of America (VVA) is very much concerned about complaints about poor care in VA facilities. Letters may be addressed to: VVA Legal Services; 2001 S St., N.W., Suite 710; Washington, DC 20009.

MEDICAL MALPRACTICE

If your health has been harmed (if you have been injured or have had an injury made worse or if you have been made ill or have had an illness made worse) due to poor diagnosis or treatment (or due to lack of treatment) at a VA health facility, you may be able to successfully make a claim against the VA in order to make it pay you money "damages" for the problems caused.

To get damages, the veteran who has been harmed (or, if he had died, his survivors) must file a claim under a law called the Federal Tort Claims Act. Filing such a claim usually requires the assistance of a lawyer, and it is best to find a lawyer who has had experience with medical malpractice claims against the VA. If you cannot find such a lawyer, phone the VVA Legal Services office at (202) 686-2599 and ask for the name of a qualified attorney in your area.

First, the lawyer (or you) must file Form SF 95, Claim for Damage, Injury, or Death. *This claim must be filed within two years of the date of the start of the problems you believe were caused by VA care, or within two years of the date you should have been aware that malpractice had occurred.*

The issue of the date on which the two years began is very complicated and often the beginning date is not the date that seems most fair. *Filing a claim for a service-connected disa-*

bility that resulted from VA medical malpractice does not keep the two year period from running out; do not believe anyone who tells you otherwise. If you have even the slightest doubt about which date applies in your case, or even if you firmly believe the two years have run out, *promptly get advice from a lawyer*. There may be a way to argue successfully that your claim is valid.

Once a claim has been filed, the VA has six months to respond. If it does not respond within six months or if it responds within that period but denies the claim, the veteran or his survivor may file suit in federal court. The suit must be filed within six months of a VA denial or, if the VA has simply failed to respond within six months, the suit must be filed within six months after the original six months has run out. Most lawyers will agree to take a VA medical malpractice case in return for a percentage (up to 25 percent) of the amount gained through trial or out-of-court settlement. This percentage is called a "contingency fee." If a lawyer is taking a contingency fee, he or she will not charge any other fee, though he or she may charge expenses. This means that if you don't win your case, you don't owe your lawyer a penny for his or her time.

7. AGENT ORANGE

Your Health and Your Money

(Dioxin is) relatively non-toxic to man and animals.
> —Army and Navy manuals used during the 1960s

The Environmental Protection Agency's Cancer Assessment Group regards (dioxin) as both an initiator and promoter of cancer.
> —*Dioxin Strategy*, 1983, by the Environmental Protection Agency

Agent Orange has been and will continue to be a highly emotional issue. Since the late 1970s, it has been a focus of intense media attention and of urgent concern among veterans. Some twenty thousand vets brought a class action lawsuit against Dow Chemical Company and six other corporations that made Agent Orange. Under that lawsuit's tentative settlement, which was reached in May 1984, veterans and their children harmed by Agent Orange will share in a fund of $180 million plus interest.

But despite all the attention to illnesses caused by Agent Orange, most vets probably don't have any of them. And despite all the attention to the huge settlement amount, you probably won't get a cent (and if you do get any money, you will probably get less than you deserve later than you deserve it).

The lawsuit, though very important, is not the best hope for the vet suffering from exposure to Agent Orange. This is because he needs health care more than he needs money and because the money value of the health care (or disability compensation) he deserves from the VA will be greater than the amount of money he will get from the suit.

WHAT IS AGENT ORANGE?

Agent Orange is a herbicide (also called "defoliant") that was used by U.S. forces in Vietnam from 1962 to 1971. It was used to kill plant life in jungle areas (to expose enemy troops) and to destroy crops. It was called Agent Orange because it came in fifty-five-gallon drums marked with an orange stripe.

U.S. forces sprayed some ninety-six million pounds of Agent Orange in Vietnam. It amounted to about 90 percent of all herbicides used by the U.S. in that country. It was sprayed primarily from planes and helicopters, but was also applied from trucks, river boats, and even backpacks.

Most veterans who were exposed to Agent Orange were exposed because they were in areas as they were being sprayed or because they entered sprayed areas shortly after spraying. In these areas, they breathed the spray directly, inhaled it from burning brush, drank or bathed in contaminated water, or ate contaminated food. Some, however, may have been exposed by taking showers with water stored in discarded Agent Orange drums or by using the drums as makeshift hibachis for cooking food.

One ingredient of Agent Orange is *dioxin*, an extremely poisonous chemical. Any vet exposed to Agent Orange was therefore exposed to dioxin.

HEALTH EFFECTS

Because it contains dioxin, Agent Orange can damage the health of people and animals. Still, there has been heated controversy—especially between veterans and the VA—as to what health problems Agent Orange causes in humans.

The two illnesses most commonly linked to Agent Orange are chloracne and porphyria cutanea tarda. Chloracne is like acne—pimples found mostly in teenagers—but much more severe. Porphyria cutanea tarda involves redness of the skin, followed by crusts and scabs, and then scarring; symptoms may also include other skin problems, excessive or abnormal hair growth, and liver damage.

Veterans filing claims with the VA for disabilities due to Agent Orange have also commonly described illnesses including other skin conditions, reduced sex drive, impotency, respiratory problems, gastrointestinal disturbances, various cancers, and miscarriages (especially by wives of exposed vets).

At the end of this chapter is a list of 135 medical conditions that *may* be caused (in some life form) by Agent Orange. This list is not "official": it comes from the lawyers representing the veterans in the class action lawsuit previously mentioned.

It is not yet known how many people have been harmed by Agent Orange. It is known that during the years the herbicide was used, some 2.4 million Americans served in Vietnam. It is also known that more than 121,000 vets have asked for and received VA examinations for possible harmful effects of Agent Orange. Although several scientific studies of Americans exposed to Agent Orange have begun, apparently no reliable studies have been made of the effects of the herbicide on the people of Southeast Asia.

THE LAWSUIT

The lawsuit against the manufacturers of Agent Orange has received far more recent publicity than any other part of the Agent Orange picture. For that reason, this book will deal with the suit early in this chapter.

The name of the lawsuit is *In re "Agent Orange" Product Liability Litigation*. It was filed in 1979 in New York State by hundreds of Viet Vets and their families. In 1983, the judge in the case, Chief Judge Jack B. Weinstein of the Federal District Court for the Eastern District of New York, determined that the case is a class action. This means the various plaintiffs (plaintiffs in a case are those who sue, defendants are those who are sued) have claims that are similar enough that the plaintiffs can join together in a single suit. By the time the suit became a class action, some twenty thousand vets and family members had joined as plaintiffs.

Trial in the case was set for May 1984. On the day the trial was to begin, attorneys representing the veterans and attorneys representing the chemical companies reached a settlement of the case. As a result, no trial has been held.

Under the settlement, which was approved by the judge in January 1985, the manufacturers of Agent Orange agreed to set up a fund of $180 million to pay claims made by veterans and family members who have been harmed due to the veterans' exposure to the herbicide. The fund has been created and is earning interest at the prime rate, about 12 percent per year.

Claim Form

Veterans and others had until January 15, 1985, to file a preliminary claim form with the court. The judge finally decided to accept all forms filed by May 28, 1985 (the date on which he approved a distribution plan).

If after the deadline you became aware of a problem you believe was caused by Agent Orange (or if this happens in the future), you must file a claim form within 120 days of your discovery of the problem.

Still, if you missed the original deadline or the 120-day deadline, it is *possible* you can share in the fund. Check with a service representative who works for a veterans organization such as Vietnam Veterans of America (VVA) or check with a lawyer familiar with veterans issues. You may be able to successfully argue that a "good and special reason" exists to excuse a late form. For example, you may argue that although you knew of the medical problem before the deadline, you did not until *after* the deadline have reason to believe the problem was *caused by Agent Orange*. Or you may argue that you did not know until after the deadline that you were affected by the lawsuit.

To get a claim form, write to Agent Orange Computer Center; P.O. Box 905; Smithtown, NY 11787; or call (toll-free), (800) 645-1355. If you are calling from New York State, phone (800) 832-1303.

To get not only a claim form but a detailed guide on how to fill out the form, write to VVA Legal Services; 2001 S St., N.W., Suite 710; Washington, DC 20009. (Simply enclose a note saying, "Please send me *VVA's Guide on Agent Orange*.")

Getting Your Money from the Lawsuit

Here is a brief summary of the 174-page distribution plan approved by the judge:

Only those who filed preliminary claim forms on time will be considered for cash payments, and then only if they also filed an application for payment. (The application was automatically sent to everyone who filed a claim form.) Two kinds of payment will be available.

1. Disability Payments: A veteran who was exposed to Agent Orange, and who now has a long-term total disability, is entitled to cash payments, unless the disability was caused in large part by a traumatic event, such as a car accident, war wound, or homicide. Regarding the exposure test, the court has adopted rules that differ from the rules the VA uses. A veteran filing a claim is required to complete a questionnaire indicating the dates and locations of service in Vietnam. Those who held a job involving direct handling of Agent Orange (such as backpack or airplane sprayers, and loaders or handlers of spraying equipment) will automatically satisfy the exposure requirement. All others will be evaluated under a computerized process that uses the HERBS tapes mentioned on page 96.

To meet the long-term total disability requirement, there must be an "inability to engage in any substantial gainful activity by reason of any medically determinable physical or mental impairment which can be expected to result in death or which has lasted or can be expected to last for a continuous period of not less than 12 months." Any veteran who is considered disabled by the Social Security Administration (for purposes of Supplemental Security Income or disability payments) will automatically satisfy the long-term total disability requirement. All others will be evaluated on a case-by-case basis.

Disability payments will be made in yearly installments. The amount will vary depending upon how old you are and how long you have been totally disabled. The court has estimated that the highest payment—which will go to a veteran who was born after 1935 and who has been totally disabled since 1970—will be $12,800, made in ten yearly payments of $1,280 starting in 1986.

2. Death Payments: The surviving spouse or children of a

deceased veteran who was exposed to Agent Orange is entitled to a death payment, unless the death was caused in large part by a traumatic event, such as a car accident, war wound, or homicide. The method of determining whether the veteran was exposed is the same as for disabled veterans.

The death payment will be made in one lump sum. The amount will vary depending upon the age of the veteran at death and when the death occurred. The court estimates that the maximum payment—which will apply to deaths occurring before 1985 to a veteran who was under 50—will be $3,400. No payment will be made for deaths occurring after December 31, 1995, or after the age of 59.

Assistance to Other Class Members: The large majority of the 245,000 who filed a claim form will *not* be eligible for a cash payment. Those ineligible include the partially disabled and children with birth defects. They may receive some assistance, however, from the Class Assistance Foundation created by the court using $45 million of the settlement fund. The Foundation will give grants to organizations to provide a variety of services to benefit all class members.

The court has not stated specifically whether you need to file a claim form in order to be eligible to receive assistance from the Foundation. Therefore, it is probably wise to file a claim form even if you are not eligible for a cash payment; you will at least get on the mailing list to receive information on what the Foundation is doing for Vietnam Veterans and their families.

At this writing, certain appeals challenging the settlement had not yet been decided. Therefore, you should check with your service representative or a veterans organization to see if the distribution plan just described has been changed.

OTHER LAWSUITS

Some veterans chose not to be part of the class action lawsuit that resulted in settlement. (The technical term is that they "opted out of the class.") Most of these veterans took this course of action because they and their attorneys chose to continue, rather than settle, their legal claims. In addition, some veterans, some veterans' families and companies that manufactured Agent Orange are suing the *government*.

All of these lawsuits were dismissed in early 1985. For a discussion of the problems of suing the government, see Chapter 16, "Claims and Appeals."

One issue of great importance to veterans who felt the lawsuit settlement was unfair was the treatment of secret government and chemical company documents that plaintiffs' attorneys requested and received in preparation for trial. These documents shed light on what the companies and the government knew about the dangers of Agent Orange before it was used in Vietnam. Vietnam Veterans of America (VVA) filed a motion in court to have the documents made public. A judge granted the motion in 1985 but an appeal to a higher court has delayed release of many of the documents.

VA HEALTH CARE

Agent Orange Exam

Since 1978 the VA has offered veterans a "special" free medical examination to check for problems caused by Agent Orange. The exam includes a medical history, a physical exam, and laboratory tests. The results of the exam and the veteran's name and address are entered in a VA computer file called the Agent Orange Registry. By early 1985, more than 121,000 vets had received Agent Orange exams.

If you think you have Agent Orange problems, you should get an Agent Orange exam. This is *not* because the exam will necessarily provide you with a lot of useful information and be one of a series of steps that ends with full and effective VA care: vets have often found Agent Orange exams unsatisfactory because they were not thorough or did not provide them with much information. Still, getting an exam will help establish whether you have problems due to Agent Orange (or some other cause). To schedule an Agent Orange exam, call the nearest VA hospital. Try to schedule the lab tests for the same day as your physical exam. At the end of the exam, ask for a copy of the exam records and the lab test results.

Treatment

In 1981 Congress passed a law authorizing the VA to provide "appropriate" medical care and treatment for illnesses and disabilities that *may* be related to exposure to Agent Orange. To refuse to treat a vet, VA doctors must conclude the vet's disease is due to a specific cause not related to Agent Orange. Under the 1981 law, thousands of vets have been hospitalized, have been admitted to nursing homes, or have received care as outpatients.

To get VA medical care for Agent Orange problems, make an appointment at the nearest VA hospital.

Avoiding Miscarriages and Birth Defects

Women exposed to Agent Orange and spouses of men exposed to it may suffer miscarriages due to the herbicide. In addition, children born to men or women exposed to Agent Orange may have birth defects.

Vets and spouses who fear that a current or future pregnancy may result in miscarriage or birth defects should take certain precautions.

Any woman currently pregnant who fears problems due to Agent Orange should inform her doctor that she or her husband was exposed to the herbicide. If the doctor is not familiar with the fact that Agent Orange may cause miscarriages and birth defects, the woman should ask the doctor to consult with physicians (or veterans groups) familiar with the effects of Agent Orange. The woman may also want to switch to a doctor who understands Agent Orange. If you would like your doctor to find out more about the health effects of Agent Orange, ask him or her to request a booklet, *The Physician's Resource: Toxic Herbicide Exposure*, from the Pennsylvania Medical Society; 20 Erford Road; Lemoyne, PA 17043.

Any vet or spouse who fears problems in a *future* pregnancy should contact the March of Dimes. That organization can refer people to doctors who provide *genetic counseling*. The March of Dimes is listed in the phone directories for most large cities.

At this writing, the VA has no programs to counsel vets and spouses concerned about miscarriages and birth defects that may result from Agent Orange, or to provide medical care to help prevent these events from occurring. Still, there is no harm in the vet or spouse calling the nearest VA hospital to ask about services it provides.

For more information on VA health care, see Chapter 6, "Medical Services."

DISABILITY COMPENSATION

Agent Orange is one of those things that make the veteran wonder whether the VA is his friend or his enemy. Regarding Agent Orange, the VA has been unresponsive about health care and especially unresponsive about disability compensation.

Through 1984, despite strong evidence that Agent Orange causes many serious health disorders, the VA *denied all veterans disability compensation claims based on exposure to Agent Orange*. The VA "justified" this by claiming that the health problems reported by the veterans could not be caused by Agent Orange.

It again took Congressional intervention to help the vet. In 1984 Congress passed the Veterans' Dioxin and Radiation Exposure Compensation Standards Act. According to *VVA's Guide on Agent Orange*, "The law . . . has the potential for providing greater help to veterans than the Agent Orange lawsuit."

The 1984 law provides that vets who developed chloracne or porphyria cutanea tarda during their service in Vietnam or within one year of leaving that country must receive temporary ("interim") VA disability benefits. The law also requires that the VA examine *other* medical conditions to determine if those conditions can be caused by Agent Orange.

That's the good news. The bad news is that under the law no interim benefits can be awarded retroactively to a time before October 1, 1984, and no benefits can extend beyond September 30, 1986. The other bad news is that in April 1985 the VA decided to drop porphyria cutanea tarda from the list of conditions caused by exposure to Agent Orange. The VA also said only chloracne (and only if it appeared within *three* months after the veteran left Vietnam) was caused by Agent Orange exposure. It remains to be seen whether the VA will change its mind (or whether Congress will force it to).

Veterans should note, however, that after the scientific studies of the health effects of Agent Orange are completed the VA may grant benefits beyond September 1986.

If you may be disabled due to Agent Orange, get the Vietnam Veterans of America (VVA) *Self-Help Guide on Agent Orange*, 1985 edition. This guide deals with disability compensation and other subjects. Write to VVA Legal Services; 2001 S St., N.W., Suite 710; Washington, DC 20009.

Remember, regarding Agent Orange disabilities or any other kind of service-connected disability, you need *not* be fully disabled (completely unable to work) to receive VA disability compensation. Compensation is provided to vets rated by the VA as being anywhere from 10 to 100 percent disabled. See Chapter 3, "Compensation."

If you were exposed to Agent Orange and are disabled due to chloracne or porphyria cutanea tarda, go ahead and apply for interim VA compensation, saying your problems are due to Agent Orange. Do the same thing regarding other conditions you have if after this writing the VA adds these conditions to its list of Agent Orange medical problems that can result in VA disability compensation.

If, however, you are disabled as a result of a medical condition other than those the VA agrees are related to Agent Orange, you must apply *very carefully* for VA disability compensation. Sure, you deserve it, but chances are the VA won't give it to you if you say your disability stems from Agent Orange. Your safest bet is to apply for VA disability compensation but *not to mention Agent Orange as the cause of your disability*. Still, you will have to give information indicating your condition is service-connected. The best way to do this is to mention a reason *other than Agent Orange* that may actually have caused the symptoms you *think* are caused wholly or partly by Agent Orange (but don't make up such a reason if none exists). Another way to establish service connection is to say (if this is true) that your symptoms first appeared while you were in the service or shortly after separation (if possible, provide evidence).

(For your disability to be service-connected, the cause of your condition need not have occurred while you were in combat or in Vietnam; it need only have occurred while you were in the service. Also, only the cause, not the symptoms, must have occurred while you were in the service. Again, see Chapter 3, "Compensation.")

The VA is supposed to give you the benefit of the doubt on the question of whether or not a condition is service-connected. If, however, you get turned down on a claim for compensation for a disability you believe was caused by Agent Orange, contact the VVA Legal Services at the address given earlier in this chapter. That office may be able to help you appeal your case.

If you are considering applying for disability compensation—or if you just want to know for sure whether you were exposed to Agent Orange—you may want to contact the U.S. Army and Joint Services Environmental Support Group. This group can provide you with a report indicating whether your unit was operating in an area that was sprayed with Agent Orange by aircraft. Write to: U.S. Army and Joint Services Environmental Support Group; 1730 K St., N.W., Room 210; Washington, DC 20006. *Use a copy of the form provided at the end of Chapter 13, "Getting Your Records."*

To file a claim for VA disability compensation due to physical or psychological problems caused by exposure to Agent Orange, read Chapter 3, "Compensation;" then file VA Form 21–526, Veteran's Application for Compensation or Pension. Attach to the form a sheet including the information on the "Attachment" that appears at the end of this chapter.

BAD PAPER VETS

Vets with bad discharges are not entirely excluded from benefiting from developments regarding Agent Orange. In particular, they have the same rights under the lawsuit settlement as all other vets. They should therefore proceed in the same way as a vet with an honorable or general discharge and are entitled to the same share of the settlement fund.

Bad discharges *do* severely limit VA benefits, including medical care and disability compensation. At the VA, bad paper

hurts Agent Orange victims just as much as it harms vets with
any other medical condition. Refer to Chapter 15, "Upgrading
Your Discharge." Note in particular that vets with undesirable
discharges are usually eligible for medical care for injuries
suffered in the service (and therefore should be eligible for the
Agent Orange exam and for treatment). Note also, however,
that vets with undesirable discharges are generally not eligible
for disability compensation; to get compensation they usually
must get a discharge upgrade. Any vet with any discharge
except one issued by a general court-martial can also ask the
VA to make an exception to its policies and grant him benefits.

STATE PROGRAMS

Vets should never forget that the federal government (which
includes the VA) is *not* the only source of services and benefits
for vets. Agent Orange is a case in point.

More than 20 states have enacted laws to help veterans
affected by Agent Orange. Most of these laws set up Agent
Orange commissions. Many of the laws also provide medical
testing and genetic counseling as well as assistance in filing
VA claims. To locate Agent Orange programs in your state,
call the state department (sometimes called "division" or
"bureau") of veterans affairs. In most cases, these departments
are found in state capitals (call directory assistance for your
capital city). In 1984, the following states had Agent Orange
commissions: California, Connecticut, Georgia, Hawaii, Illi-
nois, Indiana, Iowa, Kansas, Maine, Massachusetts, Minne-
sota, New Jersey, Ohio, Oklahoma, Oregon, Pennsylvania,
Rhode Island, Texas, Washington, West Virginia, and Wisconsin.

STUDIES OF AGENT ORANGE

In recent years, many federal and state agencies have begun
to study the effect of Agent Orange on the health of Vietnam
Veterans. The most extensive studies are being conducted by

the federal Centers for Disease Control (CDC). Results are not expected until 1988.

The results of two studies were released in 1984. A survey of parents of babies born in the Atlanta area from 1968 to 1980 concluded that Viet Vets have no more risk of having children with what the study called "major" birth defects than do non-vets. Nevertheless, the risk of fathering a child with spina bifida, cleft palate, or abnormal growths such as tumors and cysts was higher for Viet Vets than nonvets and higher still for Viet Vets who were heavily exposed to Agent Orange.

In February 1984, the Defense Department issued a press release announcing the results of a preliminary study of Air Force personnel who conducted Agent Orange spraying missions. The press release said vets should be "reassured" that the study had found no significant health problems. A close reading of the study's results, however, shows there is a greater risk of death for former enlisted personnel who handled Agent Orange than for former officers who flew the planes. The study also showed that the former enlisted personnel may be more likely than former officers to suffer liver, digestive, and endocrine disorders.

THE ENVIRONMENTAL MOVEMENT

Veterans concerned about Agent Orange have much in common with environmental groups. Just as veterans are focusing on the health effects of Agent Orange, environmental organizations are focusing on the hazards posed by a whole array of toxic substances. Among the concerns of environmental groups are the exposure of workers to dangerous chemicals and materials and the exposure of families to toxic waste dumps near their homes. Among the toxic substances that are of special concern to environmental groups is dioxin, an ingredient of Agent Orange. And, like veterans, environmental organizations are fighting for greater accountability by industry and the government.

Both veterans (and veterans organizations) and the environmental movement will benefit if veterans and environmentalists work together. One way vets can promote a common effort is to contact Citizens Clearinghouse on Hazardous Waste; P.O. Box 926; Arlington, VA 22216; (703) 276-7070.

KEEP UP TO DATE

Even after publication of this book, there may be important developments in the class action lawsuit against the manufacturers of Agent Orange. As mentioned earlier, studies are underway to determine how many vets have been affected by exposure to Agent Orange and to determine which medical conditions are caused by it. For these and other reasons, there is probably no veterans issue on which it is more important to *keep up to date*.

How do you keep abreast of what's going on regarding Agent Orange? One of the best ways is to join an organization of Vietnam Era Veterans, such as Vietnam Veterans of America (VVA). See the coupon at the end of this book. It is also helpful to stay in touch with a service representative who works for VVA or another veterans organization.

MEDICAL PROBLEMS THAT *MAY* BE CAUSED BY AGENT ORANGE

(This is not an official list of the VA or any medical organization. It is a list of medical conditions that, according to attorneys for veterans in the Agent Orange class action lawsuit, may be caused in some life form [not necessarily human] by Agent Orange.)

chloracne	DNA disturbances
porphyria cut. :ea tarda	RNA disturbances
hyperpigmentation of skin	skin eruptions and cysts
hyperkeratosis of skin	slowing of nerve impulses
hirsutism	elevated blood lipid levels
discoloration of skin	elevated cholesterol levels
various other skin conditions	prediabetic and diabetic states
asthenia	abnormal cell proliferations
weakness of extremities	organ enlargements
loss of strength	cellular atrophy
easy fatigability	decreased cell proliferation
fatigue	birth defects in offspring
headaches (including migraines)	miscarriages

peripheral neuropathy
polyneuropathy
intolerance to cold
loss of sensation
other neurological deficits
irritation to eyes
hepatitis
impairment of sight
impairment of hearing
impairment of smell
impairment of taste
impairment of touch
weight loss
weight gain
loss of appetite
anorexia
loss of libido
loss of sex drive
sleep disturbances
orthostatic hypotension
hypertension
abdominal pain
nausea
vomiting
diarrhea
rectal bleeding
other gastrointestinal disorders
neurasthenia
depression
violent behavior
uncontrolled behavior
other psychobehavioral disorders
myocardial infarction
atherosclerosis
other cardiovascular disorders
liver damage
pancreatic dysfunction
kidney disorders
urinary tract disorders
bladder disorders
pulmonary pathologies
pulmonary fibrosis
other respiratory disorders
cholangiocarcinoma
other liver cancers
kidney cancer

spontaneous abortions
neonatal deaths
increased white blood cell counts
elevation of eosinophil
decrease in IgM and IgD
alteration in B-cell and T-cell
    capabilities
skin rash
scalp tumors
neurofibrosarcoma
fibrous histiocytoma
retroperitoneal neurogenic
    sarcoma
fibrosarcomatous mesothelioma
other soft-tissue sarcomas
leukemia
angiosarcoma
other blood cancers
hepatoma
lymphoma
squamous cell carcinoma of skin
other skin cancers
thyroid cancers
other glandular cancers
cancer of tongue
cancer of hard palate
other cancers of mouth
chronic lymphocytic leukemia
various brain cancers
ischemic heart disease
loss of lymphoid tissue
atrophy of thymus tissue
increased sensitivity to
    susceptability to infections
immune system disturbances
aching muscles
blepharoconjunctivitis
porphyria
epithelial hyperplasia and
    metaplasia
various hemorrhages
increased serum triglyceride level
abnormal sperm development
chromosomal gaps, breaks, rings,
    and other aberrations
cleft palate

bladder cancer
pancreatic cancer
colon cancer
stomach cancer
other gastrointestinal cancers
lung cancer
leiomyosarcoma
liposarcoma
rhabdomyosarcoma
myofibrosarcoma
brain cancer
multiple sclerosis
testicular cancer
testicular atrophy

spina bifida
club foot
skeletal abnormalities
other reproductive defects and
    abnormalities
other organ damages
other central nervous system
    damage
other peripheral nervous system
    damage
other types of cancer and
    increased risk of all forms of
    cancer

ATTACHMENT: DISABILITY CLAIMS

Veterans applying for VA compensation for disabilities due to
Agent Orange or any other cause must file VA Form 21–526
(see Chapter 3, "Compensation"). Vets making a disability
claim based on exposure to Agent Orange should attach to the
form a sheet including the statements shown on the following
form, which was created with the help of the Vietnam Veterans
of America (VVA) Legal Services. In writing or typing your
own sheet, leave out the blank lines but add the information
introduced by the statements on the form on page 97.

The following form refers to "HERBS" tapes. HERBS tapes
are computer tapes that contain a record of all Agent Orange
spraying missions over Vietnam. Information from the HERBS
tapes may help prove you served in an area where Agent Orange
was sprayed. Although official VA policy presumes every vet
who served in Vietnam was exposed to Agent Orange, your
case will be strengthened if the VA learns from the HERBS
tapes that you served in an area that was sprayed.

ATTACHMENT TO AGENT ORANGE CLAIM

NAME: Date filed:
ADDRESS: Claim number: C-

I request that the VA, in addition to the information given here, develop pursuant to 38 CFR 3.103, evidence of my exposure to Agent Orange while I served in Vietnam. Specifically, I request the VA to match the movement of my unit in Vietnam with any spraying operations described in the HERBS tapes. I would like to be notified immediately when such development has been completed and be sent a copy of the results of such development.

This also is to request that the VA presume I was exposed to Agent Orange, as I describe below, unless the VA can affirmatively establish that I was not exposed to Agent Orange. Because military service records contain no information about veterans' exposure to Agent Orange in Southeast Asia, proof that I was NOT exposed can be established only by a cross-check of my movement with the HERBS tapes. This request, and the request that any reasonable doubt involving my claim (particularly with regard to the question of whether I was exposed to Agent Orange) should be resolved in my favor, is made pursuant to 38 CFR 3.102.

SECTION I

I served in Vietnam from the month of   , 19   , to the month of
          , 19   . I served with the following organizations: _____

_____

I was in the following provinces and towns on the dates listed below:
_____

_____

_____

I had the following duties during the dates listed below: _____

_____

_____

SECTION II

I was exposed to Agent Orange in the places and on the dates listed below:

_____

_____

_____

SECTION III.A

I request VA service-connected benefits for the following medical disabilities which I claim were caused by my exposure to Agent Orange
in Vietnam: _____

_____

_____

_____

_____

8. PSYCHOLOGICAL READJUSTMENT

Delayed Stress (PTSD), Drugs, Alcohol, and Other Problems

Are you crazy?
> —Major Danby to Yossarian
> *Catch-22*
> by Joseph Heller

Most people think the Vietnam War was over in 1975. A lot of Viet Vets know they're wrong. For hundreds of thousands of vets—and their loved ones—the psychological effects of the war are a part of everyday life. Most of these vets suffer from Post-Traumatic Stress Disorder (PTSD). Some have other war-related psychological problems or a war-related dependence on drugs or alcohol.

For many men and women who served in Vietnam, the experience there and on coming home has had a lasting and powerful effect on life. For most Viet Vets, the adjustment back to civilian life posed few or no major problems. But for others—perhaps as many as 40 percent of vets who served in Vietnam—things haven't gone well. In fact, sometimes things seem to be getting progressively worse. These and other complaints are often heard:

"I can't keep a job."

"I have no skills or training that will get me a decent job."

"Here I am thirty-five [or thirty-eight] years old and I feel my life is going nowhere."

"I can't stay in a relationship. I've been married and divorced [once or several times] and the same thing keeps happening over and over again—I go so far and that's it."

"I just can't get close to anybody. I don't trust anybody."

"Sometimes I have nightmares about the 'Nam or I wake up in a cold sweat, trembling."

"I'm always tense, wired for something to happen, can't relax."

"I thought when I left Vietnam I left all that behind me, but things keep coming back—memories, thoughts, feelings, for no apparent reason."

"I've got bad paper and I can't get any help from the VA."

"I feel so dead [or empty] inside, just numb to people and things that happen."

"I started drinking [or taking drugs] over there and now I'm doing the same thing, even though I've been through rehab programs."

"I just don't fit in anywhere in society."

"I look around, and I seem to be the only one who is having these emotional problems."

"During certain times of the year I just seem to lose it, and that's not normal."

"I feel so alone."

"I don't know what's happening to me."

"At times I think I must be going crazy."

"How can something that happened ten, fifteen, twenty years ago still be influencing my life?"

This book does not mean to paint a picture that is entirely grim. As will be explained, the feelings expressed in the quotations just given can be a normal reaction to an abnormal situation, such as war. But when the normal healing process of adjusting to terrible experiences becomes disrupted, a normal stress reaction can worsen, becoming a "stress disorder."

This is not a "mental illness," although mental health workers are trained to deal with PTSD. *The disorder can be understood by the vet and corrected*. This chapter will describe this disorder and how to get help.

PSYCHOLOGICAL PROBLEMS

Post-Traumatic Stress Disorder (PTSD) has received much more publicity than all other psychological problems of Vietnam Era Veterans combined. This is as it should be.

This part of this chapter will focus on this disorder. But this is not to say that vets do not suffer from other psychological problems. Although this book does not have the space to describe the symptoms of other psychological conditions experienced by vets (both war-related problems and conditions having little or nothing to do with the war), information is available elsewhere. VA and private psychotherapists—psychiatrists, psychologists, social workers, and others—can evaluate a vet's problems and help solve them. Countless books and articles exist on psychological conditions. The most official source on conditions and their symptoms is the *Diagnostic and Statistical Manual of Mental Disorders*, Third Edition (*DSM III*), published in 1980 by the American Psychiatric Association. People who are not trained in psychotherapy often misinterpret both their own symptoms and the information in *DSM III* and other publications. Therefore, while vets may want to refer to books and articles, they should review the information they read with a trained psychotherapist.

Post-Traumatic Stress and Post-Traumatic Stress Disorder

"Post-Traumatic Stress Disorder" is a new term for an old psychological condition. In this century it has been called by names including "shell shock," "combat fatigue," "war neurosis," and "survivor's syndrome." During and after the Vietnam War, it has been called by names including "Vietnam Stress," "Post-Vietnam Syndrome" ("PVS"), and "Delayed Stress."

The VA estimates 400,000 to 800,000 Viet Vets have readjustment problems related to their military experience (these include, but are not limited to, PTSD).

PTSD did not "officially" exist—in *DSM* and at the VA—until 1980. In that year, *DSM III* recognized PTSD as a disorder that could be diagnosed. And in that year, the VA added PTSD to its list of disabilities that could be rated and for which disability compensation could be paid.

But PTSD, by whatever name, has existed for perhaps as long as people have been exposed to horrifying or shocking events. It has been seen not only in veterans of the Vietnam War and other wars but also among accident and crime victims, survivors of the Nazi holocaust, people who lived near the Three Mile Island nuclear plant when in 1979 it nearly experienced a meltdown, residents of the Mount St. Helens area after the volcanic explosion of 1980, and those who were in the Kansas City Hyatt Regency in 1981 when a "skywalk" collapsed, killing and injuring dozens of people.

PTSD occurs in some people who experience a traumatic event and does not show up in others. It occurs in many people who did not previously have any psychological disorder. In other words, you can be "normal" and then begin to suffer from PTSD.

It is important to distinguish (1) the normal stress associated with the period of recovery from a traumatic event (Post-Traumatic Stress) from (2) a *disrupted* recovery process (Post-Traumatic Stress *Disorder*).

Normal stress during recovery typically includes the avoidance (or numbing) of feelings and the avoidance of some activities or relationships. It also commonly involves the repeated, unwanted reexperiencing of the traumatic event through thoughts, memories, or dreams.

In a normal recovery, stressful memories can keep reappearing until they are sealed over—healed. The healing process is helped by the sympathetic understanding of others, by rational explanations of the event, and by normal progress toward life's goals.

For many veterans, the Vietnam War and the homecoming made it difficult to undergo the healing process. When the normal process of recovery is delayed by the inability to seal over the memories of the traumatic event and if, as a result, the veteran's life and relationships suffer, the process may be said to be "disordered": the vet may have PTSD.

According to *DSM III*, PTSD is the experiencing of a certain set of symptoms following a psychologically traumatic event that is generally outside the range of usual human experience. A vet with PTSD generally has one or more *combinations of symptoms*. Though different vets have different symptoms, the symptoms include

- A psychological numbness, usually directly after the event, and continuing for weeks, months, or even years
- Guilt over surviving when others did not
- Anxiety or nervousness
- Depression or deep sadness
- Nightmares or flashbacks in which the veteran reexperiences the traumatic event
- Jumpiness, especially in response to sounds that remind the veteran of the event or of the war in general
- Difficulty developing close relationships with people at work, at home, or in social settings
- Difficulty sleeping
- Difficulty concentrating
- Avoidance of certain memories
- Attempts to calm down by using alcohol or drugs (sometimes called "self-medication")

For some vets the symptoms are mild and infrequent, for others they are strong and frequent. And just because you experienced a traumatic event in Vietnam and have one or more of the symptoms just listed, you don't necessarily have PTSD: you may be dealing with stress in a normal and generally successful manner. Or you may have seen friends killed in combat and may now have anxiety, but your current anxiety may be the result of something other than any wartime experience. (On the other hand, you may have symptoms that you think are *not* war-related but that really *are* connected to the war: your mind may be "masking" the painful source of your feelings.) A trained psychotherapist who is familiar with PTSD is the best judge of whether you have it.

Military experiences that may result in PTSD include, but are not limited to

- Combat
- Combat service as a medic or corpsman
- Close combat support
- Violent acts (done or witnessed) that may be accompanied

by guilt. Such acts include the killing or other brutal treatment of civilians—especially women, children, and the
elderly—and prisoners
- Confinement as a POW
- Nursing duties where serious injuries were common
- Handling the dead in a military mortuary or in a graves
  registration unit

Post-Traumatic Stress Disorder has sometimes been called
"Delayed Stress." This is because PTSD symptoms often appear years after the traumatic event connected with them. A
delay may occur for any number of reasons. A veteran at first
may have been distracted from the traumatic event by his continuing experiences in the war or by experiences directly following his service (such as school or marriage). Or perhaps
the stress the vet feels as a result of the traumatic event is
triggered or compounded by the stress that comes later (sometimes long after the war) when he takes on the many responsibilities of raising a family. Or the delay may be due partly
to a temporary "numbing" or "blocking out" of traumatic memories or feelings.

Although PTSD has been around about as long as violence
has been around, it apparently has been more common among
Viet Vets than among veterans of any other war in which the
U.S. has been involved. There are many reasons for this.

One is the age of American service members in Vietnam.
The average combat soldier in World War II was 26, the average
service member in Vietnam was just 19. Soldiers who were 26
had generally completed their adjustment to adult life. Those
who were not yet out of their teens, however, had experienced
little of life past high school, and were just beginning to become
adults. Because they were in the process of change, they were
especially likely to *feel changed* by the events of the war: they
were especially likely to come home "feeling like a different
person."

While soldiers from other wars came home slowly—such
as on troop ships—and came home together, Viet Vets often
came home suddenly and alone. Many vets were in a combat
environment and then, a shockingly short 36 hours later, were
sitting in their family's living room; they had had almost no
time for "decompression." Coming home alone, Viet Vets could

not talk over their experiences with others who would under-stand; and, instead of feeling like part of a group, they felt like outsiders.

Also, the Vietnam War was by far the most unpopular war in U.S. history. At certain points, the *majority* of the American public wanted the U.S. out of Vietnam. The U.S., and its individual soldiers, were seen by many Americans as the un-justified killers of little people who were defending their home-land. As a result, many Viet Vets—already young, already returning by plane a day after combat, and already coming home alone—also came home only to be called "murderers" by some of their fellow Americans. By contrast, the vets of World War II returned to ticker-tape parades at the end of the popular war against Hitler and the bombers of Pearl Harbor.

Nothing said here is meant to diminish the valor of American soldiers in other wars or to ignore the fact that many of them saw horrors as bad as anything experienced in Vietnam, or the fact that veterans of other combat eras have also suffered from PTSD. It is simply to say that because of certain circumstances, Viet Vets are more likely than American vets of any other war to suffer problems of readjustment.

The Treatment of PTSD

Can PTSD be treated? If you have it, can you get better? The experts say yes.

Many of the experts are Vietnam Veterans who have come out of the Viet Vet self-help movement of the 1970s. They recommend talking with a counselor (at a facility such as a Vet Center, which will be described later). If the condition is severe, they recommend more intensive treatment. Counseling and other treatment often centers on group discussions. These discussions try to help the vet understand that

- Traumatic events can produce stress symptoms in almost anyone.
- It is normal after a traumatic event to have intrusive thoughts, "numbing," rage, grief, and other symptoms. In fact, it would be unusual not to have at least some "psy-chological aftershocks."
- Some who have experienced a traumatic event continue to

have significant symptoms years or even decades after the event (this is most likely if effective counseling has not been provided).

- Following a traumatic event, it is not unusual to fear that one will lose control of some emotions.
- Once a vet starts focusing on the traumatic event and his symptoms, the symptoms usually get worse before they get better. So it's important to be patient: the worsening is temporary.
- PTSD definitely responds to treatment.
- Some symptoms may not go away completely or forever. After all, there are a number of experiences in life, both negative and positive, that a person will never forget.
- Though this may be difficult for the vet to believe at the beginning of counseling, there may turn out to be important benefits from having gone through the experiences of the war and from having faced and worked through the resulting problems.

DEPENDENCE ON DRUGS AND ALCOHOL

Viet Vets don't just have more cases of PTSD than veterans of other wars. They also apparently have more cases of dependence on drugs, and perhaps on alcohol as well. Among the reasons for this are some of the reasons for the high number of PTSD cases: a very young group of soldiers fighting a very unpopular war. Another reason is that drugs were more readily available (and their use was more acceptable) during the Vietnam War than during any previous war involving the U.S. A 1971 VA poll found that five percent of Viet Vets—some 150,000 people—had used heroin since their discharge. (And of course many of these vets started using heroin while in the service.) Abuse of cocaine and other drugs, as well as alcohol, is also widespread among Viet Vets and Vietnam Era Vets.

GETTING HELP

Vet Centers

For vets suffering from PTSD, other psychological problems, or dependence on drugs or alcohol, there has been, since 1979, a system of informal offices known as *Vet Centers*. For many vets, they are the best place to turn.

In 1979, Congress authorized the establishment of Vet Centers under what was originally known as "Operation Outreach." There are now 188 Vet Centers all over the United States. They are open to any Vietnam Era Vet—any vet who served in the period from August 5, 1964, to May 7, 1975—not just to those who served in Southeast Asia.

Vets like Vet Centers. It may therefore come as a surprise to readers that Vet Centers are part of the VA. They are. And they aren't. Although they are officially part of the VA, they are located away from VA hospitals and other VA facilities. They are found not in giant, imposing buildings, but (usually) in small, storefront facilities.

Most Vet Centers have a staff of four, including professionals and paraprofessionals. Many staff members are Vietnam Era Vets who previously have *not* worked for the VA.

Vet Centers have an informal atmosphere. Vets just walk in. Appointments usually are not needed and staff members are able to see most vets shortly after they arrive. Many Vet Centers are open in the evenings. Services are provided without charge.

Paperwork is minimal. The vet's identity is kept strictly confidential. Vet Center client folders are kept entirely separate from the VA medical record system. In reports to the VA, each vet (called a "client") is given an arbitrary number. The only link between the name and the number is a list kept in a locked place to which only the individual Vet Center's staff has access.

To help the vet deal with his experience in Vietnam and in coming home, Vet Centers provide counseling and other assistance. Counseling is available on a one-to-one basis and in groups. Counseling sometimes involves the vet along with his family or other people significant in his life. In counseling between a staff member and a vet, discussion usually focuses on what happened in Vietnam, the impact of war experiences on the vet, and how the war continues to interfere with his life.

Once in the Vet Center—surrounded by other vets, and benefiting from counseling—the vet often begins to unburden himself. He talks about the war with others who understand, and who accept what he says without being frightened and without condemning him for his statements. In many cases, the vet begins to feel no longer alone or isolated. He realizes he's not crazy, that his problems can be worked out, and that he need no longer run from these problems.

In addition to dealing directly with the vet, most Vet Centers also offer group settings in which the spouses and friends ("significant others") of vets can learn to understand the effect Vietnam has had on vets. The spouses and friends in many cases find ways to improve their relationship with vets.

Besides helping vets with problems such as PTSD, other psychological conditions, and dependence on drugs or alcohol, many Vet Centers provide other assistance. In emergencies, many help with food, shelter, and clothing. Many also assist with employment and with discharge upgrading. In addition, many Vet Centers answer questions about VA benefits, about how to file a claim for disability compensation, and about Agent Orange.

The help a Vet Center can provide is not limited to the center's four walls. Most Vet Centers have a network of contacts in local, state, and federal agencies. They can therefore help the vet find the agency that can deal with his problem and can help the vet find the right person at the agency. Some staff members at some Vet Centers will accompany a vet to a VA hospital or to appointments at other facilities, providing support and, perhaps, cutting red tape. Where appropriate and where vets desire, Vet Centers also refer vets to psychotherapists and other professionals.

Most Vet Centers also offer help to vets who never set foot in their offices. Staff members visit the homes of vets who are in a crisis. They also contact mental health professionals, law enforcement personnel, veterans groups, civic organizations, and other groups to explain the nature and treatment of PTSD and the struggle some Viet Vets are having in readjusting to civilian life. Some Vet Centers also conduct programs for vets in prison.

In some areas of the country where Vet Centers don't operate or can't handle the demand for their services, readjustment counseling is provided by groups paid by the VA to deal with the problems of Viet Vets. To qualify for assistance from one of these groups—called "private fee contractors"—you must be referred to one by a Vet Center or VA hospital.

This book cannot guarantee that every vet will be happy with every Vet Center, or even that every Vet Center is doing a good job. If you believe a local Vet Center (or private contractor) is not meeting your needs, make your views known. First, talk with the Vet Center team leader. Then, if necessary, check with the nearest chapter of Vietnam Veterans of America (VVA) to see if the chapter has investigated the center. If not, suggest an investigation. If VVA can't help, complain to the Regional Manager for Vet Centers in your part of the country. If even that does no good, write to the national Director of the VA Readjustment Counseling Service (which runs the Vet Centers). The addresses of the six Regional Managers and of the Director are listed at the end of the book (Appendix B).

To locate the Vet Center nearest you, check the list of Vet Centers at the end of this book (Appendix A). If the list includes no center near you, call the nearest Vet Center on the list and ask whether any new Vet Center has been established near you: the Vet Center system has grown rapidly, and since this book was written, a new center may have opened near you. Also ask the nearest Vet Center on the list whether there is a private contractor in your area.

Special Facilities for PTSD

For years Viet Vets with PTSD and other psychological problems have felt that VA psychiatric facilities do not understand them. Until recently, most of these facilities were little better than wards for chronic psychiatric cases and drug and alcohol abusers from earlier eras. At many facilities, Viet Vets were not wanted, felt unwanted, and received little useful treatment. Often, treatment consisted of little more than overmedication. Often, the result was violence or other conflicts between patients and against staff (at one facility, patients set punji stick traps for doctors).

Pressure inside and outside the VA has since led to the

development of inpatient and outpatient programs designed for Viet Vets. These programs focus on PTSD and related readjustment problems.

The programs are too few (at this writing there are only thirteen in the whole country). They are understaffed. They don't have enough beds. They are largely experimental. But some are run by psychotherapists who are highly skilled, who are widely respected by Viet Vet groups, and who are themselves Viet Vets.

At this writing, it is not easy to get into these facilities. Some have waiting lists. Also, different directors set different guidelines that determine who is admitted. For example, most programs will not admit active abusers of drugs or alcohol. Many will accept only vets who live in their region of the country (this makes it possible for inpatient treatment to be followed by outpatient care).

Outside pressure may help you get in. Sometimes a Vet Center can help you get admitted. If you have been convicted of a crime and a judge has given you a choice between jail and PTSD treatment, you or your attorney may be able to get you admitted to a program by bringing the judge's choice to the attention of a program director or a politician (such as your Member of Congress).

More Viet Vet psychiatric programs are needed. In fairness to the VA, it should be said that it seems finally to be *trying* in this area. And it must be understood that the VA cannot suddenly create hundreds of centers: there are not yet enough potential staff who are appropriately trained. Progress is being made.

For a list of special VA PTSD facilities, turn to Appendix C at the end of this book. Remember that, since this writing, additional "unofficial" inpatient PTSD programs have been established. To check on whether a new program has begun in your area, contact your nearest Vet Center or the Chief of Psychiatry at the nearest VA hospital.

If there seems to be strong resistance to establishing a psychiatric program in your area, political pressure can be brought to bear. In some places, chapters of Vietnam Veterans of America (VVA) have waged petition campaigns and have alerted the local media. If you want to help found a program in your area, contact your nearest VVA office. With or without VVA assistance, you may also want to contact the local media as well as local politicians (particularly your Member of Congress). (A word of caution: don't charge off into a public campaign until you have spoken with a person of authority at the VA. Hear his or her explanation before you start a public debate; otherwise, you may be made to look foolish by an experienced bureaucrat or by the disclosure of facts of which you were not aware.)

Other VA Psychiatric Facilities

If you need the sort of intense inpatient therapy not possible at a Vet Center but there is no special VA PTSD program in your area, all is not lost. Some areas have "unofficial" VA inpatient PTSD programs, such as in the "Mental Hygiene Clinic" at a Day Treatment Center or in a general psychiatric inpatient program. Check with a Vet Center, a service representative associated with a veterans organization such as Vietnam Veterans of America (VVA), or the Chief of Psychiatry at the nearest VA hospital.

If there is no official or unofficial specialized program, you still may benefit from treatment as an inpatient or outpatient within the standard VA hospital system. Check with a Vet Center or veterans organization about the quality of care for PTSD and other psychological problems at the nearest VA hospital. Some hospitals are better in this area than others. And, because of all the attention now being given to PTSD, hospitals that a short time ago did little for PTSD patients are now doing a much better job.

For more information on VA medical care, see Chapter 6, "Medical Services."

State and Private Psychotherapy

For psychiatric treatment or any other kind of medical care, vets are not limited to VA programs. VA programs do, however, have at least two advantages. One is that they are free. The other is that in many cases they involve therapists who—because they have dealt with many vets and may be vets themselves— are especially familiar with PTSD and other psychological problems of veterans.

Some states also offer free psychotherapy services. Check with a chapter of Vietnam Veterans of America (VVA), a Vet Center, your state department of mental health (sometimes called by other names), a community mental health group, or a state veterans department.

Still, private programs and private therapists do exist. In some areas, private, community-based organizations sponsor "rap groups" for Viet Vets. Also, in some areas mental health organizations run group therapy programs charging relatively low fees. Of course, there are also countless private psychiatrists, psychologists, social workers, and other psychotherapists. Some of these people are skilled in the treatment of veterans' problems and some don't know the first thing about them (but may, improperly, try to treat them anyway).

To find out whether there are helpful private programs or appropriate private psychotherapists in your area, contact your nearest Vet Center or your nearest chapter of VVA.

Self-Help for Psychological Problems

Vets with serious psychological problems should always seek help from professionals. But vets with serious problems may be able to get partial relief—and vets with minor problems may be able to get substantial relief—by helping themselves. Many people with psychological discomfort—especially anxiety—have found athletics very valuable. Many find that, in particular, *endurance athletics*—running, swimming, bicycling—can dramatically reduce stress. Some prefer competitive sports, exercise programs, or weight lifting. Other people reduce anxiety and other problems not through sport but through meditation and related techniques. An improved diet can also improve the psychological outlook. Books on all these subjects (some by experts, some by quacks) can easily be found at most any bookstore.

Programs to Treat Drug and Alcohol Dependence

The choices for the vet with a drug or alcohol problem are similar to those for the vet with a psychological condition. One option, as indicated, is a Vet Center. See the discussion of Vet Centers earlier in this chapter.

Another alternative are more traditional VA programs. Many VA hospitals have programs for the treatment of drug or alcohol dependence. For general information on VA medical care, see Chapter 6, "Medical Services."

As with PTSD, the VA has in some areas of the country arranged with private contractors to provide assistance to vets with drug or alcohol problems. The programs operated by these contractors are known as "community treatment programs."

Again, as with psychological problems, drug and alcohol conditions can be treated by state agencies or privately, by both groups and individuals.

Before choosing which course to take, it's important to get advice on which VA and private programs and individuals *in your area* are most likely to be helpful in your case. For guidance, visit a Vet Center or contact the nearest chapter of Vietnam Veterans of America (VVA).

COMPENSATION

For general information on VA compensation for disability, see Chapter 3, "Compensation." Usually, compensation is for physical problems. But vets who suffer from PTSD or other psychological problems sometimes also qualify.

For you to receive compensation for PTSD or other psychological or physical condition, your disability must be "service-connected." If you have PTSD, this means the traumatic event that resulted in PTSD must have occurred while you were on active duty.

PTSD and other psychological problems are often harder to document than physical conditions. There is no physical injury that any doctor can readily see. In the case of PTSD, symptoms often show up long after military service. The VA presumes that certain kinds of psychiatric conditions that occur more than one year after separation are not service-connected, and this doesn't help the vet whose symptoms appear five or ten years after leaving the military. Also, vets with PTSD often are in no state of mind to carefully prepare an application for disability compensation.

Therefore, if you want to claim a disability due to a psychological problem, it is important that you get help. The best person to help you is a service representative who works for a veterans organization such as VVA. Such a representative can help you gather records and other information you will need and can help fill out the necessary forms. *In filling out the forms, be sure to mention "Post-Traumatic Stress Disorder" or "PTSD."* If you fail to do this, your disability claim may be rejected.

Documentation

You and your service representative should get your complete military personnel and medical records. You or your rep should also get your VA medical records. From one source or another, it is important to document the traumatic event: what happened, when it occurred, and the names and addresses of any living witnesses. Among the records and other documents that may provide evidence of a traumatic event are "operational reports—lessons learned," "combat after action reports," casualty reports, letters to next of kin, daily journals of the battalion involved, "morning reports," Vietnam "station lists," "command post listings," "strength reports," and "situation reports." These records may be available from the U.S. Army and Joint Services Environmental Support Group. See Chapter 13, "Getting Your Records," particularly the form printed at the end of the chapter. Your service rep may have to use the Freedom of Information Act to get some of the records you need.

You may also find it useful to submit copies of newspapers or of regimental or divisional newsletters that detail specific combat actions and name you as a participant. Each service, and some divisions, have historical offices that have extensive collections of photographs. News organizations also maintain large libraries of photos. Photos that show you along with service members who were killed in action would help prove you were exposed to stressful combat. Several books are available that contain combat histories of units in Vietnam. Your service rep should be able to help you locate the kinds of evidence just described.

How hard you should work to get documents depends on your case. If a VA psychiatrist has diagnosed you as having

PTSD or if you received a Purple Heart or a medal for valor, you will probably be awarded disability compensation without providing much documentation. If there are lots of questions (in the minds of others) about whether you have PTSD or another psychological condition, you will need strong documentation of your condition and of what caused it.

Previous Diagnoses

A special problem facing Viet Vets is a false or misleading previous diagnosis. Many vets who have psychological problems today have also had them for years. As a result, many have previously been seen at a VA hospital or other facility and have received a diagnosis from a psychiatrist or other health professional. And often that diagnosis is *wrong*. There are many possible reasons. A common one is that until 1980 PTSD was not officially recognized as a psychiatric disorder. In addition, vets with PTSD often have problems with drugs or alcohol that may make it difficult for a doctor to come up with a correct diagnosis. And some psychiatrists and psychologists simply make a lot of mistakes.

Before granting disability compensation for PTSD, the VA requires that any past diagnoses be "reconciled." This means an application must explain how it can be that the vet was once diagnosed as having another psychological problem (or as having no problem) but now has PTSD.

The VA is supposed to give vets claiming PTSD the "benefit of the doubt" on all claims for disability compensation, but legitimate claims are sometimes denied. If your claim is denied because of a previous diagnosis, you should promptly appeal the denial and should get an independent examination by a psychiatrist or psychologist who is experienced with PTSD cases (the results of this examination can be used in your appeal). Nevertheless, it is extremely important that a VA psychiatrist diagnose you as having PTSD. For help with your appeal, contact your service representative. Also see Chapter 16, "Claims and Appeals."

Using the PTSD Attachment

Vietnam Veterans of America (VVA) has prepared a form on PTSD that you can adapt to your specific case and attach to your claim for disability compensation (or any other VA claim). It may be found at the end of this chapter. Do not tear out the page that includes the attachment: start with your own blank, letter-size sheet of paper. It will probably help your application if you *type or print* all applicable information you find in the form and all information you add to fill in the blanks. Do not type up parts of the attachment that do not apply to your case.

In creating your own attachment, be sure to explain in Section I just how severely a particular event upset you (how badly stressed you were). Give a detailed description of the stressful event(s) on one or more sheets separate from the attachment. Be sure to include the date(s).

In Section II, estimate how many times the various problems have occurred. Regarding Section IID, remember the VA will not agree you have PTSD unless you have at least two of the first six symptoms that are listed.

In Section IIIA or on a separate sheet, give names and places of employment, the dates you worked there, the type of work you did, how well you performed and how you felt about your performance, and whether you had to leave your employment because it reminded you of your war experience. If you were fired or got bad work evaluations, attach copies of documents indicating these facts.

Regarding social problems, you may want to include letters from your parents, other relatives, spouse, friends, or lover that describe the difference between your behavior before you served in the military and your behavior after service.

Be sure everything on your attachment accurately applies to you and does not make it look like you just copied something prepared as a sample.

Now you have your own attachment. Staple it to your VA claim.

Remember that PTSD is treatable. So expect your disability rating to be reevaluated from time to time and reduced as you get better.

Social Security Benefits

The Social Security Administration operates the Supplemental Security Income program and the Social Security Disability Program. These programs provide payments to disabled persons. If PTSD has interfered with your ability to hold a job, you may qualify for payments from the Social Security programs. You can receive these payments in addition to any VA disability compensation you may be getting. Payments from the Social Security programs may, however, reduce the amount of the VA pension for which you may qualify.

Disability Compensation for Drug or Alcohol Dependence

Although the VA provides *treatment* for dependence on drugs or alcohol, it is difficult to get VA approval for *compensation* for disability due to dependence. In many cases, the VA will say such dependence is "willful misconduct" or is not service-connected. It is possible, however, to receive compensation for the physical results of the abuse of drugs or alcohol if the abuse is directly related to a service-connected disability such as PTSD.

For more information, check with your service rep and see Chapter 3, "Compensation."

Appealing VA Decisions

If you apply for disability compensation on the basis of a psychological disability and receive a denial, think about appealing it to the VA regional office or the Board of Veterans Appeals. You will have an especially good chance of winning an appeal if your claim was based on PTSD. Ask your service representative for advice and see Chapter 16, "Claims and Appeals."

Suicide

In several highly publicized cases, veterans have committed suicide apparently due to despair over their belief that life would never improve. Some of these veterans had been to VA facilities and had ended their lives by consuming a month's supply of VA-provided medication. Some had never sought help from the VA.

It is possible for the vet's survivors to receive financial benefits, including Dependency and Indemnity Compensation (DIC). To do so, survivors must establish that the vet's death was service-connected. Also, in some cases, medical malpractice claims (or lawsuits) have resulted in large awards of money damages.

For information on compensation for survivors, see Chapter 3, "Compensation." For information on lawsuits, see Chapter 16, "Claims and Appeals."

More important than compensating survivors is avoiding more suicides. It is important to communicate to vets suffering from PTSD or other psychological conditions that these problems can be treated: impossible as it may seem to some veterans, they can—and in almost all cases will—get better. If you know a vet who needs help, be sure he gets it.

SELF-HELP GUIDE

The Veterans Education Project has published *The Veteran's Self-Help Guide on Stress Disorder*. This eight-page guide provides a good summary of what a vet with PTSD needs to know. It should be noted, however, that it includes much of the same information that is contained in this chapter. Vets can get a copy by writing to: Veterans Education Project; P.O. Box 42130; Washington, DC 20015.

MINORITIES AND THE DISABLED

Minority Vietnam Era Vets have special problems, many of them relating to psychological readjustment to civilian life. Although most published information about minority vets is about black vets, it is reasonable to assume that some of what is true about blacks is also true for members of other minority groups.

Black Veterans

Blacks, vet-for-vet, have many more cases of PTSD than vets in general. According to *Legacies of Vietnam*, a 1981 study commissioned by Congress and prepared by Arthur Egendorf, Ph.D., Robert S. Laufer, Ph.D., and others, nearly 70 percent of blacks who were in heavy combat suffer some degree of PTSD. The figure for whites is "only" 23 percent. The percentage may be so much higher for blacks partly because blacks as a group were more sympathetic than whites toward the Vietnamese people and were more opposed to the war. As a result, they presumably suffered more guilt in connection with the killing and brutalization of Vietnamese soldiers and civilians.

Blacks also had special problems behind the lines, where racism against them was often much more pronounced than in combat. Due to racism and other causes, blacks, vet-for-vet, received far more bad discharges than vets in general. And bad discharges sometimes add to psychological problems.

In addition, blacks, even more than whites, returned to a society that made them feel different, made them feel alone. As discussed earlier, all Viet Vets suffered because of the unpopularity of the war and because they generally came home rapidly from Vietnam and came home by themselves. But blacks felt even more alienated because, war or no war, they represented a small minority of the society and belonged to a minority group that had always been subjected to racism and discrimination.

What can the minority veteran do about his psychological problems and other problems? Mostly, he can do the same thing all other vets can do: get help from the same organizations. Vietnam Veterans of America (VVA) has been at the forefront in assisting minority vets. Vet Centers, which have many minority employees, and the other facilities mentioned in this chapter can also help. Joining minority veterans groups can make these groups stronger and can help them get more attention from politicians and the media for the special problems of minority vets.

For this book, three Viet Vets—two from minority groups and one who is disabled—have written articles on the readjustment problems facing minority and disabled veterans. The articles follow.

Hispanic Veterans

By Richard L. Borrego, Assistant Regional Manager for Counseling,
Readjustment Counseling Service (the Vet Centers)

In discussing Hispanic veterans, it is important to point out that this is a very heterogeneous population. In this group are Mexican-Americans, Puerto Ricans, Cubans, and Latin Americans. Hispanics may be almost totally submerged into traditional Hispanic culture, or nearly completely assimilated into the predominant Anglo culture.

In spite of this heterogeneity, a majority of Hispanics have had to cope with a triple oppression: poverty, racism, and cultural oppression. Such oppression has resulted in fewer opportunities for good jobs or careers which require higher education. Military service became the alternative for many Hispanics.

While in Vietnam, Hispanics often served in the infantry. In many cases this was by choice, because of the value Hispanics place on pride and courage.

Upon return from Vietnam, Hispanics found that the triple oppression, coupled with what was often a combat role in the war, complicated their reintegration into society. Generally, human service agencies have not been utilized by Hispanic Veterans to facilitate the reintegration process. There is a need for such agencies to evaluate their services in terms of how to make them more responsive to Hispanics.

Fortunately, the strong family and extended family network among Hispanics provided support for readjustment. Also, many Hispanics have a strong Catholic background and may find peace through their religion.

For some, the survival skills learned in dealing with oppression helped. On the other hand, the added stress of war, and the racism involved in the war, increased anger and the desire to remain isolated from the main culture. Given the war experiences, it is important for Hispanic Veterans to channel their anger into adaptive behaviors as opposed to self-destructive behaviors. This can be done by joining or developing Hispanic Veteran organizations which serve as a forum for the ventilation and resolution of their unique problems.

Such organizations could serve as a link to existing resources such as VVA, the Disabled American Veterans (DAV), and the Vet Centers.

The key to survival for the Hispanic veteran, or for any war veteran, is to reach out to those you feel most comfortable with. For Hispanics, this is often *la familia* or other Hispanic community resources. In addition, our comrades in arms can provide a supportive role.

Hispanics have traditionally been enthusiastic about meeting the call to duty. In the Vietnam war they served with honor and suffered heavy casualties. Those who returned deserve nothing less than the utmost respect and support in their quest for successful reintegration into "the World."

Native American Veterans

By Frank Montour, Chairman, Readjustment Counseling Service (the Vet Centers), National Working Group on American Indian Vietnam Veterans

The interesting thing about American Indians (Native Americans if you prefer) in Vietnam is that each nonIndian vet we in the Vet Centers talk to had an Indian in his unit. That Indian was invariably called "Chief" and usually walked point. But even after spending a year or more with him in Southeast Asia, after coming home, there remained a general feeling of never really having known the Indian dude called Chief, who walked point.

The mysteriousness about Indian vets, unfortunately, is not limited to their service in Vietnam. It seems to prevail, even now, in the VA and other service-providing agencies. The Department of Defense can't tell us how many Indians served in Vietnam. The 1980 Census states 82,000 American Indians are Vietnam Era Veterans but makes no estimate of how many were in Vietnam.

In September 1983, a number of Indian vets, already working in Vet Centers, were pulled together to form the National Working Group on American Indian Vietnam Veterans. It was the Group's charge to find answers to a great many questions concerning service delivery to this unique population.

The Group devised a fairly comprehensive survey/

questionnaire and distributed it through various Vet Centers and the Vietnam Era Veterans Inter-Tribal Association, the largest national organization of Indian veterans.

The number of completed questionnaires returned was far greater than the Working Group had imagined, including results from some 55 tribes in the U.S. and Canada.

According to the survey, close to 90 percent of the Indian vets had enlisted (many before their 18th birthday, with parental consent). Most chose combat-arms military occupations in the Marines or Army and felt that being Indian helped in securing positions in combat specialty or elite groups. A significant number felt their "Indianness" made them better prepared for Vietnam service. Close to half were counseled, spiritually prepared, or ceremonially protected by their individual tribes before passing into the madness of war. Upon return to their communities, many were counseled, spiritually cleansed, or ceremonially reaccepted as proven warriors with varying degrees of special status or regard. Very few entered the military for reasons of national patriotism. The reason in most cases was related to tribal or family honor. Most Indians who served in the war have felt sorrow that "other Viet Vets" have been treated so poorly by their own people.

Does the American Indian Vet have service-related problems?

Yes. Even with the special family and tribal support mechanisms remaining intact within the Indian culture, more than half of those surveyed report having dealt with (or continuing to deal with) the same problems of night terrors, sleep disturbances, and the like noted by so many other Viet Vets. But many Indians perceive their combat residuals to be a part of the price one pays to become a warrior.

For various reasons, Indians have not much used Vet Centers, other VA facilities, or the Indian Health Service. IHS facilities are located in or near Indian communities, so why don't Indian vets take advantage of their services?

They do, to some extent, for medical problems. But Indian Vietnam Vets, while reporting the IHS to be more culturally sensitive than the VA, find that when it comes to dealing with warrior issues, such as PTSD, Agent Orange, and veterans benefits, IHS personnel have little specialized insight.

The Working Group has recommended that the two agencies

(VA and IHS) form an interagency agreement in the near future. The Group hopes the agreement would allow for joint or shared training, or some other mechanism through which Vet Centers might gain an understanding of the culture of the Indian world while contributing special insights from the problems of Vietnam Vets.

Inter-Tribal Association membership is open to all Vietnam Era Veterans (regardless of discharge status) of all tribes in North America. As of this writing, membership is free and provides a quarterly newsletter highlighting Indian Vietnam Veteran news, announcements, and a calendar of coming events, such as Pow Wows, ceremonials, and unit reunions. To join this organization, drop a note with your name, address, and tribal affiliation to: Vietnam Veterans Inter-Tribal Association; 4111 North Lincoln, Suite 10; Oklahoma City, OK 73105.

Disabled Veterans

By Steven N. Tice, Chairman, Readjustment Counseling Service (the Vet Centers), National Working Group on Physically Disabled Vietnam Veterans

There are special factors associated with Post Traumatic Stress Disorder cases among physically disabled Vietnam veterans. The nature of the war, homecoming, hospitalization, and the rehabilitation process, as well as "living disabled" in America had impact upon and continue to influence the stress recovery process of those who were injured in Vietnam.

Vietnam, with its booby traps and rocket-propelled grenades, its snipers and sappers, lent itself to the likelihood of serious injury. Modern technology, replete with rapid helicopter evacuation by Medevac and corresponding superior emergency medical care, assisted in prolonging lives that in past wars would have ended.

The legacy of Vietnam includes 303,704 wounded American soldiers of whom over half required hospitalization. The Vietnam War created an unprecedented wave of seriously disabled individuals (some seventy-five thousand) in America. The probability of incurring a permanently disabling injury was far greater for soldiers in that war than for previous warriors. In

Vietnam G.I.s suffered amputation or crippling wounds to the lower extremities at a rate 300 percent higher than in World War II.

Once he was stateside, the soldier's hospital experience was focused on the healing of physical wounds. Certainly for those in an emergency condition, this focus seems appropriate. However, as the individual's physical condition improved, a corresponding emphasis on the emotional stress recovery process too often did not emerge.

While the quality of stateside medical care varied, attention to the psychological components of rehabilitation appears to have been minimal. Instead the focus was on physical, vocational and monetary issues. Many veterans failed to receive adequate emotional preparation for living disabled in America.

Some writers attribute to hospitalized warriors an advantage over their unscathed counterparts, who quickly separated and were essentially denied an opportunity to process their wartime experiences. This popular theory hails disabled veterans as achieving an earlier and often more complete readjustment in large part due to peer support during hospitalization.

Certainly, in the hospital, the camaraderie borne of battle was fortified by the continuing struggle to survive. The primary group was intact; soldiers continued to aid their comrades. This care most often took the form of physical assistance, with those with appropriate working body parts supporting those without.

Impromptu rap groups emerged, but outside of building camaraderie, they completed little work of substance. This is not meant to minimize the value of the hospital relationships. Powerful feelings were expressed. However, little direction was provided by staff, family, or veterans themselves in the processing of those feelings.

Instead, the hospital setting provided the means to deny or numb the emotions associated with combat and recovery. Drugs and alcohol were used, and indeed, sanctioned, to numb physical as well as emotional pain. The attitude changed very little during the ongoing rehabilitation process.

The regimen of rehabilitation is often so intense and prolonged that the veteran's focus becomes preoccupied with the process. It is when this effort is perceived as completed or is interrupted that the veteran may experience psychological distress. It is when the physical "rehab" battle subsides that the unfinished business of emotional stress recovery often emerges. The return to "routine" can be accompanied by the surfacing of unresolved feelings associated with combat and disability.

Physically disabled Vietnam Veterans experienced multiple losses. Comrades were killed in battle; the soldier's belief in his own immortality often was a casualty; and, importantly, individuals lost body parts and/or functioning. Many have not grieved for those losses and carry an untold, unspent sadness through their lives. Anger, both internalized and/or externalized may be a regular dynamic of that life. Frustration is a routine feature of the ongoing rehabilitation process. The injured veteran may experience depression, pain, guilt, dependency, as well as difficulties with intimacy and sexuality. These are often aggravated by the lack of mobility, by isolation, and by substance abuse. While many disabled veterans have worked or are working through these issues others have found the process blocked.

There is a reluctance for the disabled to seek assistance from the temporarily-able-bodied population. The stereotype of the "problematic" Vietnam Veteran is heightened by prevailing stigmas surrounding the disabled. Racial, gender and cultural factors increase the probability of prejudgment. Disabled veterans hesitate in drawing any further negative attention to themselves. The result is an atmosphere that discourages the disabled vet from soliciting help when difficulties arise.

Outreach, education and participation are paramount in the healing process. Veteran organizations are important tools for the breaking down of negative public views and for building positive, useful ones. A number of national and local veterans organizations represent specific disabled populations, while Vietnam Veterans of America and other organizations focus on all disabled veterans. The Vet Center program is addressing the issue through a National Working Group on Physically Disabled Vietnam Veterans.

The myth of the "adjusted" disabled Vietnam Veteran prevails today. Although disabled vets have, through personal sacrifice, made enormous strides in the readjustment process, the time to finish the work is now. The task for disabled Vietnam Veterans is to take on the pain of working through the stress recovery process. The task for America is to encourage them to do so.

SPOUSES

Spouses (usually wives) of Vietnam Veterans sometimes have special problems too. One problem is that *their* spouses often have problems connected with the war, such as PTSD, illnesses, injuries, and bad discharges. And of course these problems affect the relationships between the vet and his spouse and any children. For example, some vets have trouble controlling their impulses and their anger, and, as a result, the spouse or children may suffer physical abuse. Or a vet may find it difficult to share or express feelings, causing his spouse or children to feel that the vet has little interest in them or affection for them.

Another problem is that in many cases the veteran returned from the war a seemingly different person from the one who left for Vietnam. A third problem for spouses is that *their* problems are largely ignored: the problems of vets are often greater and get much more media attention, and as a result many people view the problems of spouses as small.

But the problems are substantial, and the spouses need help. The programs described in this chapter are designed for vets, and some are available only to vets. But some are open to spouses (and some to other family members and friends too). In particular, many Vet Centers and some VA hospitals counsel family members along with vets and also offer counseling and "rap" sessions exclusively for families of vets.

Some spouses are also eligible for traditional VA psychiatric care. Those eligible are generally the spouses of vets who are permanently and totally disabled or who are deceased. For more information, see Chapter 6, "Medical Services."

Spouses are also eligible for free care from some state and private mental health facilities. Some Vet Centers can provide information on programs available to spouses.

Of course spouses can also—if they can afford it—get help from psychiatrists, psychologists, and other therapists who are in private practice. Just because their psychological problems have a lot to do with their relationship with another person (a vet), spouses who are suffering should not hesitate to get help for themselves.

Regarding psychological problems and most any other kind of problem having to do with a spouse's relationship with a veteran, veterans groups can sometimes provide assistance. Some chapters of Vietnam Veterans of America (VVA) have special "rap" groups for the spouses of Vietnam Vets.

BAD PAPER

Many vets got bad discharges because of PTSD or other psychological problems (or due to use of drugs or alcohol). Bad discharges in most cases prevent vets from getting VA benefits, including disability compensation and medical care (although in some cases vets with undesirable discharges can get medical treatment).

If you have a bad discharge, you can try to get it changed. If your bad discharge is due to PTSD, you have a fairly good chance of getting an upgrade—if your upgrade application is supported by evidence. A typical applicant who has a strong chance of upgrade is a veteran who, as a service member, had a good record in Vietnam followed by a series of petty offenses during stateside service. Some Discharge Review Boards understand PTSD and are often sympathetic to vets with PTSD who apply for an upgrade.

For more information on bad discharges and on how to get them upgraded, see Chapter 15, "Upgrading Your Discharge."

VETS IN PRISON OR CHARGED WITH A CRIME

Some vets are in prison because they committed a crime for reasons relating to PTSD. Others are there for reasons unconnected to PTSD or any other reason related to military service, but still need treatment for the disorder. And still other vets with PTSD have been arrested for a crime but have not yet stood trial. All of these vets may benefit from special legal procedures or special programs for vets with PTSD who have been charged with or convicted of a crime. See Chapter 18, "Veterans in the Criminal Justice System."

VETS WITH EMPLOYMENT PROBLEMS

In some cases Vets who have PTSD have been fired or had other employment problems due to conduct associated with their disorder. In some cases these vets have a right to get their jobs back or to get a better job than they currently have. See Chapter 9, "Employment."

A PARTING WORD

This chapter—and this whole book—is designed to help the veteran. But the book is here to help the vet who deserves help, not the occasional vet who may be trying to get benefits for which he doesn't qualify or which he doesn't need, and not the occasional vet who may be trying to shirk his responsibilities to others and to himself.

These points are especially important to make in a chapter that focuses on PTSD. This chapter will therefore approach its end with a quotation from Arthur Egendorf. Egendorf, a Viet Vet, is also the clinical psychologist who began the largest study yet completed on veterans of the Vietnam War, *Legacies of Vietnam*, which this chapter previously mentioned. Here's what he says:

> It's one thing for a vet to speak up about real troubles. It's another thing when guys make themselves out to be sickies to avoid responsibilities to themselves, to people who love them, or to society. Veterans should be warned that fake claims don't work in the long run. Somebody else might fall for it. But you lose self-respect—something we veterans need too much to throw away.

The great majority of vets who claim to have PTSD or other psychological problems are telling the truth, are genuinely suffering, and deserve help from specific programs and from their country at large. This chapter is for them.

ATTACHMENT TO PTSD CLAIM

[Staple to pertinent VA application]

NAME:
ADDRESS:
Date Filed:
Claim number: C-

I request that the VA, in addition to the information given here, develop evidence of my duties while I served in Vietnam, pursuant to 38 C.F.R. § 3.103. I would like to be notified immediately when such development has been completed and be sent a copy of the results of such development. This also is to request that the VA presume I was exposed to the traumatic event described below, unless the VA can affirmatively establish otherwise. Any reasonable doubt involving my claim (particularly with regard to the severity of the traumatic event) should be resolved in my favor pursuant to 38 C.F.R. § 3.102.

SECTION I

I served in Vietnam from the month of   , 19 , to the month   , 19 . I served with the following organizations:

_____

_____

I had the following duties during this time:

_____

_____

The military experiences I found most terrifying, life-threatening, or stressful include the following:

___ armed combat or enemy action
___ bombed or shelled or tripped booby-trap
___ shipwrecked or in airplane or vehicle accident
___ captured
___ grave registration duty
___ other action that threatened my life
___ other

I have attached a detailed description of the stressful events and have attached portions of military records or other evidence that are objective proof of or support the existence of the stressful event.

SECTION II

A. Since the event described above, I have reexperienced the event in nightmares, flashbacks and over and over again in my mind.

____ Nightmares have occurred ____ times each month over the past ____ year(s).

____ I have thought about the event ____ times each month over the past ____year(s).

____ Flashbacks have occurred ____ times each month over the past ____ year(s).

B. I felt numb after the event, or had difficulty "feeling."

C. I have much less interest in my family, friends, and activities like

_____

_____

that used to be important to me. I don't feel close to anyone anymore.

D. The following problems were not present before the event described above but are now:

____ I'm jumpy or hyperalert.
____ My sleep is disturbed; I can't get to sleep or stay asleep; I wake up too early; or I have nightmares.
____ I feel guilty that I survived when others did not; and guilty about what I had to do or not do to survive.
____ I have trouble concentrating on things or remembering things.
____ I avoid activities that remind me of the event.
____ Certain activities that resemble the event and remind me of it make me more nervous or anxious.
____ I avoid getting close to anyone in my family, or on my job, or among my friends.
____ I have no interest in getting close to anyone in my family, or on my job, or among my friends.
____ OTHER (specify): _____

SECTION III

A. I request service-connected benefits and believe I have been and continue to be unable to function in social settings like I used to or to work to my fullest capacity because of Stress Disorder and that it had its origin in my active duty service. The following information explains my social and employment history since I was discharged (see attached letters and documents):

B. I have received psychiatric treatment for my nervous condition:

___ in the military in ___ while stationed at _____.
___ within one year following discharge from service at _____.
___ more than one year following discharge from the service at _____.

9. EMPLOYMENT

Getting a Job, Starting a Business

> Come back home to the refinery
> Hiring man says, "Son, if it was up to me"
> Went down to see my VA man
> He said, "Son, don't you understand now?"
> —*Born in the U.S.A.*
> by Bruce Springsteen

Many veterans returning from Vietnam found that "Jody" (the boy back home) had not only taken their girls; he had also taken their jobs. And many vets found that finding a good job is the hardest job of all.

For many years, the federal government wasn't much help. Vets coming back to "the World" found themselves lumped together with all other unemployed people in programs that didn't suit the special needs of veterans.

Thanks to veterans organizations such as Vietnam Veterans of America (VVA), the situation is improving. But finding suitable employment is still a hard job.

In many areas covered by this book, there is one major system that concerns the veteran. For instance, in medical services, it's the system of VA hospitals; in disability compensation, it's the VA disability rating program.

The subject of employment presents an entirely different picture. There are as many routes to employment as the vet can imagine, and there are many different programs that may provide help.

Despite the number of programs, many are administered by

just two agencies: the U.S. Department of Labor and the U.S. Small Business Administration. So you will have some success locating programs to help you if you simply contact these agencies, found in the "United States" listings in your phone directory.

You will have more success, however, if you contact the very same person already recommended over and over in this book. That is the service representative who works for a veterans organization such as Vietnam Veterans of America (VVA). The service rep will be particularly well equipped to help you if he or she has a copy of the 640-page *Service Representatives Manual*, first published in October 1983 by the VVA. This manual contains a chapter on employment, which itself includes a thick appendix featuring federal agency addresses all over the country, rules, forms, and other useful information.

GETTING A JOB—AND KEEPING IT

Training and Related Services

Two recent federal laws are designed to provide training to veterans who want to learn new job skills.

The *Job Training Partnership Act*, passed by Congress in 1982, was created to assist unemployed persons, including vets who lack skills needed to get good jobs. This law provides federal funding to state and local governments to set up training programs in local communities.

The law is administered by the Department of Labor. Contact the Veterans' Employment and Training Service (VETS) office in the nearest U.S. Department of Labor office, or check with the nearest office of your state employment service. (For the employment service, look in your phone book under the name of your state.) Ask about organizations in your area that are providing training and other services under the Job Training Partnership Act.

The *Emergency Veterans' Job Training Act* was passed by Congress in 1983. It provides on-the-job training for vets of the Vietnam Era and the Korean War. Under this law, the federal government pays an employer to hire vets for permanent positions that require significant training. Training may be for up to fifteen months for veterans with at least a 30 percent disability and for veterans with a 10 or 20 percent disability who have a serious employment handicap. For other veterans, payment is limited to nine months.

The goal of the "emergency" law is to place forty thousand vets in jobs.

To qualify for training under this law, you must be unemployed (you must have no regular, full-time job) at the time you apply for training. You must also have been unemployed for fifteen of the twenty weeks before you apply.

To apply for training under this law, get VA Form 22–8932, Application for a Certificate of Eligibility, from the nearest VA regional office or state employment service office. After completing the form, return it to the same office. The state employment service office will assist you in finding an employer who is participating under the law. At the state employment service office, be sure to ask for the Veterans Employment Representative or the Disabled Veteran Outreach Program Specialist.

At this writing, the programs of the Emergency Veterans' Training Act were scheduled to be terminated. Organizations such as Vietnam Veterans of America (VVA) are working to keep these programs alive.

Job Placement

Job placement assistance is a part of some training programs. The main source for job placement, however, is the state employment service office.

State employment service offices have Veterans Employment Representatives and Disabled Veteran Outreach Program Specialists. These employees provide job counseling and placement services.

State offices also can provide information about job marts, training programs, and other services. Most veterans qualify for priority at such offices in referrals to job openings and to training programs. Among veterans, disabled vets get special priority.

Veterans organizations, including some chapters of Vietnam Veterans of America (VVA), also assist vets looking for work.

Other sources of jobs include those that exist for vets and nonvets alike. Among these are unions, private employment agencies, help-wanted ads in newspapers (check out-of-town papers as well as local ones), and, perhaps most effective, friends, relatives, and other contacts. Ask as many people as possible if they know of openings where they work or elsewhere. Remember that many jobs are neither available through government or private employment services nor advertised in the want ads. And remember that *persistence pays off*: many people have found a job only after contacting many dozens of potential employers.

Employment Preference for Vets

As mentioned, veterans have priority in referrals from state employment service offices. They also benefit from other types of preference.

Federal Government Preference: In applying for federal jobs, veterans have advantages over nonveterans, and Vietnam Era Vets have special advantages.

Veterans may be eligible for advantages including points added to passing scores on civil service exams, not having to fulfill certain physical requirements, and having first consideration for being able to keep a job in the event of a layoff.

Vietnam Era Vets who have completed no more than fourteen years of education may in some circumstances be hired by a U.S. government agency without having to take a civil service exam. To qualify to be hired without an exam, the vet must agree to participate in a program of education or training. A job obtained in this way is called a Veterans Readjustment Appointment. The fourteen-year limit on education does not apply to vets who have disabilities that qualify for compensation or to vets who were discharged due to service-connected disabilities.

For more information on veterans preferences for federal jobs (and for information on federal job openings that exist in your area) contact a Federal Job Information Center. The nearest center may be found in the "United States" listings in the phone book, under "Office of Personnel Management."

State and Local Government Preference: Most state and local governments also provide hiring preferences for veterans.

To find out about the preferences that may apply to you, call the personnel offices for your city and county, nearby cities and counties, and your state. Look in the phone book in the listings for a particular city, county, or state, under the word "personnel" or "employment."

Affirmative Action: Affirmative action is not limited to women and minorities. It also helps veterans of both sexes and every race and ethnic group.

Federal law requires employers who have federal contracts or subcontracts for $10,000 or more to take affirmative action to employ and advance Vietnam Era Vets and vets who have a disability of 30 percent or more or who were discharged due to a service-connected disability.

If you believe a federal contractor or subcontractor is failing to take affirmative action to hire and promote vets, you may file a complaint with the Veterans Employment Representative at your state employment service office. Generally, the complaint must be filed within 180 days of the date of violation of the law.

Discrimination Against the Handicapped

Federal law requires employers with federal contracts for more than $2,500 to take affirmative action to employ and advance qualified handicapped persons. The law also prohibits discrimination based solely on handicap by any employer receiving federal funds.

Veterans protected by the law include not only those with physical disabilities but also those suffering from Post-Traumatic Stress Disorder (PTSD). In fact, a postal employee suffering from PTSD got his job back because of the law. The employee had drinking problems and was fired for a series of absences. After an appeal to the U.S. Merit Systems Protection Board, he was reinstated. The Board ruled that in this case PTSD was a handicap the Postal Service should have tried to accommodate.

If you believe an employer has discriminated against you due to a handicap, file a complaint with the Merit Systems Protection Board. For information on how to file a complaint, phone the nearest office of the Office of Personnel Management, found in the phone book in the "United States" listings. If you are in a union, also ask your union for assistance.

REEMPLOYMENT

In most cases, federal law required that the employer you had before serving in the military give you back your old job—or one with similar seniority, status, and pay—when you returned from service. In most cases you were also entitled to all benefits you would have earned through seniority if you had not left your job for the military. (These benefits generally include credit toward pension.)

To have been eligible for legally required reemployment, you must have left a job that was not temporary and must have served in the military after August 1, 1961, but for no more than five years. If you served more than *four* years, your additional service must have been rendered because the government required it. You must also have received an honorable or general discharge. And you must have been qualified to perform your old job or, if you were disabled in the military, you must have been qualified to perform another job of similar seniority, status, and pay with your old employer.

And there are still more rules. You must have applied for reemployment within ninety days of separation from active duty. If you were hospitalized immediately after active duty, you were eligible for reemployment if you were in the hospital for one year or less and if you applied for reemployment within ninety days after separation.

If you were attempting to return to a job in state or local government, you must have been released from the military after December 2, 1974.

If you were eligible for reemployment but your former employer refused to hire you back (or hired you back but did not provide you with the seniority, status, and pay to which you believe you were entitled), you may report the refusal to the Office of Veterans' Reemployment Rights in the nearest office of the U.S. Department of Labor. If you applied for reemployment within ninety days of separation, it generally is *not* too late now to complain to the Veterans' Reemployment Rights Office.

If that office does not resolve the problem, the U.S. Attorney's office, in cooperation with the U.S. Department of Labor's Regional Solicitor's office, may file a lawsuit against the employer to enforce your rights. By law, the U.S. Attorney is required to represent veterans in most reemployment rights cases. Sometimes, however, even though the Labor Department favors bringing suit, the U.S. Attorney is reluctant.

If neither the Reemployment Rights office nor the U.S. Attorney can help you, ask your service representative whether you should hire a private attorney to sue your old employer. In considering a particular private attorney, carefully check his or her reputation and his or her experience in cases such as yours. Ask for a written estimate of the fees and expenses you will have to pay, of how likely it is that you will succeed, and of how much you will win if a court decides in your favor or if the case is settled out of court.

National Guard and Reserve

If you have joined the National Guard or a Reserve unit, you have a legal right to take time off from your job to attend training sessions or to perform military service. You must request leave from your employer and your employer must grant your request. Your leave is *unpaid*, but you may use paid vacation time you have earned. Federal law requires that you not be denied a promotion or any other employment advantage (such as benefits) because of your military obligations.

If your employer discriminates against you because of these obligations, contact the Office of Veterans Reemployment Rights at the nearest office of the U.S. Department of Labor.

UNEMPLOYMENT COMPENSATION

If you have been separated from military service for less than a year, you may qualify for up to thirteen weeks of unemployment compensation through the federal Unemployment Compensation Program for Ex-Servicemembers. The abbreviation for this program is UCX. To be eligible for UCX benefits, you must have been separated with an honorable or general discharge and, in most cases, must have completed your first full tour of duty.

To apply for UCX compensation, go to your nearest state employment office. If possible, take a Form DD 214 (your separation papers).

If you are unemployed but have been out of military service for more than one year you may still be eligible for regular state unemployment compensation. Generally, you will be eligible if you did not voluntarily quit your last job. For information, phone the nearest state employment office.

STARTING A BUSINESS

If a veteran is going to decide to go into business for himself, he usually does so between the ages of thirty-five and forty-five. This book therefore comes at a time when many vets are making a choice between remaining as employees of someone else and becoming their own bosses.

If you want to start a business, it is important that you understand from the beginning that no one is going to hold your hand, perfectly explain every step you should take, and guarantee that you will succeed. Most of the responsibility will fall on your shoulders. You will have to learn a lot, work hard, and have at least a little luck. And still you may fail: a very large percentage of new businesses do just that.

Still, there is a lot of reason for hope and lot of available assistance. And special assistance is available to veterans.

Small Business Administration

By far the main source of government assistance to veterans who want to start a business is the U.S. Small Business Administration. The SBA has about one hundred offices, with at least one in every state. It assists people who have a small business and people who want to start one. The SBA provides management counseling, training, and limited financial assistance. It also helps small businesses get government contracts.

The SBA has an Office of Veterans Affairs and an Office of Veterans Business Enterprise. In each district and regional office of the SBA, there is a Veterans Affairs Officer (VAO). The job of the VAO is to be sure that SBA services are provided to vets, especially those from the Vietnam Era and those who are disabled.

Each SBA office is required to have a Veterans Business Resource Council (VBRC). The VBRC's purpose is to establish communication and cooperation between SBA offices and the veterans community.

In addition to having various officials who work with veterans and maintaining various programs to assist veterans, the SBA was directed by Congress in 1974 to give "special consideration" to vets in all SBA programs.

SBA Loans

In the year ending September 30, 1983, the SBA made or guaranteed $641 million in loans to veterans, including $292 million to Vietnam Era Vets. Still, the SBA should be seen only as a *lender of last resort*: the SBA will make or guarantee a loan only if a vet has already been turned down by private lenders. To qualify for an SBA loan, a vet must also own and operate at least 51 percent of the firm for which the loan is requested, must have enough capital (money to invest) to operate the firm on a sound financial basis, and must show he is able to successfully run the business. In these and other ways, he must demonstrate he will be able to pay back the loan.

Most loans involving the SBA are made not by the agency itself but by a private lender, with the SBA guaranteeing part of the loan (up to 90 percent). Guaranteed loans cannot exceed $500,000. They may be paid back over as many as twenty-five years. (The average guaranteed loan is $155,000, payable over about eight years.)

Loans made directly by the SBA are limited to $150,000. The SBA has a $25 million program for direct loans only to Vietnam Era Vets and disabled vets.

Veterans are not *entitled* to loans under any SBA program, but are supposed to receive preference over nonvets. If you expect to apply for an SBA loan, first make a careful and sincere application to private lenders: if your application to a bank or other private lender is poorly prepared, it will harm your chances at the SBA.

In preparing to apply for an SBA loan, your focus should be not on the money itself but on establishing a solid plan for your business. There are two reasons for this. First, the loan money won't do you any good in the long run if your business fails. Second, to get an SBA loan, you must first be turned down by at least two private lenders. Most vets turned down by private lenders are rejected because of lack of money to invest and lack of collateral. And if you don't have enough money or collateral, about the only way you're going to qualify at the SBA is with a solid business plan.

So come up with such a plan. As with applications to the VA, it is much easier to succeed with a strong original application to the SBA than to be denied and then go back hoping for a change in decision. To prepare your best possible business plan for your SBA application, go to the SBA for advice and management assistance.

SBA Management Assistance

To succeed in business and to get an SBA loan, you must have a business plan that includes a marketing plan and a variable cash flow analysis. (For explanations of these and for advice on preparing them, check with the SBA.) You must firmly know what you are going to do, how you are going to do it, and who your customers are going to be. You must understand how money, material, and labor will flow through your business.

To help you come up with a business plan that incorporates these factors, the SBA provides management assistance. It furnishes this help through individual counseling and through courses, conferences, workshops, problem clinics, and a wide variety of films and publications.

Counseling is available through the SBA Management Assistance staff; the Service Corps of Retired Executives (SCORE); the Active Corps of Executives (ACE), which is like SCORE except that its members aren't retired; and many professional associations.

The Veterans Business Resource Council (VBRC) at each SBA office can also help. Training sessions may be available through the VBRC as well as the SBA in general, nearby Chambers of Commerce, and veterans organizations.

In addition, many colleges and universities provide management assistance. The SBA has helped organize Small Business Institutes (SBIs) at colleges and universities in more than thirty states. In each SBI, business administration faculty and students provide management counseling at business sites.

Another source of management help are the Small Business Development Centers (SBDCs). These centers, based at universities, draw from government programs, businesses, and university programs to provide managerial and technical help, research, individual counseling, and practical training.

Not all programs exist in all areas. Also, the quality of a program varies from area to area: for instance, some SBDCs are very active and very effective, while others are weak. Check with friends, veterans organizations, and SBA staff about programs in your area that have a good reputation.

SBA Surety Bond Guarantees

Once you have established a small business, the SBA can help you get surety bonds for contracts. Many contracts, especially large ones in construction and other fields, require these bonds, also called performance bonds. A surety bond is like an insurance policy, paying the party with whom you enter a contract if you end up not doing what you have agreed to do.

Under its Surety Bond Guarantee Program, the SBA can guarantee up to 90 percent of performance bonds and other kinds of bonds required to get a contract. The vet applies to a participating surety company, which in turn applies to the SBA. Contracts must not exceed $1 million.

Your local SBA office can provide a list of participating companies. Under the SBA surety bond program in the year ending September 30, 1983, Vietnam Era Vets received some $24 million in contracts.

Procurement Assistance

The SBA assists vets who own small businesses and who want to get contracts with the federal government. You can register your firm with the computerized SBA Procurement Automated

Source System (PASS). PASS has registered more than ninety thousand small firms, of which more than eight thousand are owned by Vietnam Era Vets. When federal agencies are ready to award a contract, they may use PASS to find a firm with which to do business. To register with PASS, get SBA Form 1167 from any SBA office.

To increase your chances of getting a federal contract, regularly consult the *Commerce Business Daily* (*CBD*). You may subscribe to it or look at it at a public library. Federal law requires all government procurement solicitations to be printed in *CBD*. This periodical can notify you of contracts for which you may want to apply.

All contract *awards* must also be printed in *CBD*. If you see a large contract awarded in your area, you may want to approach the contractor and propose that your firm become a subcontractor.

Another route to federal contracts is for you to meet and stay in contact with procurement officers at federal agency offices in your area. Tell them your firm is interested in bidding on contracts and subcontracts.

8(a) Company Contracts

"8(a)" is the common term for section 8(a) of the Small Business Investment Act. This section requires that 10 percent of most federal government contracts be set aside for businesses owned by minorities and women. Minority and women vets should register for the 8(a) program at their SBA office. In the year ending September 30, 1983, more than $82 million in government contracts was awarded under this program to firms owned by veterans.

SBA, VA, and VVA

You didn't think this book would get through a whole chapter without a VA program, did you?

Each VA Regional Office has a Veterans-in-Business Coordinator (VIBC). His or her job is to work with the SBA to refer veterans to appropriate agencies and programs for small business assistance. VIBCS also sit on VBRCs. In English, this means Veterans-in-Business Coordinators also sit on Veterans Business Resource Councils.

Some chapters of Vietnam Veterans of America (VVA) provide advice about the SBA. If the chapter in your area cannot, you may contact the national VVA office at (202) 332-2700.

General Advice

Starting a small business and keeping it healthy and growing is no activity for the meek. If you want somebody to tell you exactly what to do and to pay you every couple weeks, stay an employee.

If you want to succeed in small business, check into every office, official, and program mentioned in this chapter and use all those that look promising to you. Visit the nearest SBA office and talk with the Veterans Affairs Officer, and visit the nearest VA regional office and talk with the Veterans-in-Business Coordinator (phone ahead to each office to see if an appointment is needed). When you meet with people who may help you, be active, imaginative, and assertive (but not hostile).

In addition to joining appropriate management assistance programs, do what you can on your own. Read books and trade journals on the specific type of business that interests you. If you have not already worked in the type of business you plan to start, consider doing so in order to learn all the details you will eventually have to know. Determine whether there is room in your community for a business of that type (or for *another* business of that type). Carefully assess possible locations for your business.

Learn as much as you can about trends within your business field and related business fields: these trends will help determine whether your business will succeed or fail (delivering ice is no longer a major growth industry; computers are). Try to think of everything you will need to succeed (plant/store, materials/inventory, employees, office supplies, insurance, advertising, . . .) and how much it will cost. Learn not only about your own type of business but about business in general: find out about accounting methods, banking procedures, and tax laws. Consult not only businesspersons but also, where appropriate, one or more accountants and lawyers.

The majority of jobs created in the United States each year

are in firms employing one hundred people or less. Many Vietnam Era Vets are unemployed. Many Vietnam Era Vets who found firms will hire their fellow veterans. So by establishing a small business you may end up helping not only yourself but your fellow vet as well. Good luck.

10. EDUCATION AND REHABILITATION

The G.I. Bill and Other Programs

Feelin' strong now
Won't be long now

> —*Gonna Fly Now* (theme from *Rocky*)
> by Bill Conti, Carol Connors, and Ayn
> Robbins

After a brief detour to employment programs run by the Department of Labor and business programs handled by the Small Business Administration, it's time to return to the main highway of veterans affairs: the VA. That's because the VA is in charge of federal education and rehabilitation programs for veterans.

EDUCATION

Veterans education is covered by perhaps the most prominent veterans program of all, the G.I. Bill. The G.I. Bill is the popular name for Chapter 34 of Title 38 of the U.S. Code. This chapter contains many laws providing educational benefits for vets. So the G.I. Bill is in reality many bills. And these bills cover most any kind of responsible educational program you can imagine—from universities to vocational training to remedial education at the elementary school level.

But the G.I. Bill does not cover the vet like a blanket. It

covers him more like a moth-eaten sheet: in many areas where you would think the veteran would be heavily covered, he is in fact covered very thinly; in some other areas, he's not covered at all.

The biggest hole has nothing to do with the kind of education the vet wants to undertake. It has to do with time. This hole is called the "ten-year delimiting date." It means that with few exceptions the vet must use his G.I. Bill benefits within ten years of separation from active service. More on that later. But keep it in mind. Also keep in mind that for all Vietnam Era Vets the G.I. Bill expires on December 31, 1989.

When many Vietnam Era Vets were discharged, going back to school was the furthest thing from their minds. Getting a job and supporting their families was more important than sitting in a classroom. Colleges didn't have programs to help the vet reenter school.

In addition, the climate on most college campuses in the lates 1960s and early 1970s did not make many vets feel comfortable, much less welcome. Those suffering from what was then called the Post-Vietnam Syndrome (now known as Post-Traumatic Stress Disorder, or PTSD) were particularly reluctant to attend school with their antiwar peers.

The result of all this was that many vets did not use their G.I. Bill benefits before the ten-year deadline had passed. So many Vietnam Era Vets have missed the deadline, and for such good reasons, that Vietnam Veterans of America (VVA) has urged Congress to extend the period of time for Vietnam Era Vets to use the G.I. Bill.

Eligibility

To be eligible for G.I. Bill benefits, you must fulfill *one* of these requirements:

1. Served on active duty for more than 180 continuous days any part of which occurred after January 31, 1955, and before January 1, 1977, and discharged "under conditions other than dishonorable." (See Chapter 15, "Upgrading Your Discharge.")
2. Enlisted or contracted (for instance, through a delayed

entry program or ROTC program) before January 1, 1977, for service and began active duty for training for more than 180 days, any part of which began within twelve months of January 1, 1977.

3. Continued on active duty on or after January 1, 1977, if the requirement of more than 180 days was met before that date.

4. Discharged for a service-connected disability, if service was after January 31, 1955, and before January 1, 1977.

Education Covered

If you served eighteen or more continuous months after January 31, 1955, and before January 1, 1977, you are entitled—if otherwise eligible—to forty-five months of educational assistance.

If you served seventeen or fewer months, you are entitled to one and a half months of educational assistance for each month or fraction of a month served.

The monthly amount you can be paid under the G.I. Bill varies depending on whether you are attending a program full time and how many dependents you have. For instance, a vet who has no dependents and is attending school half-time gets $188 a month. A vet with two dependents who is attending school full time gets $510.

For you to receive G.I. Bill payments, your educational institution must be "VA-approved." Among institutions that may be VA-approved are public and private elementary, junior high, and high schools; junior or community colleges; four-year colleges and universities and their graduate and professional programs; vocational institutions; scientific and technical institutions; teachers colleges and normal schools; correspondence schools; business schools; and professional schools that are independent of other institutions. Other institutions may also be approved.

Be sure the institution you want to attend is VA-approved. To be sure it is, check with the nearest VA regional office. Do not depend on the institution itself or on the fact that the VA has been paying G.I. Bill benefits to you or any other student at the institution you choose: the VA routinely (by mistake) pays benefits for schools it has not approved. Once it learns of its error, the VA will label the benefits an "overpayment" and will demand its money back. (See Chapter 4, "Overpayments.") Even if your institution is VA-approved now, the VA will stop paying benefits if it drops its approval of the institution.

To continue receiving G.I. Bill payments, you must maintain a certain standard of academic progress toward your educational goal (for instance, you cannot change majors at will). The exact standards vary from institution to institution (check with a counselor at yours). In most cases, however, a student on academic probation will continue to receive benefits until the end of the term. Students who drop a course or who receive a "nonpunitive grade not used in computing their graduation requirements" (such as an "incomplete") can be denied continued G.I. Bill benefits unless certain "mitigating circumstances" (excuses) exist. If certain mitigating circumstances do not exist, the VA may determine these students have received an "overpayment."

Special G.I. Bill Programs

Cooperative Education: Cooperative education combines formal education with training in business or industry. The emphasis is on training. If they are VA-approved, cooperative education programs qualify for G.I. Bill payments.

Farm Cooperative Training: Eligible veterans will also receive G.I. Bill benefits if they enroll in a VA-approved farm cooperative program. In such a program, vets must be working full-time in agriculture and must take agricultural courses relating to their employment. If the vet is scheduled for at least forty-four weeks a year of courses, he may receive payments for the full year.

Apprenticeships: VA-approved apprenticeship programs and on-the-job training programs also qualify for G.I. Bill benefits. To receive payments, the vet must be in a full-time program. For on-the-job training programs to qualify, the vet's wages at the beginning of the program must be at least half of the wages paid for the job for which he is training. The vet's wages must increase on a regular schedule until he is receiving at least 85 percent of the wages for the job. And the 85-percent level must be reached no later than the last full month of training. On-the-job training must take two years or less.

Correspondence Courses: Vets may also receive G.I. Bill payments for VA-approved correspondence courses. Vets receive reimbursement for 55 percent of the cost of courses.

Elementary and Secondary Education: The G.I. Bill covers elementary and secondary education (secondary education is junior high and high school). In most cases, G.I. Bill payments for elementary and secondary education will be made *without a reduction of the vet's G.I. Bill entitlement*. In other words, even after payments, the vet will still have available his full period (for instance, forty-five months) of G.I. Bill benefits. These cases include the vet who must finish high school, who must pass a General Education Development (G.E.D.) exam to qualify for post-high school education, or who has not completed the eighth grade. The G.I. Bill may also cover secondary education such as refresher courses or remedial skills courses—if these courses are needed for the vet to qualify for admission to a school or other institution. As with all other types of education, all elementary and secondary education must be VA-approved if the vet is to receive benefits.

Veterans Educational Assistance Program (VEAP)

Chapter 34 of Title 38 of the U.S. Code is called the G.I. Bill. Chapter 32 is called the Veterans Educational Assistance Program (VEAP). VEAP participation requires service members on active duty to contribute money toward their future education; each $1.00 contributed is matched by a larger amount from the government.

VEAP covers vets who enlisted after December 31, 1976. For this and other reasons, vets who qualify for G.I. Bill benefits *do not* qualify for VEAP. As a result, VEAP applies to very few Vietnam Era Veterans.

If you think VEAP may apply to you, check with a service representative who works for a veterans organization such as Vietnam Veterans of America (VVA). The service representative can explain the rules of this program. If you mistakenly contributed money to VEAP, request a refund at the nearest VA Regional Office.

Extensions of the Ten-Year Delimiting Date

As stated earlier, the biggest hole in the G.I. Bill is the "ten-year delimiting date." Generally this date means that the vet must use his G.I. Bill benefits within ten years of separation from active service.

But most every rule has an exception. There are at least three kinds of veterans for whom the delimiting date may be extended beyond ten years:

Vets who had physical or mental disabilities that prevented them from attending educational programs: If you could not start or continue your education due to a physical or psychological condition, you may qualify for an extension. It is not yet clear whether the VA will grant an extension if you were disabled by PTSD. It *is* clear that the VA will *deny* an extension if it determines your disability resulted from your own "willful misconduct." The VA considers most drug and alcohol abuse as falling into this category. Recently, three federal courts have said the VA rule that alcoholism is willful misconduct violates federal law. Veterans denied an extension because of alcoholism should contact the VVA Legal Services for help. Write to VVA Legal Services; 2001 S Street, N.W., Suite 710; Washington, D.C. 20009.

The VA will not extend the delimiting date for vets who could not attend school because they were in jail. (In some cases, however, a vet may be able to successfully argue that PTSD caused him to get in trouble with the law and that he should therefore get an extension.) If you receive an extension, it will be limited to the amount of time for which your disability prevented you from attending an educational institution.

Vets who have received an upgraded discharge: If you had a bad discharge that prevented you from qualifying for G.I. Bill benefits, you usually will start a ten-year period of eligibility on the date your discharge is upgraded. You will not receive payments for time spent in school before this date.

If you have a discharge other than an honorable or general one, do not *assume* you do not qualify for the G.I. Bill. Check with your service representative. This is important particularly for vets who due to homosexuality have an undesirable or bad conduct discharge. Generally, these veterans *do* qualify for G.I. Bill benefits. Such veterans may get a discharge upgrade and may assume they are starting a ten-year eligibility period, only to find that they are eligible for no G.I. Bill benefits at all: they may learn that under their old discharge they qualified for benefits but that their ten years have run out.

For more information on discharge upgrading, see Chapter 15, "Upgrading Your Discharge."

Remember: Whether or not you get an extension, the G.I. Bill expires for all Vietnam Era Veterans on December 31, 1989. Plan so that all of your education and training for which you expect G.I. Bill benefits is completed by that date.

Some members of Congress have proposed legislation to change the deadline from ten years to twenty. Check with your service representative on the progress of this legislation. You may want to write to your Senator or Member of Congress, saying you recommend extending the deadline.

How to Apply for G.I. Bill Benefits

Generally, you should apply for G.I. Bill benefits through the school or other educational or training program in which you want to participate. The application is a two-part process. First, you apply at your institution or program. Second, your institution or program certifies to the VA that you have been accepted for study or training.

When you apply, be sure to determine that your institution or program is VA-approved. Also, ask whether it provides tutorial assistance or work-study programs for veterans.

Educational Assistance for Dependents and Survivors

Dependents and survivors of certain veterans are entitled to essentially the same educational payments as those a veteran himself can get under the G.I. Bill. The monthly rates are the same.

Spouses and children and surviving spouses and children of veterans and service members are eligible for educational benefits if one of the following is true:

1. The veteran is permanently and totally disabled due to a service-connected disability.
2. The service member has been classified for at least ninety days (and is still classified) as missing in action, captured in the line of duty, or forcibly detained or interned in the line of duty by a foreign power.
3. The veteran died due to a service-connected disability.

Generally, a spouse or child is eligible for ten years from the date the veteran was found to have a service-connected permanent and total disability, or ten years from the date of death or the date the VA determines death was due to a service-connected disability, whichever is later.

For spouses and children of service members missing in action, captured, detained, or interned, eligibility is for ten years after the date the service member was listed as missing, captured, detained, or interned.

Assistance for dependent and surviving children extends from ages eighteen through twenty-five. Children may continue to receive benefits even after marriage.

To receive benefits, a dependent child must fill out VA Form 22–5490, Application for Educational Assistance (Son or Daughter). For a spouse, the form is VA Form 22–5490w, Application for Educational Assistance by Spouse or Surviving Spouse. Applications should be submitted to the nearest VA regional office.

To learn more about eligibility, the dependent or survivor should check with the nearest VA regional office or with a service representative. Dependents and survivors should also check with community colleges, four-year colleges, and universities about state programs for veterans' survivors and dependents.

TRAINING AND VOCATIONAL REHABILITATION

Some disabled veterans qualify for VA training or vocational rehabilitation programs, under which the VA will pay a monthly subsistence allowance (for minimal living expenses) as well as all costs for tuition, books, fees, and supplies. Rates are based on the individual vet's program and on the number of dependents he has. Subsistence rates range from $155 for a vet in a half-time training program who has no dependents to $452 for a vet in a full-time training program who has two dependents ($33 more per month is granted for each additional dependent).

Programs that may qualify the vet for payments include schools, colleges, on-the-job and apprenticeship training programs, institutional and on-farm training programs, and programs that combine school and job training. Other programs that may make the vet eligible include programs that, due to the vet's serious disability, are located in special rehabilitation facilities or in the vet's home.

After a vet has completed a training or vocational rehabilitation program, the VA will help him to find and hold a suitable job. The VA in some cases will also grant no-interest loans to vets who experience unexpected financial problems during training. In addition, the VA may pay for tutorial assistance and for unusual transportation expenses.

For a veteran to qualify for training and rehabilitation benefits, *all three* of the following must be true:

1. He suffered a service-connected disability in active service, and that disability entitles him to compensation, or would entitle him to compensation if he were not receiving military retirement pay.
2. He was discharged or released under "other than dishonorable conditions."
3. The VA determines he needs vocational rehabilitation to overcome the handicap to employment caused by his disability.

Generally, the vet must complete a rehabilitation program within twelve years of the date he is notified that he is entitled to VA disability compensation. If the vet has been unable to enter or continue a training program because he has had medical problems, the VA may grant an extension of the twelve-year deadline.

Eligible veterans may receive up to four years of full-time training or an equivalent amount of part-time training. The VA will generally approve training of more than four years if the vet required remedial training to prepare for post-high school education.

To apply for training or rehabilitation benefits, fill out VA Form 28–1900, Disabled Veteran's Application for Vocational Rehabilitation. File the form with the nearest VA Regional Office. Generally, the VA requires that disabled vets undergo VA educational counseling before it will approve a specific program of rehabilitation.

If you are a disabled vet, you may qualify for benefits under the rehabilitation program just described and also under the G.I. Bill; you must choose one or the other. In most cases, you will do better under the rehabilitation program. Although its monthly payment rates are slightly lower than those for the G.I. Bill, it also covers *all* educational costs. Under the G.I. Bill, you must pay all costs that are not met by your monthly check.

If you are disabled, but your disability has not been rated by the VA as service-connected, you may still be eligible for vocational rehabilitation at the vocational rehabilitation agency run by your state government. Check in the phone directory listings for your state, under "rehabilitation" or "vocational rehabilitation." Also check with your service representative. For information on VA disability compensation, see Chapter 3, "Compensation."

11. HOUSING

VA Loans and Other Programs

VA LOANS

For many veterans, the most helpful VA program of all is the one that provides VA home loans. Getting a VA loan can be the critical step in buying a home. And buying a home can be the critical step in improving the financial picture of a family or single person.

There are many advantages—and some dangers—in buying a home. The chief advantage is that you can stop making rent payments and can start making mortgage payments. When you pay rent, you have nothing to show for it but a receipt or canceled check. When you get a loan and buy a home, your mortgage payments build up your equity (share of ownership) in the property. And the interest portion of mortgage payments can amount to a very large tax deduction.

There are pitfalls too. One is that you may pay more for a home than it's worth. In particular, a property may be priced higher than similar homes in the area or may have hidden structural or other defects. So it may pay to have a property appraised and to have it inspected by an engineer. Also, you may face discrimination. Lenders participating in the VA loan program are required by the Civil Rights Act of 1968 to act on loan applications without regard to the veteran's race, sex, religion, or national origin. Other laws also prohibit discrimination. If you suspect discrimination by a builder, broker, or lender, get VA Form 26–8827, Housing Discrimination Complaint, from a VA Regional Office and file the form there.

A VA loan makes the purchase of a home possible for many vets who otherwise could not make such a purchase. This is partly because a VA loan often requires no down payment. Down payments on homes usually are 10 to 30 percent of the purchase price. (So on an $80,000 home, the down payment would usually be $8,000 to $24,000.)

Also, VA loans are usually made at slightly lower interest rates than standard loans.

A VA loan, as the term is generally used, is not a loan from the VA. It is a home loan (also called "mortgage") made by a private lender (such as a bank or savings and loan) and *guaranteed* by the VA. If the vet fails to keep up the payments, what generally happens is that the lender forecloses (the vet loses the property) and the VA bids at a sheriff's sale and buys the home. If the lender loses money through the sheriff's sale, the VA, under its guarantee, must make up the loss to the lender. And the amount paid by the VA must be paid *to* the VA by the vet.

The VA makes its guarantee under the VA Home Loan Mortgage Program. The VA guarantees the lower of two amounts: (1) 60 percent of the loan or (2) the veteran's available "entitlement." A veteran starts with an entitlement of $27,500, but the *available* entitlement is $27,500 minus any amount of the entitlement used in any previous VA home loans. (For veterans purchasing a *mobile* home, the VA guarantees 50 percent of the loan or $20,000, whichever is lower.)

Although they are most commonly used to buy houses, VA loans can be used to purchase, build, or improve a house, mobile home and lot, condominium (but generally not a cooperative apartment), or farm residence. They can also be used in some cases to refinance an existing home loan or to buy solar heating devices or other equipment or materials used to conserve energy.

Loan Rules

For the VA to guarantee a loan, all of the following must be true:

1. The loan must be used to pay for the purchase, construction, or improvement of residential property. (In other words, don't apply for a VA home loan expecting to use the money to buy a Buick.)
2. The terms of the proposed mortgage—such as the size of monthly payments—are appropriate to the vet's current and anticipated income and expenses. (If you make $1,000 a month, the VA isn't going to guarantee a loan calling for monthly payments of $800.)
3. The vet is a satisfactory credit risk.
4. The property is suitable to use as a place to live.
5. If the loan is for construction, repairs, or alterations, the loan must not exceed their reasonable value.
6. If the loan is for repairs, alterations, or improvements, the work must substantially protect or increase the value or usefulness of the property.

Energy Conservation Improvements

Among the kinds of energy conservation measures for which a VA loan may be used are:

1. Caulking and weatherstripping of exterior doors and windows
2. Certain modifications of furnaces to improve their efficiency
3. Clock thermostats
4. Insulation of ceilings, attics, walls, and floors
5. Insulation of water heaters
6. Storm windows and doors
7. Heat pumps

Eligible Vets

Almost all veterans discharged under "other than dishonorable conditions" are eligible for VA loans. Eligible vets include:

1. Veterans who served on active duty at any time during World War II, the Korean War, or the Vietnam Era *and* were on active duty for at least 90 days or were discharged due to a service-connected disability.
2. Vets who served during the periods of July 26, 1947, to June 26, 1950; February 1, 1955, to August 4, 1964; or May 8, 1975, to September 7, 1980 (if enlisted) or to October 16, 1981 (if an officer) *and* were on active duty for at least 181 continuous days or were discharged due to a service-connected disability.

Eligible Surviving Spouses

For the surviving spouse of a veteran to qualify for a VA loan, all of the following must be true:

1. The spouse must not have remarried. Or, if the spouse has remarried, the later marriage(s) must have ended.
2. The veteran died in the service, due to an injury or illness caused by or made worse by service in the line of duty.
3. The surviving spouse is not eligible *as a veteran* for a VA home loan.

How to Apply

To get a VA loan, a veteran must have a certificate of eligibility from the VA. Many veterans automatically received a certificate shortly after discharge. If you do not have a certificate, get VA Form 26–1880, Request for Determination of Eligibility and Available Loan Guaranty Entitlement. You can get this form from a VA Regional Office; also, many real estate agents have them. You or your real estate agent must file this form with the regional office; attached to it must be a copy of your DD Form 214 (your separation document).

A surviving spouse must fill out VA Form 26–1817, Request for Determination of Loan Guaranty Entitlement—Unmarried Surviving Spouse.

A vet who was not honorably discharged can apply for a certificate of eligibility by completing VA Form 26–8261a, Request for Certificate of Veteran Status.

Be sure to apply for your certificate as soon as you begin hunting for a home.

Not So Simple

Unfortunately, a vet does not simply get a VA loan, buy a house, sell it at a profit, and move on to something else. If you get a VA loan and then sell your home to somebody who takes over the loan, you remain liable (legally responsible) for the loan. If your buyer defaults (fails to make required payments) on the loan, *you* must take over the payments.

But you can avoid liability by getting a *release* from the VA. For a veteran to get a release, the buyer need not be a veteran. The VA must issue a release if all of the following are true:

1. Both you and the buyer have applied for it.
2. The loan is current: all payments that have come due have been made.
3. The buyer is obligated by contract to assume full liability for the loan and the buyer is a satisfactory credit risk. (So ask your real estate agent or lawyer to include in the sales agreement a clause stating that the sale is contingent on—depends on—the VA providing a release. Because real estate agents don't like contingencies, you may have to be firm about this.)

To get a release, apply to the Loan Guaranty Division at a VA Regional Office.

Direct VA Loans

Usually the term "VA loan" does not mean a loan from the VA; it means a loan *guaranteed* by the VA. But there are some true

VA loans; loans made directly by the VA to a veteran. Since 1980, however, these have been made only to severely disabled vets who need to adapt their homes for use by the disabled.

Help in Finding a Home

VA Regional Offices can help you find a home. They can give you a list of housing—new and under construction—in your area that is for sale with VA financing. Also, in many areas, the VA sells homes it has repossessed (and some are very good deals). To get a list of housing or to find out about repossessed homes that are for sale, contact the VA Home Loan Mortgage Guaranty Officer at a VA Regional Office or check with a real estate agent.

Foreclosure

If you fall behind in your mortgage payments, you may lose your home. Whether you have a VA loan or a standard loan, the lender may foreclose: undertake a legal proceeding to take away your ownership of the property.

If you begin to find it difficult to make your payments, take immediate action. See your lender (and, if you have a VA loan, your VA loan officer) and ask if an easier payment schedule can be arranged. Once you are several months behind in your payments, there may be little anyone will be willing to do to help you.

If you have a VA loan, you have certain rights and hopes that home owners with other loans generally do not possess. A lender may not foreclose on a VA loan unless the veteran is three months late in payments. Before foreclosing, the lender must give the VA thirty days notice. Under some circumstances, the lender must accept partial payments rather than foreclose. And lenders are supposed to give the veteran "all reasonable forbearance": they are, as much as possible, supposed to avoid foreclosure. If your lender does not make efforts to avoid foreclosure, you may want to complain to the Loan Guaranty Division of a VA Regional Office. It may also help to complain to a chapter of a veterans organization.

Even if the lender wants to foreclose, the VA may help you out. The VA may arrange for an "assignment"—taking over the loan itself. This procedure is called "refunding," and is pronounced "re-FUNDING." In an assignment, the VA pays off the loan and the veteran begins making payments to the VA rather than to the original lender. But these payments are usually *higher* than the original ones. The VA says it considers assignment in every case where a vet is threatened with foreclosure. Whether or not this is the case, assignment rarely occurs. It seems to occur most often with vets with service-connected disabilities who have fallen behind in payments because their monthly disability compensation checks have been delayed.

There is no standard application for the veteran to fill out if foreclosure threatens. He may, however, arrange a meeting with a loan officer in the Loan Guaranty Division of the VA Regional Office. Before such a meeting, the vet should get advice from a service representative associated with a veterans organization such as Vietnam Veterans of America (VVA).

If the VA provides no help and the vet wants to fight the foreclosure on his home, he should consult an attorney. A lawyer can advise the veteran of state laws that protect homeowners in general (not just vets). A lawyer should also be helpful in analyzing and explaining VA and other regulations as well as the various legal documents involved in foreclosure.

VA Pamphlet

For more information on VA home loans, ask a VA Regional Office for a copy of VA Pamphlet 26–4, *VA-Guaranteed Home Loans for Veterans*. This twenty-three-page pamphlet is written clearly and explains most of what you must know if you want to buy a home with a VA loan.

Lawsuit on Mobile Homes

In April 1985, Vietnam Veterans of America (VVA) filed a lawsuit over a problem it had discovered involving mobile home manufacturers and dealers. Since about 1977, many such manufacturers and dealers apparently had padded invoices they sent to the VA as part of the process to arrange for guaranteeing a home loan. Criminal charges had been brought over this problem and over kickback arrangements.

Here is the key point for veterans who bought a mobile home in or after 1977 using a VA-guaranteed loan (including veterans who no longer live in the mobile home): contact the VVA national office as soon as possible. Such veterans may be able to join the lawsuit, and joining it may be worth several thousand dollars for each victimized vet. Write to: VVA; Attn.: Mobile Home Investigation; 2001 S St., N.W., Suite 700; Washington, DC 20009.

STATE LOAN PROGRAMS

California, Texas, and some other states operate home loan programs for vets. The programs vary a great deal from state to state. Some are more generous than the VA program. Some require that the vet was a resident of the state when he entered the service. Check with your state department of veterans affairs.

VETERANS HOMES AND DOMICILIARY FACILITIES

One route to finding housing is to buy a home with a VA or state veterans loan. Another route, especially for older vets, is to apply for admission to a VA domiciliary facility or a state veterans home. See Chapter 6, "Medical Services," in the section titled "Domiciliary Care."

12. OTHER BENEFITS

Programs of the VA, Other Federal Agencies, and the States

> The mission of the Veterans Administration is to serve America's veterans and their families efficiently and with compassion.
> —Dorothy Starbuck
> Former Chief Benefits Director
> The Veterans Administration

There are benefits programs for veterans and their families that have not been covered in previous chapters. This chapter will discuss the more important ones.

LIFE INSURANCE

Veterans insurance is one of many areas where Vietnam Era Vets are not treated as well as veterans of earlier wars. While in the service, all vets were given an opportunity to buy life insurance. Vets of World War II and Korea were allowed to keep their armed forces insurance as a term policy with low rates. Vietnam Era Vets, however, can continue with a term policy for only five years after service. If the policy has not lapsed (or has lapsed, but is eligible for reinstatement), the vet can convert from term to whole life.

The whole-life policies are part of the Veterans Group Life Insurance (VGLI) program. Some VGLI policies are issued directly by the VA, while others are handled by private insurance companies that are supervised by the VA. VGLI rates usually are lower than rates available to nonvets.

There are at least eleven types of VGLI policies. They have various codes: "T," "RH," and so on. Most do not apply to Vietnam Era Vets. The only type that is important for many Vietnam Era Vets is the "RH" type. "RH" refers to the National Service Life Insurance policies (NSLI). These policies have been issued since 1951 directly by the VA to vets with service-connected disabilities. This is the only kind of life insurance currently being issued by the VA.

Getting National Service Life Insurance

To qualify for an NSLI ("RH") policy, a vet must have a service-connected disability. In most cases he need not prove he is healthy or take a medical exam.

The right to an RH policy is very important: without the RH program, the disabled vet would have to apply for insurance with private companies, which in general would either require a higher premium than they require of nondisabled applicants or would reject him entirely. The RH policy is even more valuable for the totally disabled vet: if he has a continuous total disability for six or more consecutive months, he will not have to pay any premiums. The waiver of premiums continues as long as he remains totally disabled.

Eligibility: To qualify for RH coverage, all of the following must be true:

1. The vet was released from active service after April 23, 1951.
2. The vet was separated under "other than dishonorable conditions." (This is different from having other than a dishonorable discharge. See Chapter 15, "Upgrading Your Discharge.")
3. The vet must have a service-connected disability that has been rated by the VA. If the disability is dental, it must have a rating of at least 10 percent; if it is medical, it can be rated as low as 0 percent. For more information on disability ratings, see Chapter 3, "Compensation."

If you are eligible for RH coverage, you must apply within one year of the date you receive notice of a disability rating. If you reopen or amend a disability claim and you are found to have a "new" service-connected disability, you may apply for RH coverage within one year of being notified of a rating for a "new" disability.

Different RH Plans: The veteran may select any of ten plans. These include term insurance, convertible term, ordinary life, endowment policies, and modified life.

How to Apply: Fill out VA Form 29–4336, Application for National Service Life Insurance (Medical) (RH). Especially because some medical conditions might cause your application to be rejected, get help from a service representative. This form is available at VA Regional Offices. Send the form, along with a copy of the VA's letter to you that establishes that your disability is service-connected, to the VA Insurance Center that deals with your area of the country. Ask the VA Regional Office for the address of the insurance center.

If you are also applying for a waiver of premiums because you have had a total disability for six or more consecutive months, also file VA Form 29–357, Claim for Disability Insurance Benefits.

BENEFITS FOR FUNERALS AND BURIALS

In death, as in life, the veteran is the subject of VA programs that do not cover all situations, that provide payments that are often inadequate, and that are tied up with yards and yards of red tape known as regulations. Because this book is directed at Vietnam Era Vets, most of whom have several decades of life ahead of them, it will not go into great detail on death benefits.

Survivors of deceased veterans should get detailed information from a service representative who works for a veterans organization such as Vietnam Veterans of America (VVA). Funeral directors, who run funeral homes, are also often helpful: they often are familiar with programs, have the applicable VA forms, and will file the forms for the family of the deceased veteran.

Although benefits are not generous, they are extensive. They include free headstones and grave markers (but not their erection or placement) and reimbursement for privately purchased headstones and markers (but only up to the average cost of a VA headstone or marker). They also include plot allowances: payments (but only up to $150) toward the purchase of a grave plot. There are also burial allowances: payments (but only up to $300 for most vets, $1,100 for those who die of a service-connected disability) toward the cost of a funeral and burial.

Nearly all vets (and their spouses and children) qualify for burial in a national cemetery. Most vets who died in active duty qualify for burial at Arlington National Cemetery, across the Potomac River from Washington, D.C. Certain other veterans may also be buried at Arlington; for example, those who received the Medal of Honor, the Distinguished Service Cross or Medal, the Silver Star, or the Purple Heart. Spouses and children of vets eligible for burial at Arlington may also be buried there.

The VA may pay for transporting a veteran's remains, particularly if they are to be transported to a national cemetery. Also available are United States flags with which to drape coffins, and Presidential Memorial Certificates, which are issued to the next-of-kin.

Generally, for benefits to be made available, the deceased veteran must have been discharged under "other than dishonorable conditions." Some benefits vary depending on whether the death was service-connected.

FEDERAL AGENCIES OTHER THAN THE VA

Throughout this book are descriptions of programs of the Veterans Administration. Chapter 9, "Employment," also explains programs for veterans that are operated by the Department of Labor and the Small Business Administration.

Many other federal agencies also maintain programs that

may provide critical assistance to the veteran. Most of these programs are open to all citizens, but others are designed specifically for veterans.

This book does not have space to present detailed information on these programs. You can obtain further information by contacting your service representative or the agencies themselves. For phone numbers of federal agencies, look in the "United States" listings in your phone book.

Here is a quick sketch of some federal agencies that offer programs of value to many vets:

Department of Agriculture

Programs include many types of loans, such as loans to buy or improve farms and to buy livestock, equipment, and supplies. Rental assistance is offered to low-income rural residents of housing projects financed by the Department's Farmers Home Administration (FmHA).

Department of Education

Programs include loans and work-study plans for students in colleges and professional schools.

Department of Health and Human Services

Programs of the Department's Social Security Administration include

Social Security payments made to workers retiring at age sixty-two or later. Also, wage credits for members of the armed forces: veterans are treated as though they received wages of $300 per calendar quarter in addition to basic pay actually paid for each quarter in the service from 1957 through 1977; for service beginning in 1978, the veteran receives a credit of $100 for each $300 of military pay (up to a maximum credit of $1,200 per year).

Supplemental Security Income (SSI), which sends monthly checks to people who are disabled, blind, or sixty-five or over and who have limited income and assets. For a single person,

SSI can pay as much as $314 a month. (Many states supplement SSI with their own funds.)

Aid to Families with Dependent Children (AFDC), a federal-state program that helps needy families that include children. AFDC assistance varies from state to state but may include welfare payments, food stamps, and medical and social services. (The Department of Labor operates the WIN program to help parents of AFDC families to get jobs and receive training and education for jobs.)

Medicare, a health insurance program for people sixty-five and over and for some disabled people under sixty-five (generally those disabled people who have been receiving SSI checks for at least twenty-four months). (Because Medicare does not fully pay for health care, most disabled veterans will save money by getting care in the VA system rather than through Medicare.)

Medicaid, a federal-state program providing medical care to the needy. Eligibility varies from state to state. (Check with an office of your state welfare, social services, or human services department.)

Department of Housing and Urban Development

Programs include mortgage insurance through the Federal Housing Administration (FHA), programs to assist low- and moderate-income families to purchase homes, and a special home mortgage insurance program for veterans.

Treasury Department

Programs of the Department's Internal Revenue Service (IRS) include

The elimination of income tax on any compensation received while missing in action or while a POW during the Vietnam Era.

The cancellation of income tax for service members or veterans who die in a combat zone (such as Vietnam and certain adjacent waters) or who die elsewhere as the result of wounds, illness, or injury that occurred while the service member or veteran was in a combat zone. (The tax is canceled for the tax year in which the death occurs and for any previous tax year ending on or after the first day the member served in a combat zone after June 24, 1950. If tax was collected, the amount collected will be credited or refunded as an overpayment by the veteran. Survivors of a deceased vet may apply, but generally must do so within three years of the date the tax return was filed or two years of the date the tax was paid. There are exceptions to this rule for certain veterans and their survivors. To claim a refund, check with an IRS office for the forms and documents you will be required to provide.)

STATE PROGRAMS

Veterans sometimes think so much about VA and other federal programs that they barely notice state programs for veterans. Certainly, VA programs are generally more important to the veteran and provide greater benefits. And most of this book focuses on VA programs. But all states have laws providing benefits for veterans, and some states have extensive programs. California and Ohio, for example, each have a network of county employees to serve veterans. Some state programs require honorable or general discharges, some do not.

Programs and benefits vary tremendously from state to state. Among those you may find in your state are

1. Help in applying for VA benefits
2. Educational benefits, such as tuition waivers
3. Preferences in hiring for state jobs
4. Home and farm loans
5. Exemptions from certain taxes and certain license fees
6. Veterans homes
7. Burial allowances
8. Cash bonuses for service during the Vietnam Era (but most bonus programs have expired)

This short list is only a rough summary. A recent publication of the Committee on Veterans Affairs of the House of Representatives contains *306 pages* of fine print listing the benefits provided to vets, state by state.

For more information on state veterans programs, check with your service representative. Also check with the veterans affairs office in your state. (Depending on the state, it may be called a "department," a "division," or a "bureau.") Every state except Utah and Wyoming has a veterans office, and even these two states provide some benefits for veterans.

States, like the federal government, also offer many programs that are not designed specifically for vets but that may assist vets, particularly the disabled and the poor. For more information on programs for these groups, check with the nearest office of your state welfare, social services, or human services department. For information on state employment programs, see Chapter 9, "Employment."

13. GETTING YOUR RECORDS

Getting Your Files from the Military and the VA

I hereby authorize release of the requested information/documents to the person indicated at right (item 7).
—Standard Form 180

There are many cases in which it is useful for the veteran to have a copy of his records. There are many other cases in which having a copy of records is not just useful but absolutely necessary. Among the vets for whom copies of records are a necessity are those who are filing a claim for disability compensation, those claiming injuries or illnesses associated with Agent Orange or Post-Traumatic Stress Disorder (PTSD), those who believe their records contain mistakes that should be corrected, and those wanting to upgrade their discharges.

Your records can help you prove what happened to you and when it happened—in the military, at VA facilities, and in other settings. Records can also help refresh your memory.

Even if you have no current, specific need to get your records, it may help you to get them now. You may need them in the future, and if you get them now you won't have to wait for them then. Also, your records may contain negative information about you—information that could hurt you if, for instance, you apply for a job, a security clearance, or credit and you are required to sign a release for your records. If your records contain harmful information that is inaccurate, you can, under the federal Privacy Act, request that your side of the story be included in your records.

Records can also be corrected—or simply changed in order to help a veteran—through application to a Board for Correction of Military Records (BCMR) or a Discharge Review Board (DRB). BCMRs handle matters such as correcting or removing information about disciplinary actions including court-martials, changing the reason given for discharge, removing SPN (Separation Program Number) codes and RE (eligibility for reenlistment) numbers, and upgrading discharges. They can correct most any error in records and can consider certain applications for upgrade. DRBs deal with most upgrade applications. For more information, see Chapter 14, "Correcting Your Records," and Chapter 15, "Upgrading Your Discharge."

The chapter you're now reading will help you get your records (and help you get them for free).

Getting records is yet another area in which you will probably have the best results if you get help from a service representative who works for a veterans organization such as Vietnam Veterans of America (VVA). Unfortunately, getting your records is not an easy matter; you don't fill out one simple form and send it to one address. In fact, submitting a form that seems to request your complete records may result in getting only a few of the documents you need. Service representatives are familiar with which records you need, which forms to use, which words to use in filling out the forms, where to send forms, and what to do if the military or the VA refuses to give you the copies you want.

MILITARY RECORDS

What you want is your Official Military Personnel File (OMPF). This is the file of records of your service in the military. After your discharge, this file was forwarded to the National Personnel Records Center (NPRC) in St. Louis, where it will be stored permanently.

In most cases, all you will need to do to get a copy of your OMPF is to fill out Form SF 180 and send it to NPRC. You can get this form at any VA Regional Office or from your service representative. The form includes the address of various records centers, including NPRC (9700 Page Blvd., St. Louis, MO 63132).

In filling out Form SF 180, be sure to use the same name you used during the service. In the space titled "SECTION II—REQUEST," in block number 1, write, "Complete service and medical records." (If you need only a Form DD 214—report of separation—or a discharge certificate, leave block 1 blank and check box "a" or "b" below it.)

The only medical record this sort of request will generally get you is a copy of the record of your final separation medical exam. If you need additional military medical records, specifically list them in block 1. You will probably want additional records if you have a medical problem that affected your military performance, if you saw a psychotherapist, or if you had problems with drugs or alcohol. In requesting additional medical records, describe the records as well as you can, including the type of record (for example, sick call or inpatient), the medical facility visited, and the approximate dates of your visit(s). To improve your chances of getting all your medical records as soon as possible, you not only should file an SF 180 form with NPRC but you should also send a letter to the medical facilities that treated you. In the letter you should write something along the lines of "Please send me all your medical, nursing, and other records pertaining to my leg injury, for which I was treated at your hospital in April 1972."

NPRC's policy is that medical records will be released to a veteran "unless it appears that such release might prove detrimental to his/her physical or mental health." If, when you get your records from NPRC, you believe NPRC has withheld some records because of this policy, ask your service representative for assistance. It is possible that NPRC will release certain records to a doctor or service rep that it will not release to you.

In addition to medical records, other records you may need may include court-martial transcripts, reports of investigations, pay records, personnel rosters, ships' logs, and morning reports (head counts). Your personnel file (OMPF) will not usually contain all these records. If you need these records, specifically list them in block 1 of the "request" section of the SF 180. If NPRC does not provide all the files you request, it may at least tell you where you can get them. If, after you hear from NPRC, you don't know where to find all your files, check with your service representative.

In block 4 of the "request" section of the form, write, "To confirm accuracy and completeness of records under Freedom of Information and Privacy Acts; request fee waiver."

In block 6b, sign the form.

In block 7, write your complete address. If you want the information sent to your service rep or other person instead of yourself, fill in not your name and address but the name and address of that person. That person then signs in block 6b and you sign in block 5.

Be sure to put the date of your request in the box in the upper right corner of the form.

You should hear from NPRC in four to eight weeks. If after eight weeks you have received no reply, send a second request. On the second SF 180 write, "SECOND REQUEST."

On pages 178–79 is an example of a completed Form SF 180. Do not tear out this copy of the form and do not copy all the hand-printed information included in this example. Get a regular, full size form and fill in the information that deals with *your* case.

After applying to NPRC for their records, some Army veterans discharged in the period from January 1 to July 12, 1973, will receive a reply stating that their records were destroyed in a fire that occurred at NPRC in 1973. This kind of reply *should* be accompanied by a questionnaire. The veteran is expected to fill out the questionnaire to help NPRC search for records that would provide the information that was destroyed. If NPRC informs you that your records were destroyed, be sure you get the questionnaire. If, eight weeks after sending back the questionnaire, you have not heard again from NPRC, write NPRC a letter asking what progress has been made and asking that it complete its search as soon as possible.

If your records have been destroyed by fire or are for any other reason not available, other sources may have the information you need. One is the Vietnam War Collection, described later in this chapter. Another is the files of your hometown newspaper, if that newspaper published articles on your enlistment, your promotion(s), or any other event in your military service.

Another problem that may occur is that NPRC will send you not a paper copy of your records but one on *microfiche*. Microfiche is a sheet of film containing information far too tiny to be read except with an expensive machine called a microfiche reader. Paper copies can be made only with a special kind of microfiche reader.

You can attempt—not necessarily successfully—to avoid microfiche by writing on your form SF 180 (in block 1 of the "request" section), "PLEASE PROVIDE PAPER COPIES, NOT MICROFICHE." Still, you may be sent microfiche. If you are in a rush to read and copy your records, try to find a library or other facility that has a microfiche reader/copier. If you can wait, write again to NPRC and ask for a paper copy. Do not return the microfiche unless requested to do so: until NPRC sends you a paper copy, the microfiche could prove valuable.

VA RECORDS

The VA may have as many as three files on you. If you have ever made an application to the VA—for instance, for G.I. Bill benefits, a home loan, or disability compensation—the VA will have a Claims File on you. It is called a "C" file. It will include every form, letter, and other document about you that has been received or sent by the VA. It may, for instance, include military records (if, for example you have filed a claim for disability compensation) and inquiries by Members of Congress (if, for instance, you have requested assistance from a Congressman). The only exception to the rule that the file will contain every document the VA has sent or received about you is that VA employees are authorized to destroy letters they believe have nothing to do with a veteran's rights to benefits.

In addition to the claims file, there may be as many as two medical files. One would be for inpatient treatment, one for treatment as an outpatient. Although the claims file contains a summary of medical exams and treatment, the inpatient and outpatient treatment files are more detailed. They are especially useful in claims for disability compensation.

To get your VA records, file VA Form 00–3288 (sometimes numbered 70–3288). Copies are available at VA Regional Offices; your service rep should also have copies. You can submit this form in person to a VA Regional Office (if you want claims records) or to a VA Medical Center (if you want medical records), or you may send it there by mail. (If you want both claims records and medical records, you must submit one form to a VARO and another to a VAMC.)

In the block near the bottom of the form, where it says, "PURPOSES FOR WHICH THE INFORMATION IS TO BE USED," write, "To confirm accuracy and completeness of records under Freedom of Information and Privacy Acts; request fee waiver."

As with NPRC and your military records, the VA may refuse to release certain medical records to you (especially psychiatric records) if it believes release to you would have a "serious adverse effect on the individual's mental or physical health." If you believe the VA has withheld medical records from you, check with your service rep for advice. It is possible that special arrangements can be made with the VA, such as having records released to a doctor or having your service rep visit a VA facility to meet with a physician who treated you.

On pages 182–83 is an example of a completed VA Form 00–3288 (sometimes numbered 70–3288). As with form SF 180, get a regular, full size form and fill in the information that applies to you.

THE VIETNAM WAR COLLECTION

This is a collection of reports prepared by various levels of command in Vietnam. It occupies some forty thousand feet of shelves. This collection can be used to determine where a particular veteran was on a particular day during the war. This information can be critical in determining whether a veteran was exposed to Agent Orange or experienced a traumatic event that may have resulted in Post-Traumatic Stress Disorder

REQUEST PERTAINING TO MILITARY RECORDS

Please read instructions on the reverse. If more space is needed, use plain paper.

DATE OF REQUEST

PRIVACY ACT OF 1974 COMPLIANCE INFORMATION: The following information is provided in accordance with 5 U.S.C. 552a(e)(3) and applies to this form. Authority for collection of the information is 44 U.S.C. 2907, 3101, and 3102, and E.O. 9397 of November 22, 1943. Disclosure of the information is voluntary. The principal purpose of the information is to assist the facility servicing the records in locating and verifying the correctness of the requested records or information to answer your inquiry. Routine uses of the information as established and published in accordance with 5 U.S.C. 552a(e)(4)(D)

include the transfer of relevant information to appropriate Federal, State, local, or foreign agencies for use in civil, criminal, or regulatory investigations or prosecution. In addition, this form will be filed with the appropriate military records and may be transferred along with the record to another agency in accordance with the routine uses established by the agency which maintains the record. If the requested information is not provided, it may not be possible to service your inquiry.

SECTION I—INFORMATION NEEDED TO LOCATE RECORDS (Furnish as much as possible)

1 NAME USED DURING SERVICE (last, first, and middle)	2 SOCIAL SECURITY NO	3 DATE OF BIRTH	4 PLACE OF BIRTH
Smith, John Doe	999-50-1111	2-13-50	Norfolk, Virginia

5. ACTIVE SERVICE, PAST AND PRESENT *(For an effective records search, it is important that ALL service be as shown below)*

BRANCH OF SERVICE	DATES OF ACTIVE SERVICE		Check one		SERVICE NUMBER DURING THIS PERIOD
(Also, show last organization, if known)	DATE ENTERED	DATE RELEASED	OFFICER	ENLISTED	
USN - USS Intrepid	01-19-68	12-8-72	✓		B55 99 11

6. RESERVE SERVICE, PAST OR PRESENT If "none," check here ▶ ☐

a BRANCH OF SERVICE	b DATES OF MEMBERSHIP		c Check one		d SERVICE NUMBER DURING THIS PERIOD
	FROM	TO	OFFICER	ENLISTED	

7. NATIONAL GUARD MEMBERSHIP (Check one): ☐ e ARMY   ☐ b AIR FORCE   ☑ c NONE

d STATE	e ORGANIZATION	f DATES OF MEMBERSHIP		g Check one		h SERVICE NUMBER DURING THIS PERIOD
		FROM	TO	OFFICER	ENLISTED	

8. IS SERVICE PERSON DECEASED ☐ YES ☑ NO   *If "yes," enter date of death.*

9. IS (WAS) INDIVIDUAL A MILITARY RETIREE OR FLEET RESERVIST ☐ YES ☑ NO

SECTION II—REQUEST

1. EXPLAIN WHAT INFORMATION OR DOCUMENT IS NEEDED OR, CHECK ITEM 2; OR, COMPLETE ITEM 3

Complete service and medical records

2. IF YOU ONLY NEED A STATEMENT OF SERVICE ☐ check here

3. LOST SEPARATION DOCUMENT REPLACEMENT REQUEST		YEAR ISSUED	
☐	a. REPORT OF SEPARATION (DD Form 214 or equivalent)		This contains information normally needed to determine eligibility for benefits. It may be furnished only to the veteran, the surviving next of kin, or to a representative with veteran's signed release (item 5 of this form).
☐	b. DISCHARGE CERTIFICATE		This shows only the date and character of discharge. It is of little value in determining eligibility for benefits. It may be issued only to veterans discharged honorably or under honorable conditions; or, if deceased, to the surviving spouse.

(Complete a or b.1 and c)

c. EXPLAIN HOW SEPARATION DOCUMENT WAS LOST

4. EXPLAIN PURPOSE FOR WHICH INFORMATION OR DOCUMENTS ARE NEEDED

To confirm accuracy and completeness of records under Freedom of Information and Privacy Acts; request fee waiver.

6. REQUESTER

a. IDENTIFICATION (check appropriate box)
☐ Same person identified in Section I
☐ Next of kin (relationship) _____ ☐ Surviving spouse
☐ Other (specify) _____

b. SIGNATURE (see instructions 3 and 4 on reverse side)

John Doe Smith

5. RELEASE AUTHORIZATION, IF REQUIRED (Read instruction 3 on reverse side)

I hereby authorize release of the requested information/documents to the person indicated or right (item 7).

VETERAN SIGN HERE ▶ _____

(If signed by other than veteran, show relationship to veteran)

7. Please type or print clearly — COMPLETE RETURN ADDRESS

Name, number and street, city, State and ZIP code

John D. Smith
3716 Dupont Street
Kenmore, MD. 20899

TELEPHONE NO. (Include area code) ▶

STANDARD FORM 180 (Rev. 5-78)
Prescribed by GSA, FPMR (41 CFR) 101-11 410-7

180-105

180 THE VIET VET SURVIVAL GUIDE

INSTRUCTIONS

1. **Information needed to locate records.** Certain identifying information is necessary to determine the location of an individual's military service. Please give careful consideration to and answer each item on this form. If you do not have and cannot obtain the information for an item, show "NA," meaning the information is "not available." Include as much of the requested information as you can. This will help us to give you the best possible service.

2. **Charges for service.** A nominal fee is charged for certain types of service. In most instances service fees cannot be determined in advance. If your request involves a service fee you will be notified as soon as that determination is made.

3. **Restrictions on release of information.** Information from records of military personnel is released subject to restrictions imposed by the military departments consistent with the provisions of the Freedom of Information Act of 1967 (as amended 1974) and the Privacy Act of 1974. A service person has access to almost any information contained in his own record. The next of kin (see item 4 of instructions) if the veteran is deceased and Federal officers for official purposes are authorized to receive information from a military service or medical record only as specified in the above cited Acts. Other requesters must have the release authorization, in item 5 of the form, signed by the

veteran or, if deceased, by the next of kin. Employers and others needing proof of military services are expected to accept the information shown on documents issued by the Armed Forces at the time a service person is separated.

4. **Precedence of next of kin.** The order of precedence of the next of kin is: unremarried widow or widower, eldest son or daughter, father or mother, eldest brother or sister.

5. **Location of military personnel records.** The various categories of military personnel records are described in the chart below. For each category there is a code number which indicates the address at the bottom of the page to which this request should be sent. For each military service there is a note explaining approximately how long the records are held by the military service before they are transferred to the National Personnel Records Center, St. Louis. Please read these notes carefully and make sure you send your inquiry to the right address. (If the person has two or more periods of service within the same branch, send your request to the office having the record for the last period of service.)

6. **Definitions for abbreviations used below:**

NPRC—National Personnel Records Center PERS—Personnel Records
TDRL—Temporary Disability Retirement List MED—Medical Records

SERVICE	NOTE	CATEGORY OF RECORDS	WHERE TO WRITE ADDRESS CODE	▼
AIR FORCE (USAF)	Air Force records are transferred to NPRC from Code 1, 90 days after separation and from Code 2, 30 days after separation.	Active members (includes National Guard on active duty in the Air Force), TDRL, and general officers retired with pay.		1
		Reserve, retired reservist in nonpay status, current National Guard officers not on active duty in Air Force, and National Guard released from active duty in Air Force.		2
		Current National Guard enlisted not on active duty in Air Force.		13
		Discharged, deceased, and retired with pay (except general officers retired with pay).		14
COAST GUARD (USCG)	Coast Guard officer and enlisted records are transferred to NPRC 3–6 months after separation.	Active, reserve, and TDRL members.		3
		Discharged, deceased, and retired members (see next item).		14
		Officers separated before 1/1/29 and enlisted personnel separated 1/1/15.		6
MARINE CORPS (USMC)	Marine Corps records are transferred to NPRC 4 months after separation.	Active and TDRL members, reserve officers, and Class II enlisted reserve.		4
		Class III reservists and Fleet Marine Corps Reserve members.		5
		Discharged, deceased, and retired members (see next item).		14
		Officers and enlisted personnel separated before 1/1/1896.		6

		Code
ARMY (USA) — Army records are transferred to NPRC as soon as processed (about 30 days after separation)	Reserve, living retired members, retired general officers, and active duty records of current National Guard members who performed service in the U.S. Army before 7/1/72.*	7
	Active officers (including National Guard on active duty in the U.S. Army).	8
	Active enlisted (including National Guard not on active duty in the U.S. Army) and enlisted TDRL.	9
	Current National Guard officers not on active duty in the U.S. Army.	12
	Current National Guard enlisted not on active duty in the U.S. Army.	13
	Discharged and deceased members (see next item).	14
	Officers separated before 7/1/17 and enlisted separated before 11.1.12.	6
	Officers and warrant officers TDRL.	8
NAVY (USN) — Navy records are transferred to NPRC 6 months after retirement or complete separation.	Active members (including reservists on active duty)—PERS and MED	PERS only 10 / MED only 10
	Discharged, deceased, retired (with and without pay) less than six months, TDRL, drilling and nondrilling reservists	10, 11
	Discharged, deceased, retired (with and without pay) more than six months (see next item)—PERS & MED	11, 14
	Officers separated before 1/1/03 and enlisted separated before 1/1/1886—PERS and MED	6

* Code 12 applies to active duty records of current National Guard officers who performed service in the U.S. Army after 6/30/72.
Code 13 applies to active duty records of current National Guard enlisted members who performed service in the U.S. Army after 6/30/72.

ADDRESS LIST OF CUSTODIANS (BY CODE NUMBERS SHOWN ABOVE)—Where to write / send this form for each category of records

1 USAF Military Personnel Center, Military Personnel Records Division, Randolph AFB, TX 78148	**8** USA MILPERCEN, Attn: DAPC-PSR-R, 200 Stovall Street, Alexandria, VA 22332
2 Air Reserve Personnel Center, 7300 East 1st Avenue, Denver, CO 80280	**9** Commander, U.S. Army Enlisted Center and Evaluation Center, Ft. Benjamin Harrison, IN 46249
3 Commandant, U.S. Coast Guard, Washington, DC 20590	**10** Chief of Naval Personnel, Department of the Navy, Washington, DC 20370
4 Commandant of the Marine Corps, Headquarters, U.S. Marine Corps, Washington, DC 20380	**11** Naval Reserve Personnel Center, New Orleans, LA 70146
5 Marine Corps Reserve Forces Administration Center, 1500 E. Bannister Road, Kansas City, MO 64131	**12** Army National Guard Personnel Center, Columbia Pike Office Building, 5600 Columbia Pike Boulevard, Falls Church, VA 22041
6 Military Archives Division, National Archives & Records Service, General Services Administration, Washington, DC 20408	**13** The Adjutant General (of the appropriate State, DC, or Puerto Rico)
7 Commander, U.S. Army Reserve Components Personnel & Administration Center, 9700 Page Boulevard, St. Louis, MO 63132	**14** National Personnel Records Center, (Military Personnel Records), 9700 Page Boulevard, St. Louis, MO 63132

STANDARD FORM 180 BACK (Rev. 5-78)

☆U.S. Government Printing Office: 1981—341-488/4830

Form Approved
OMB No. 76-R0194

REQUEST FOR AND CONSENT TO RELEASE OF INFORMATION FROM CLAIMANT'S RECORDS

NOTE: The execution of this form does not authorize the release of information other than that specifically described below. The information requested on this form is solicited under Title 38, United States Code, and will authorize release of the information you specify. The information may also be disclosed outside the VA as permitted by law or as stated in the "Notices of Systems of VA Records" published in the Federal Register in accordance with the Privacy Act of 1974. Disclosure is voluntary. However, if the information is not furnished, we may not be able to comply with your request.

TO	Veterans Administration	NAME OF VETERAN (Type or print) John Doe Smith	
	Regional Office	VA FILE NO. (Include prefix)	SOCIAL SECURITY NO.
	94 N. Capitol	C28-501-999	999-50-1111
	Washington, D.C. 20421		

NAME AND ADDRESS OF ORGANIZATION, AGENCY, OR INDIVIDUAL TO WHOM INFORMATION IS TO BE RELEASED

John D. Smith
3716 Dupont St.
Kenmore, MD. 20899

VETERAN'S REQUEST

I hereby request and authorize the Veterans Administration to release the following information, from the records identified above to the organization, agency, or individual named hereon:

INFORMATION REQUESTED (Number each item requested and give the dates or approximate dates—period from and to—covered by each.)

Complete claims file

PURPOSES FOR WHICH THE INFORMATION IS TO BE USED

To confirm accuracy and completeness of records under Freedom of Information and Privacy Acts; request fee waiver.

NOTE: *Additional items of information desired may be listed on the reverse hereof.*

DATE	SIGNATURE AND ADDRESS OF CLAIMANT OR FIDUCIARY, IF CLAIMANT IS INCOMPETENT
02-13-85	John D. Smith 3716 Dupont St; Kenmore, Md. 20899

VA FORM
DEC 1975 **00-3288**   EXISTING STOCKS OF VA FORM 07-3288, FEB 1974, WILL BE USED.

(PTSD). The collection can also be of great value for veterans whose records are not available from NPRC because they are missing or were destroyed by fire or other cause.

To get records from the Vietnam War Collection, write to U.S. Army and Joint Services Environmental Support Group; 1730 K St., N.W., Room 210; Washington, DC 20006. Use a photocopy of the form provided at the end of this chapter.

OTHER RECORDS

When you are making a claim for VA benefits or are applying for a discharge upgrade, you may need records that are not in the hands of either the military or the VA.

If you are applying for disability compensation, records of treatment by private physicians or psychotherapists may be critical. These records may be the key to proving you have a service-connected injury or illness and to demonstrating the degree to which you are disabled.

Any number of records outside the military and the VA may help in convincing a Discharge Review Board to upgrade your discharge. Among useful records may be records of treatment by private doctors or psychotherapists, high school transcripts, juvenile arrest records, welfare department records, records of participation in programs of rehabilitation or therapy for drug or alcohol problems, and statements from service "buddies" as well as from family and friends.

Here are some examples of the use of nonmilitary, non-VA records:

1. If you went AWOL due to a family crisis or hardship, but did not first request an emergency leave or a hardship discharge, there may be no military records on the problems you were facing. But if while AWOL you turned for help to the Red Cross or a community organization, one of these groups may have records of your visits to their facilities.

2. If you abused drugs or alcohol during the service, your abuse may have contributed to your violation of military law. Your disciplinary problems, in turn, may have resulted in your getting a less-than-honorable discharge that you now want to have upgraded. And in applying for an upgrade you may want

to argue that your disciplinary problems resulted from problems with alcohol or drugs. But if your abuse of drugs or alcohol was not detected by the military, the military will have no record of it. So your best chance of proving the connection between drug or alcohol abuse and your disciplinary record may be to get records of your participation after military service in a private rehabilitation or therapy program.

3. If you need to prove your earnings during the military, first try to get records from the military finance centers. There is one for each service. To get these records, get Form DD 827, Application for Arrears in Pay, from a VA Regional Office. Send the form to the address for your service that is printed on the form. If you cannot get records from a military finance center, you may be able to get records of your earnings by checking your old tax returns (if you still have them) or by contacting the Internal Revenue Service or the Social Security Administration.

GENERAL NOTE

Records you have requested because they are important now may become important again. If they do, you will not want to have to request them again and wait for them again. Also, records that seem insignificant now may turn out to be very useful in future years. Therefore you may do yourself a favor by getting some file folders from a stationery store and keeping files of your military and VA records. You should also keep copies of records of medical treatment (records such as medical bills) and of other events that may be helpful in current or future claims for VA benefits or for other purposes. In addition to keeping copies of formal documents such as military records and medical bills, make your own notes of events and information (such as your symptoms of injuries and illnesses) that may not be carefully recorded in formal documents.

REQUEST FOR SERVICE INFORMATION

TO: US Army & Joint Services   FROM:
     Environmental Support Group
     Room 210
     1730 K Street, NW
     Washington, DC 20006

The veteran's record has been checked for the existence of decorations indicating exposure to life-threatening stressors. None has been found. We request that a records search be made to locate and forward combat action reports and other pertinent data to support the veteran's claim to compensation based on Post-Traumatic Stress Disorder and/or Agent Orange exposure. The following information is provided:

VETERAN'S NAME: _____
                 Last   First   Middle

SOCIAL SECURITY NUMBER: _____
MILITARY SERVICE NUMBER: _____

BRANCH OF SERVICE: ☐ USA ☐ USN ☐ USMC ☐ USAF ☐ USCG

UNIT(S) OF
ASSIGNMENT: 1. _____
                  Company   Battalion   Regiment   Division

                  2. _____
                  Company   Battalion   Regiment   Division

                  3. _____
                  Company   Battalion   Regiment   Division

DATES OF
ASSIGNMENT: 1. ___ to ___ 2. ___ to ___ 3. ___ to ___

SPECIFIC
INCIDENT: (Type, place, date; if possible, names of close friends killed or wounded in action.)

                  _____

                  _____

ADDITIONAL
INFORMATION: _____

                  _____

REQUESTED BY: _____

SIGNATURE: _____

PLEASE RETURN ALL INFORMATION TO THE SENDER

14. CORRECTING YOUR RECORDS

Correcting Records, SPN Codes, and Court-Martial Convictions

SPN 461: Inadequate personality
> —Official Department of Defense List of Separation Program Numbers

There are countless types of military records. They range from medical records to Separation Program Numbers (SPN codes) to court-martial convictions. Military records can do the veteran a lot of good or a lot of harm, especially when he applies for a job or for VA benefits.

This chapter will concentrate on the correction of military records, which generally is handled by the Boards for Correction of Military Records. The next chapter will deal with the upgrading of discharges, which generally is considered by the Discharge Review Boards.

Both of these areas are full of technicalities. For this and other reasons, it is important that vets who want to correct their records or upgrade their discharge get advice from a service representative who works for a veterans organization such as Vietnam Veterans of America (VVA) or from an attorney with experience in veterans issues. The service rep or lawyer will be especially well equipped to help the vet if the rep or lawyer has access to two extensive manuals. One, published by the Veterans Education Project, is *Military Discharge Upgrading and Introduction to Veterans Administration Law*. The other, published by Vietnam Veterans of America (VVA), is the VVA *Service Representatives Manual*.

BOARDS FOR CORRECTION OF MILITARY RECORDS

The Army, Air Force, and Coast Guard each have a Board for Correction of Military Records (BCMR). The Navy (including the Marines) has a board that functions in the same way, called the Board for Correction of Naval Records (BCNR). When this chapter refers to "BCMRs" it will mean both BCMRs and the BCNR.

BCMRs are composed of high-ranking civilian employees of a military department (such as the Army). Many BCMR members are veterans.

Under federal law, BCMRs have the power to "correct any military record" when "necessary to correct an error or remove an injustice." As a result, BCMRs have authority to resolve almost any dispute—except for most attempts to overturn a court-martial conviction—between a veteran and a military service.

For instance, BCMRs have the power to:

- Remove the effect (such as a bad discharge and forfeiture of pay) of a court-martial conviction (though they can only rarely erase the conviction from the vet's records)
- Void a discharge by changing its date of issue to a date showing the vet completed the normal term of service (this may result in back pay and allowances)
- Reinstate a vet into military service (this is rarely done)
- Remove disciplinary actions from a vet's records or change the vet's performance marks (A vet may want to request this before or at the same time as applying for a discharge upgrade.)
- Credit a vet with service time or otherwise change a record to qualify a vet for VA benefits
- Correct performance reports and order promotion
- Correct records to show that medals have been awarded
- Grant disability and retirement benefits

- Overrule the results of line of duty investigations or overrule reports of survey
- Correct any other error in a vet's service record
- Remove other problems that stand between a vet and benefits provided by the VA and other agencies
- Upgrade any bad discharge, including a dishonorable discharge or a bad conduct discharge issued by a general court-martial (While Discharge Review Boards deal with most cases involving discharges, only BCMRs can upgrade the two discharges just mentioned.)
- Change the reason given for a discharge (such as from misconduct to medical reasons or from homosexuality to expiration of enlistment)

"Deadline" and Exhausting Your Remedies

Technically, a BCMR can correct military records only if an application is filed within three years of the date the veteran discovers an error or injustice—unless the BCMR in the interest of justice excuses the vet's failure to meet the deadline. In reality, however, most BCMRs almost never reject an application because it fails to meet the three-year deadline. (The exception is the Army BCMR, which requires a good explanation of why the vet missed the deadline.)

If there is an agency other than the BCMR that can give the vet what he wants, the vet must apply there and be turned down before applying to the BCMR. This is called "exhausting other remedies." For instance, if the vet is seeking the sort of discharge upgrade that Discharge Review Boards can grant, he must apply first to a DRB. Unlike the deadline rule, the rule requiring the vet to exhaust other remedies is a rigid one.

How to Apply for Correction of Records

To apply to a BCMR, you must send a Department of Defense Form 149 to the address shown on the form. (Although all BCMRs are in Washington, D.C., the addresses are sometimes elsewhere.) You can get a Form DD 149 from a VA Regional Office, your service rep, or the Vietnam Veterans of America (VVA) Legal Services. You may address your request to VVA

Legal Services; Attn.: Forms; 2001 S St., N.W., Suite 710; Washington, DC 20009.

Do not file the DD 149 until you have filed an SF 180 (a request for your military personnel and medical records) and have received an answer. See Chapter 13, "Getting Your Records."

If you are anxious to get your case decided by a BCMR, file your DD 149 as soon as you get an answer to your SF 180, even if you are not yet ready to send documents and other materials you would like the BCMR to consider. You can submit your material later because it usually takes a BCMR several months to get to a case. To be safe, though, send your additional materials within two months of the date you send your application. With your additional materials, attach a letter or note saying, "Please attach these materials to my application dated _____ ."

You should also write a letter to send along with your original application. This letter is to request copies of the materials the BCMR will consider in deciding your case. If you are not happy with the BCMR decision, you will need these copies to decide what to do next and to prepare for any further step, such as a request for reconsideration or the filing of a lawsuit.

Your letter should include this statement:

> Prior to the BCMR's consideration of such documents, please furnish me copies of any (1) advisory opinions, (2) staff briefs or memoranda, and (3) military investigative reports (such as CID or OSI reports) obtained or prepared for use and consideration by the BCMR on petitioner's application. Upon receipt of this material, I will determine if a rebuttal is to be submitted. This request is made pursuant to the Privacy Act, 5 U.S.C. Sec. 552a, and the Freedom of Information Act, 5 U.S.C. Sec. 552.

If the veteran is deceased or is otherwise physically or mentally unable to file the application, it may be filed by the spouse, parent, heir, or legal representative of the veteran. When filing the application, such a person should file proof of the relationship with the veteran (and, if the veteran is deceased, should also file a copy of the death certificate).

Service representatives can be of great assistance to the veteran or other person completing the application to be sent to a BCMR.

In filling out the application, you must indicate whether or not you want a hearing in which you would appear in Washington, D.C., before the BCMR. BCMRs grant hearings in fewer than five percent of cases. Still, just requesting one may help show your sincerity. If you are granted a hearing but cannot currently afford to travel to Washington for it, the BCMR in most cases will grant you a "continuance"—a delay in the case—until you can get the money you need to get to Washington. Even if you have to raise money to do so, it is important to attend a hearing if you have the opportunity to have one. If you have a hearing, be sure to get a service representative or lawyer to attend with you as your counsel.

The only document you are *required* to file is the application itself. But your probability of getting what you want will be dramatically better if you also file

1. A typed argument explaining the reasons you should get what you are requesting. Write very clearly: BCMRs are very busy and will pay more attention to cases "laid out" for them.
2. Evidence of good conduct after leaving the service and evidence of your other characteristics and experiences that may help the BCMR form a good impression of you. You may, for instance, get a statement from your local police department saying that you have no arrest record, a statement from the president of a community organization saying that you are a member in good standing, and a statement from your employer saying you are a reliable employee. You may also attach other kinds of documents, such as newspaper articles.

If you have already been turned down by a Discharge Review Board or other agency and the agency has not given specific reasons for rejecting your application, you can simply photocopy (or retype) the argument you used in your previous application. If, however, the previous agency *has* given specific reasons for denying your application, you should change your argument so it effectively argues against the reasons given.

If, in response to your request to the BCMR, you have received copies of staff briefs, advisory opinions, or other documents that the BCMR will use in deciding your case, carefully check over these documents. If you find any error or incomplete statement in them and the BCMR has not yet decided your case, immediately send a letter to the BCMR to point out the error(s) or incomplete statement(s). Because the BCMR relies heavily on staff briefs and certain other documents, your correction of documents can provide critical help to your case. Don't be alarmed if the BCMR has asked for a legal opinion from the Judge Advocate General and the JAG opinion just says "applicant's contentions are without merit." *Do* be concerned if a JAG opinion specifically states *why* the JAG thinks your application should not be granted: if you can, respond to the JAG statement point-by-point.

Your application to the BCMR will be kept confidential: only you and the BCMR will know about it.

BCMR Decision Process

Once a BCMR is ready to act on an application, it will consider the application, materials you have sent, and military records it has obtained. It then will make one of three decisions:

1. To authorize a hearing
2. To recommend that the records be corrected without a hearing
3. To deny the application without a hearing

Hearings: If the BCMR authorizes a hearing, *you* will have three choices:

1. To appear without counsel
2. To appear with counsel
3. Not to appear yourself but to have counsel represent you at the hearing

If you want to be assisted by counsel, you can select a lawyer, service representative, or any other person to act as your counsel. Because the hearing does not directly concern VA benefits, the rule limiting legal fees to $10 does not apply to hearings, assistance in preparing an application, or any other part of trying to get your records corrected. Your service representative may be able to advise you about lawyers and others who are well qualified to act as your counsel. Your service rep should also be able to help you prepare for your hearing.

If a lot of money (for instance, in VA benefits) is involved, seriously consider finding an attorney who is an expert on the correction of records. VVA Legal Services (whose address was given earlier in this chapter) may be able to represent you. If not, its staff should be able to refer you to a qualified lawyer in your area.

If you have a hearing, you can ask witnesses to appear on your behalf. But the BCMR cannot require them to appear and will not pay the expenses needed to get them to Washington.

BCMR Recommendations: After it has completed its work, the BCMR in some cases sends its recommendations—for or against the requested correction(s)—to the Secretary of the branch of the military in which the veteran served, or to another official designated by the Secretary. In some cases, however, the BCMR has final say.

If the BCMR denies your application without a hearing, it will mail you a brief statement of its reasons for denying your request. If, after receiving a favorable or unfavorable recommendation from the BCMR, the Secretary or other official ends up denying part or all of the application, the Secretary or official will send you notice of the decision and a brief statement of the grounds for denial. (The Secretary or offical need not explain the grounds for denial if he or she uses the same grounds as the BCMR.) BCMRs take about a year to decide cases.

Changing a Bad Decision

You have two main alternatives if you want to challenge a BCMR decision that you think is wrong.

Reconsideration: A BCMR decision denying an application does not mean it is impossible for you to prove your case. It means only that you have not yet presented enough evidence to demonstrate that an error or injustice has occurred. Anytime after the BCMR decision, you may submit a new application along with evidence you did not submit before (and along with any evidence you *did* submit before that you want to submit again). If it agrees to reconsider your case, the BCMR will treat the application as though it were on a case it has never considered.

In their first applications to BCMRs, many vets have done little more than submit a Form 149: they have provided little argument and little evidence. These vets may succeed if they ask for a reconsideration. This is true especially because BCMRs apply *current* standards, and in many cases current standards are more favorable to the vet than the standards under which a case was originally considered. Vets who previously did little more than submit a Form 149 should make a special effort to supply a complete argument and substantial evidence when they submit the Form 149 for reconsideration.

Court Review: Federal District Courts (and sometimes the U.S. Claims Court) will under certain circumstances review BCMR denials of applications. They will do so on:

1. Denials of money claims (such as claims for back pay) if the application was filed within six years of the date on which the error first existed (this is usually the date of discharge)
2. Denials of "equitable relief" (requested action such as a record change, rather than requested money), usually without any limit on when the application was filed

Requesting court review means you have to sue the branch of service with which the BCMR is connected. Anytime you're thinking about suing anybody about anything, check with a lawyer. See Chapter 16, "Claims and Appeals."

BCMRs and Courts-Martial

BCMRs can help the vet who has a less-than-honorable discharge due to a court-martial decision. But if you want to appeal the court-martial decision *itself*, you must appeal to the Judge Advocate General of the service branch in which you served (see later in this chapter).

Although Discharge Review Boards have jurisdiction over

applications for upgrades of most types of discharge, BCMRs deal with discharges that result from general courts-martial. This is actually good news for the vet with such a discharge, because BCMRs grant a much higher percentage of upgrade applications than do Discharge Review Boards. While the rate at DRBs is about 10 percent, the rate of BCMRs is 30 to 50 percent.

In evaluating an application for a discharge upgrade, the BCMR will generally not concentrate on a single event or a single time period. Instead, it will look at many factors over many years. As a practical matter, it is looking for whether the vet is a "good guy" or a "bad guy" and whether the offense he committed was "serious." If the BCMR thinks you're a "good guy" and that the offense was not "serious," it will in most cases grant you a discharge upgrade.

If you are requesting a discharge upgrade, the BCMR will evaluate not only your accomplishments and other experiences while in the service but also your civilian life both before and after the military. It will weigh your positive qualities and achievements against the offense that led to the bad discharge. The BCMR will generally try to do what it thinks is fair, taking into account that you may already have suffered for years due to the stigma of a bad discharge.

Your chances of an upgrade will be greatest if your offense did not occur in a combat zone, if it did not involve violence, if it happened a long time ago, and if you served for a substantial time in the military without any other problems.

Disability Separation and Disability Retirement

The Secretary of a service branch may determine that a member of the service has a physical or psychological disability that disqualifies him from active military duty. If the Secretary makes such a decision, he or she will choose one of four alternatives for the service member:

1. Permanent disability retirement
2. Temporary disability retirement
3. Disability separation with severance pay
4. Disability separation without severance pay

Disability retirement pays monthly benefits as long as the vet remains disabled. Severance pay is a one-time payment: it is two months' basic pay for the highest active duty grade achieved, multiplied by the number of years the service member has served (to a maximum of twelve years).

If you were not separated from the service due to a disability but you have a physical or psychological condition that should have been detected on or before the date you were separated from the service, you can apply to the BCMR to change your discharge to disability retirement or disability separation with severance pay. Note, however, that for enlisted personnel who served only one term, VA disability compensation is usually higher than armed forces disability compensation (you must choose to receive either VA compensation or armed forces compensation; you can't have both). Armed forces disability retirement, however, includes some benefits that are better than those from the VA, and some of these benefits may be received even if you are getting VA benefits.

Getting armed services retirement is a complicated area. You must prove that at the time of separation you were unfit to perform military duties. But the military does not like to recognize it made a mistake, partly because of the amount of retirement pay that may be due the vet. (Of course, any retirement pay is reduced by the amount of VA compensation the vet has already received.) So consult a service representative on issues including whether it would be worthwhile to apply.

When you consult your service rep, suggest that he or she read Chapter 10 of the VVA *Service Representatives Manual*: it contains seven detailed pages on who qualifies for disability retirement or separation.

If you have a disability, you should also read Chapter 3 of this book, "Compensation," and Chapter 6, "Medical Services."

CHANGING OR DELETING SPN AND RE CODES

Many citizens who have not served in the military think the only kind of "bad paper" that can hurt a vet is a bad discharge.

Many vets, however, have learned that "bad paper" can include
a discharge form (Form DD 214, Report of Release or Discharge from Active Duty) that reports a good discharge but a
bad—or seemingly bad—SPN code or RE code.

SPN Codes

"SPN" means Separation Program Number. A "SPN code,"
pronounced "Spin code," is the series of numbers or letters,
often beginning with "SPN," that appears on the DD 214 form
in the block titled "reason and authority." As a matter of commonly used slang, codes similar in function to codes starting
with "SPN" but beginning with other letters are also called
"SPN codes." These include codes beginning with "SDN" (Separation Designator Number), "TINS" (Transaction Identification Number), and "SPD" (Separation Program Designator).

Beginning in May 1974, SPN codes have been deleted from
the veteran's copy of the DD 214. (The veteran's copy is copy
1; if the veteran requests it, he can also get copy 4, which,
like all other copies, includes the SPN code.) But even veterans
with discharges in May 1974 or later can be harmed by bad
SPN codes, because copies of the DD 214 that are sent to the
VA, the Department of Labor, the military records center in
St. Louis, and the state department of veterans affairs *do* include
the SPN code (as well as the RE code and the reason and
authority for discharge; these will be explained later).

Vets usually must show their DD 214 when applying for
VA benefits. The form must also be shown when applying for
a job with the federal government. Also, many private employers ask to see the form.

All this would be fine if SPN codes were a big secret: if
nobody but the Secretary of Defense and his chauffeur had a
list of what the codes mean. Unfortunately, however, *lots* of
people have lists.

Worse still, most lists in the hands of people outside the
military contain inaccuracies. SPN codes have been revised
over the years so that in some cases numbers that used to mean
a favorable reason for separation have been re-assigned so they
now mean something bad; most lists outside the military have
not been changed to keep up with the new codes. So a vet who

got what at the time of separation was a good number may now have a bad number.

There are other ways a SPN code can hurt a vet. Some employers are confused and think having *any* SPN code means the vet was discharged for unfavorable reasons. In addition, due to typographical or other error, wrong SPN codes sometimes appear on the DD 214.

To get a quick idea of what *your* SPN code means, check with a service representative who has a copy of *Military Discharge Upgrading and Introduction to Veterans Administration Law*, a thick manual published by the Veterans Education Project. A list of SPN codes appears at the end of Chapter 7 of the manual. But even this list is not complete. To be sure what your code means, file Form SF 180, Request Pertaining to Military Records. In block 1 of the "Request" section, write, "Please supply narrative description of SPN (SDN/TINS/SPD) code(s) on Form DD 214." You can get this form at any VA Regional Office or from your service rep. Send the form to the National Personnel Records Center, 9700 Page Blvd., St. Louis, MO 63132.

To give you a sense of how good or bad a SPN code can sound, here are a few "good" ones, followed by several "bad" ones:

Good:

SPN 41C: To accept a teaching position

SPN 202: Expiration of term of enlistment

SPN 414: To accept or return to employment

Bad:

SPN 46B: Sexual deviate

SPN 263: Enuresis (bed-wetting)

SPN 280: Misconduct, fraudulent entry (enlistee not revealing criminal record)

SPN 287: Unclean habits, including VD many times

SPN 385: Pathological lying

SPN 464: Schizoid personality

SPN 489: Disloyal or subversive (Military Personnel Security Program)

Having one of these "bad" SPN codes would not exactly do wonders for your chances of getting a job.

There are also some SPN codes that would strike some people (such as employers) favorably and others unfavorably. These include SPN 318—conscientious objection—and eight different SPN codes relating to homosexuality.

If your SPN code is inaccurate, you can apply to have it changed. When you are preparing your application, it is best to get help from your service representative. And it is best for the service rep to consult Chapter 25 of the *Military Discharge Upgrading* manual. In summary, what you do is write a letter in which you say you are applying under the Privacy Act and that you are requesting that your SPN code be changed because it is inaccurate. And you give reasons and information to demonstrate its inaccuracy. You may attach documents to support your case. You are not likely to succeed if you simply say your SPN code is unfair; it is better to argue the SPN code is illegal, contrary to regulations, or a mistake. Also give your name, Social Security number, and military service and identification number, and your dates of service, and attach a copy of your DD 214.

You have the best chance of getting your SPN code changed if it was assigned by mistake. Your next best chance is if there has been a change in the reason for your discharge. To request a change in the reason for discharge, you must first apply to a Discharge Review Board or a Board for Correction of Military Records. See Chapter 15, "Upgrading Your Discharge."

After preparing your request for a change of SPN code, send it to one of the following addresses, depending on your branch of service:

Army: Commander, Reserve Components Personnel and Administration Center; Box 12479; Olivette Branch; St. Louis, MO 63132.

Air Force: Air Force Military Personnel Center (DPMDR); Randolph Air Force Base, TX 78148.

Navy: NPRC (Military Personnel Records); Navy Reference Branch; 9700 Page Blvd.; St. Louis, MO 63132.

Marine Corps: Commandant; U.S. Marine Corps (MSRB-10); Headquarters; Washington, DC 20380.

Coast Guard: Commandant; U.S. Coast Guard (G-PS); Washington, DC 20590. (Or apply to a local base personnel office.)

Whether or not your SPN code is "bad" and whether or not it is inaccurate, you may simply want to get it *removed* from your copy of the DD 214. To do so, write to one of the offices whose addresses were just given. Simply ask the office to remove your SPN code (and, if you want, also your RE code and the information in the "reason and authority" block). Be sure to say you want a new DD 214, not a photocopy of the old DD 214 with the codes blocked out.

If you are applying for a job and have a bad, but mistaken or misleading, SPN code, the employer may learn about it from your DD 214 or by requesting information from the military. If this happens, tell the employer the code is wrong and give him or her a copy of your application to get it changed.

RE Codes

RE codes deal with eligibility for reenlistment. RE codes are the letters "RE" followed by a number or a number and letter. Each RE code indicates how well qualified—in the eyes of the branch in which the veteran served—the vet is for reenlistment in that branch. Just like SPN codes, RE codes can be inaccurate and are often misunderstood by employers. For instance, some employers mistakenly think any code other than RE-1—the code given to almost all vets eligible to reenlist—is bad. (RE-2 codes, for instance, may be given to service members separated due to family hardship.) And, as with SPN codes, RE codes (and the regulation and paragraph giving the reason and authority for discharge), have, since May 1974, been deleted from the vet's copy of the DD 214 separation form.

Here are some examples of RE codes (in all, there are 10 common Army RE codes, ranging from RE-1 to RE-4A, and 23 common Navy and Marine codes, ranging from RE-1 to RE-4):

Army:
    RE-1: Fully qualified for immediate reenlistment
    RE-2: Fully qualified for immediate reenlistment; separated for convenience of the government under a separation which does not contemplate immediate reenlistment
    RE-3: Not eligible for reenlistment unless a waiver is granted

RE-4: Not eligible for reenlistment. Disqualification is un-
waivable

Navy and Marine Corps:
   RE-1: Recommended for reenlistment
   RE-2: Recommended for reenlistment but ineligible because
of status: Fleet Reservist Retired (except for transfer
to TDRL), Commissioned Officer, Warrant Officer;
Midshipman, Cadet
   RE-3: Recommended for reenlistment except for disquali-
fying factor
   RE-4: Not recommended for reenlistment

(There are also Air Force RE codes, but no Coast Guard
ones.)

A complete list of common reenlistment codes appears at
the end of Chapter 7 of the *Military Discharge Upgrading*
manual.

If you simply want to have your RE code *removed* from
your copy of the DD 214, apply just as you would to have a
SPN code removed and apply to the same address (see earlier
in this chapter). Again, be sure to say you want a new DD
214, not a photocopy of the old one with the codes blocked
out.

If you want to have your RE code *changed*, what you should
do depends on the circumstances. If you want to have it changed
so you can reenlist, ask a recruiter for assistance. Recruiters
can get certain codes changed, especially those that are temporary—those that can be waived after a specified period or
after a particular cause no longer exists.

If you want to have your RE code changed because it is
inaccurate, consult a service representative and suggest he or
she consult Chapter 25 of the *Military Discharge Upgrading*
manual. Write a letter, saying you are applying under the Privacy Act and that you are requesting that your RE code be
changed because it is inaccurate. Give reasons and information,
attaching documents if you want. You will be more likely to
succeed if you convincingly argue the RE code is illegal,
improper under regulations, or a mistake. Arguments about

fairness rarely work. Give your name, Social Security number, any military service and identification number, and your dates of service, and attach a copy of your DD 214. Apply to one of these addresses:

Army: U.S. Army Enlisted Eligibility Activity; 9700 Page Blvd.; St. Louis, MO 63132.

Navy: Commander; Naval Military Personnel Command (N-03); Department of the Navy; Washington, DC 20370.

Marine Corps: Headquarters; U.S. Marine Corps CMC (CODE MMCP); Washington, DC 20380.

Air Force: Headquarters; U.S. Air Force Recruiting (ATC); Attn.: RSOEA; Randolph Air Force Base, TX 78148.

As with SPN codes, you'll have your best chance for a code change if your RE code is simply a mistake, and your next best chance if there has been a change in the reason for your discharge. To get a change in the discharge reason, you must first apply to a Discharge Review Board or a Board for Correction of Military Records. See Chapter 15, "Upgrading Your Discharge."

Before going to the trouble of applying for an RE code change, carefully evaluate the strength of your case: though it is easy to get an RE code removed from your copy of the DD 214, only rarely will the service grant an application to change an RE code.

Other Errors on Form DD 214

If your DD 214 contains a routine error, such as a misspelling of a name or a failure to mention decorations that you have received, you should have little trouble getting it corrected. Simply write to the National Personnel Records Center; 9700 Page Blvd.; St. Louis, MO 63132. Explain what is incorrect and how it should be corrected. Attach a copy of your DD 214. In some cases, the records center will change the DD 214; in others, it will issue a correction on a DD 215.

Other errors—errors other than mistakes in SPN code, RE code, or regulatory authority—can be corrected by filing a Form DD 149. See the discussion of BCMRs earlier in this chapter. Also apply to a BCMR if you want to change the DD

214's statement of your name or the dates or place of your service.

APPEALING OLD COURT-MARTIAL CONVICTIONS

The set of laws that govern members of the armed services is called the Uniform Code of Military Justice (UCMJ). This is Title 10 of the U.S. Code (the U.S. Code is the set of all federal laws). As a result of a change made in 1968 in Article 69 of the UCMJ, many old court-martial convictions can be appealed. Appeals are made to the Judge Advocate General (JAG) of the service in which the veteran served. All this may be of interest to many Vietnam Era Veterans, because from 1964 through 1975 courts-martial issued some thirty-seven thousand bad conduct and dishonorable discharges.

There are, of course, limits. In particular, to be appealed, a decision must never have been reviewed by a Board of Review or a Court of Review. What this means is that the following kinds of court-martial convictions can be appealed:

1. Almost all decisions before 1951 (before the UCMJ existed)
2. All decisions in or after 1951 in which the sentence did not include a bad conduct discharge or dishonorable discharge (or dismissal) or a period of more than one year in jail

Under these requirements, about *90 percent of all court-martial convictions of Vietnam Era Veterans can be appealed* under Article 69.

But there still are problems. One is that in 1981 Congress amended Article 69 so it requires that an appeal be filed within two years of a conviction or by October 1, 1983, whichever is later. The same article allows an exception to the time limit if the applicant "establishes good cause for failure to file within that time." The armed services have not explained what "good cause" is, but the Army has said informally that if the applicant has not previously filed an appeal under Article 69, "good cause" will be interpreted liberally. The other services have not commented. If you are applying more than two years after conviction (as of course would be the case with almost all court-martialed Vietnam Era Vets), be sure to specify why you should be excused from the time limit. Reasons that might be useful to mention are that you did not have assistance of counsel or that you had assumed that no appeal was possible (the latter reason is especially appropriate for discharges occurring before 1968).

Grounds for Appeal

Under Article 69, there are only four grounds on which you can appeal a court-martial conviction. They are

1. Newly discovered evidence.
2. Fraud on the court. (This would be the rare case where you can prove someone lied or presented false evidence to the court with the result that you were convicted.)
3. The court did not have jurisdiction over you or over the offense with which you were charged.
4. The court committed an error that was harmful to important rights you had as an accused person.

The fourth category—legal error—is the source for almost all successful appeals. It is not enough to say that you were innocent or that other people should have been charged with an offense instead of you or in addition to you or that the trial was unfair.

But there are countless arguments you might make to convince the Judge Advocate General that the court made an error. The most general argument would be that the evidence in the record of the trial does not support the court's findings *beyond a reasonable doubt*. (As with criminal trials outside the military, the prosecutor must prove more than that it is more likely than not that the charged person is guilty; the prosecutor must prove it to the extent that the average person would not have a reasonable doubt about the person's guilt.)

Other possible court errors include, but are by no means limited to, the following:

- The court permitted the consideration of evidence that was seized improperly.
- The court allowed improper morning reports to be used to prove you were AWOL.
- The court failed to excuse your show of disrespect for a superior even though the show of disrespect was in response to behavior that was inappropriate for a person of the superior's rank.
- The court failed to excuse your action even though it was taken in self-defense.
- The court failed to excuse your action in disobeying an order even though the order was illegal.
- The court gave incorrect instructions to the jury.

Showing that the court made an error is a way to *reverse* its decision: to change its decision from guilty to not guilty. If you cannot change a conviction to an acquittal, you may still be able to get a reduction in sentence. This is not easy to do. The Judge Advocate General usually will not reduce a sentence just because it is too harsh. It can, however, reduce a sentence and authorize you to receive pay you would have received if you were not in jail. But you must show *the sentence was illegal*. One way to do this is to show that the court made an error and if it had not made the error it would have convicted you of a lesser offense (for instance, assault rather than assault with a deadly weapon), which carries a shorter sentence.

Consult a Lawyer

If you want to appeal a court-martial conviction, it's time to consult a lawyer. This is no place for people not trained in the law. In fact, it's no place for lawyers not familiar with *military* law: so find a lawyer who has handled a number of court-martial appeals. The VA rule limiting lawyer fees to $10 does not apply to such appeals. Be sure the lawyer gets a copy of the transcript of your court-martial (if it is still available). And suggest that the lawyer refer to Chapter 10 of VVA *Service*

Representatives Manual. You may be able to get a referral to a qualified attorney and your attorney may be able to get legal advice by calling the VVA Legal Services, (202) 686-2599.

Special Cases

Discharge Review: If your discharge was issued by a court-martial, you can try to get your discharge upgraded by a BCMR or possibly by a Discharge Review Board or the Secretary of your service. See Chapter 15 of this book, "Upgrading Your Discharge."

Other Courses of Appeal: BCMRs and federal courts can review any type of court-martial conviction, but reversals of convictions are rare. If you believe the court that found you guilty clearly did not have jurisdiction over your case, you may be successful in overturning its decision if you file a "writ of error *coram nobis*" with the appropriate Court of Military Review. This, too, rarely works. Check with your lawyer.

Pardons: You may want to apply for a Presidential pardon. A pardon does not reverse a conviction, but it removes some of its consequences. To have a chance for a pardon, you must have completed your sentence at least five years ago and you must have had a clean criminal record since the conviction.

To apply for a pardon, write a letter to the Office of the Pardon Attorney; Department of Justice; 5550 Friendship Blvd., Suite 208; Bethesda, MD 20814.

In your letter, request a petition. Give the date and place of your conviction, type of court-martial, nature of the offense, sentence imposed, date of sentence, place you were in custody (if you were), date you were released (if you were in custody), and date you completed your sentence (if you were sentenced, as opposed to receiving a suspended sentence). If the Pardon Attorney's office decides you are eligible to apply for a pardon, it will send you forms and instructions for completing your petition. The completed petition should be sent to your service. On the envelope, write "Executive Clemency Petition." Processing takes at least a year.

FAULTY DRUG TESTS

In 1985, it was becoming apparent that in 1982–83 each branch of service had used faulty procedures to detect drug abuse. Vets who were disciplined or discharged for alleged drug abuse supposedly detected by urinalysis conducted in 1982–83 may be able to get their records corrected. Some vets have received notices from the military regarding the faulty tests; others have not. The notices fail to fully advise vets of their rights. If you were disciplined or discharged due to a 1982–83 drug test, you should write to VVA Legal Services; 2001 S Street, N.W., Suite 710; Washington, D.C. 20009.

GETTING YOUR MEDALS

Some veterans never received the medals or decorations to which they were entitled. Sometimes the Form DD 214 indicates a medal was issued, but the veteran never got it. Other vets want to replace awards that were lost or destroyed. To request medals that were not received or to request replacement medals, veterans can write to these addresses:

Army:
   AGUZ-PSE-AW
   9700 Page Blvd.
   St. Louis, MO 63132
Navy, Marine Corps, Air Force:
   Director
   National Personnel Records Center
   9700 Page Blvd.
   St. Louis, MO 63132

No special form is required. Still, be sure to include your full name, Social Security number, service number (if you served before 1970), date and place of birth, approximate dates of service, and medals or decorations requested. Because there is a long backlog of requests, you can expect to wait several months for a reply.

15. UPGRADING YOUR DISCHARGE

Getting Rid of Bad Paper

Been down so long it looks like up to me
—Book and movie of the same name
By Richard Fariña

A CASE HISTORY

(To protect the privacy of the veteran involved in this case, a false name has been substituted for his. This false name is Naretev, which is Veteran spelled backwards.)

Before going to Vietnam in 1967, Mr. Naretev had no police record, was active in high school sports and other activities, and had no psychiatric symptoms.

Mr. Naretev served his first tour of duty, 1967–69, and was discharged honorably. He had difficulty readjusting to civilian life and reenlisted in 1970, desiring to return to Vietnam. When he was not stationed in Vietnam, Mr. Naretev became depressed and irrational and went AWOL from active duty.

After a long period of being AWOL, Mr. Naretev turned himself in to military authorities. He was discharged through involuntary administrative discharge proceedings and was given an undesirable discharge.

Following his return to civilian life, Mr. Naretev was estranged from family and friends, could not hold a job for more than several weeks, and eventually faced criminal charges and served time in prison.

In 1978, with the aid of psychiatric counseling, Mr. Naretev began to understand that his emotional problems were related to his service in Vietnam. He applied to the VA for disability compensation on the basis of a service-connected psychiatric condition, but the VA denied his claim. At that point Mr. Naretev got help from the Public Interest Law Clinic (PILC) at the American University Law School and from attorneys at Vietnam Veterans of America Legal Services.

Represented by a PILC law student (who was supervised by a lawyer), Mr. Naretev applied to the Army Discharge Review Board for a discharge upgrade. His law student counsel contended, with psychiatric evidence, that Post-Traumatic Stress Disorder (PTSD) harmed Mr. Naretev's second tour of duty. The ADRB agreed, finding evidence of PTSD in Mr. Naretev's record as early as 1970. Mr. Naretev's discharge was upgraded to honorable.

Armed with the discharge upgrade and the Army's finding of PTSD, Mr. Naretev pursued his VA disability claim on the basis that he had service-connected PTSD. His claim was denied by a VA Regional Office. On appeal to the Board of Veterans Appeals, however, Mr. Naretev's law student counsel successfully argued that Mr. Naretev was suffering from service-connected PTSD. The case was remanded (sent back) to the regional office for a determination by a rating board. A rating board granted Mr. Naretev a 100 percent disability rating for PTSD.

Because he had been AWOL more than 180 days, Mr. Naretev, to get VA benefits, had to prove that his AWOL period was based on "compelling circumstances." He was required to do so even though he had received a discharge upgrade. With the assistance of counsel, Mr. Naretev was successful here too.

INTRODUCTION

For many vets, there is no veterans issue as important as the upgrading of discharges. Upgrading a "less than honorable discharge" can make a veteran eligible for VA benefits and other benefits from federal and state agencies—even many years after discharge. A discharge upgrade can dramatically improve his employment opportunities. And, for many, it can significantly increase self-esteem.

More than 650,000 Vietnam Era Veterans have "less than honorable" discharges (including "general" discharges, which usually do not keep veterans from getting VA benefits). Yet relatively few apply for upgrades and far fewer get them.

Most veterans discharged before 1970 can apply for discharge upgrades to Boards for Correction of Military Records (BCMRs). See Chapter 14, "Correcting Your Records." These boards approve a percentage of upgrade applications that is acceptable to most veterans organizations.

Some vets, however, must apply to a Discharge Review Board (DRB). Each service has a DRB, made up of panels of five career military officers. In the six months ending September 30, 1984, DRBs acted on only 3,885 requests. And though Vietnam Veterans of America (VVA) believes some 25 to 40 percent of upgrade applications deserve approval, only 11.9 percent (463) of the applications were approved.

What these figures mean is that more vets should apply for upgrades and a greater percentage of applications should be approved. Two factors would increase the percentage approved. One would be a more conciliatory, humane attitude on the part of the Discharge Review Boards. Another would be veterans who apply in a more effective manner.

This book can't do a lot to change the attitude of the DRBs. It can, however, help vets to apply more effectively.

It is unfortunate that the veterans issue that is for many vets the most important—discharge upgrading—is also perhaps the most complex. It is a highly technical area, full of laws and regulations and court cases.

The area is so complex that you could write a book about it. In fact, somebody already has. In 1981, five military law experts at the National Veterans Law Center (now VVA Legal Services) published *Military Discharge Upgrading and Introduction to Veterans Administration Law*. This manual is more than seven hundred pages long, and the pages are letter size, not book size. It contains twenty-eight highly specific chapters—"Preparing a List of Contentions," "Alcohol Abuse," "Homosexuality," "Discharges for Good of Service (in Lieu of Court-Martial)," "Retroactive Application of Current Standards," "The Privacy Act," and so on. It also includes a thirty-two-page bibliography of books, articles, and other materials.

The manual is so heavily detailed that it calls into question the mental health of those who wrote it. Still, *this* book is not about to come to any conclusions on the psychological status of the authors of *that* book, because three of its coauthors are coauthors of this one too.

This book will, however, say that for any veteran to *read* all of *Military Discharge Upgrading*, *he* would have to be crazy. To benefit from it, however, he would only have to be *smart*.

Because discharge upgrading is so complicated, in most cases you should not venture into it alone. You should get help from a service representative associated with a veterans organization such as Vietnam Veterans of America (VVA) or from an attorney experienced in discharge upgrading. And you will be served best if your representative or lawyer has a copy of *Military Discharge Upgrading* (*MDU*) and is familiar with it. All Legal Services and Legal Aid offices have a copy, as do some VVA service reps.

One way your rep or lawyer can get the most out of *MDU* is to use *SRM*. *SRM* stands for the VVA *Service Representatives Manual*. Its Chapter 11, *Discharge Upgrading*, is a fourteen-page (plus appendices) introduction to discharge upgrading that includes references to *MDU* sections that apply to specific cases. *SRM* can be ordered from VVA Legal Services; 2001 S St., N.W., Suite 710; Washington, DC 20009; *MDU* from the Veterans Education Project; P.O. Box 42130; Washington, DC 20015.

The rest of this chapter will sketch the basic areas of discharge upgrading.

TYPES OF DISCHARGES

During the Vietnam Era, the military services issued the following discharges:

- *Honorable (HD)*. Honorable discharges were issued at separation or after "administrative proceedings." (Administrative proceedings are actions *other than court-martial* taken by the military.)

- *General (GD)*. This is also called "Under honorable conditions." General discharges were issued at separation or after administrative proceedings.

- *Undesirable (UD)*. (Now this is called "under other than honorable conditions.") Undesirable discharges were issued through involuntary administrative proceedings. Some were also issued as a form of clemency after a court-martial that sentenced a service member to a worse type of discharge.

- *Clemency (CD)*. Clemency discharges were issued to some participants in President Ford's Clemency Program. These discharges replaced undesirable, bad conduct, and dishonorable discharges given to participants for offenses having to do with absence from the military. Clemency discharges are basically the same as undesirable discharges.

- *Bad Conduct (BCD)*. Bad conduct discharges were issued only to enlisted service members and were issued as the result of a special or general court-martial.

- *Dishonorable (DD)*. Dishonorable discharges were issued to enlisted service members as the result of a general court-martial. Officers discharged as a result of a general court-martial received a "dismissal." (For the purposes of benefits, a dismissal is treated as a dishonorable discharge.)

DISCHARGES AND BENEFITS

The benefits available to you and your family depend on the kind of discharge you have. This is true not only for VA benefits but also for benefits administered by the Department of Defense. Your discharge also helps determine your eligibility for certain programs of the Department of Agriculture, the Civil Service Commission, the Department of Labor, the Department of Justice, the Immigration and Naturalization Service, and the

Social Security Administration. Some state programs also require certain types of discharge.

Rules about eligibility for benefits *after an upgrade* are somewhat complex. Generally, if you get an upgraded discharge, you will have eligibility identical to that of a veteran who received the same discharge without upgrade. In a few special situations, an upgrade will not improve your eligibility for benefits. All upgrades, however, will make it easier for you to get a job.

Despite the complexity of the world of discharges, here are a few general rules:

- A veteran with an honorable discharge or general discharge—even if it is the result of an upgrade—is automatically eligible for benefits, unless a federal law prohibits benefits because of the reason for the original discharge.

- If his discharge was issued by a general court-martial, a vet with a bad conduct discharge or dishonorable discharge is not eligible for benefits. (There are a few exceptions to this rule.)

- A vet with an undesirable discharge, or a bad conduct discharge issued by a special court-martial, must, to get benefits, get a determination from the VA that his discharge is under "other than dishonorable conditions."

- A vet with a clemency discharge has the same eligibility he had under the original discharge that the clemency discharge replaced.

- As of October 8, 1977, a vet with an undesirable discharge *can* get VA medical treatment for injuries suffered "in the line of duty." Treatment may include counseling at Vet Centers for problems of psychological readjustment (as of mid-1985, eligibility at Vet Centers was in dispute). See Chapter 8, "Psychological Readjustment."

- If you get a favorable decision from a Discharge Review Board (DRB) or a Board for Correction of Military Records (BCMR), the VA usually will accept a document from a DRB or BCMR that shows its decision. The VA will use the document as "proof of character of service." This will allow you to qualify for benefits before you receive a new Form DD 214 (separation document), which might take months.

There are many other rules, some general, some highly specific. For guidance on your specific case, check with your service rep or your attorney. For general guidance, refer to the chart "Eligibility for Benefits Based on Character of Discharge," at the end of this chapter.

Delimiting Dates

Once a veteran, as a result of a discharge upgrade, becomes eligible for benefits, any time period in which the benefits must be used (for instance the ten years in which G.I. Bill benefits must be used) begins on the date of upgrade.

If, however, a vet becomes eligible for benefits only because of a decision *within the VA*—and not due to a discharge upgrade or a correction of records—the period for using benefits begins with the date of discharge.

APPLYING FOR AN UPGRADE

Who May Apply

To have a discharge reviewed, almost any veteran may apply at any time. If the veteran is deceased or is incompetent, application may be made by the veteran's surviving spouse, next of kin, or legal representative.

Where and When to Apply

In some cases, it is difficult to decide whether it is best for the vet to apply to a DRB for a discharge upgrade, a BCMR for a discharge upgrade, or to the VA for a determination of character of service. In some cases, it is best to apply to two or all three of these institutions. In cases where it may be useful to apply to more than one, it is sometimes hard to determine to which institution the vet should apply first. If you have a bad discharge and *want to get G.I. Bill educational benefits*, it is especially important that you consider where and when to apply.

As a general rule, however, veterans should apply first to a DRB; if no upgrade results, apply to a BCMR; and if still no upgrade is granted (and if the vet is not already entitled to veterans benefits), apply to the VA for a character of service determination.

There is an important deadline for Vietnam Era Veterans: if you want to apply to a DRB, you must do so within *fifteen years* of the date of discharge.

The difficulty of deciding the issues just discussed is one of many reasons to consult a service representative or a lawyer who is familiar with discharge upgrading. The two books mentioned earlier in this chapter—*MDU* and *SRM*—will help your rep or attorney on these issues.

A DRB or a BCMR?

Each service has both a Discharge Review Board and a Board for Correction of Military Records. Officially, all DRBs and BCMRs are supposed to use the same policies in considering applications for discharge upgrades. In fact, however, different boards often decide very similar cases very differently.

Normally, a vet with a bad discharge must first apply to a DRB. DRBs, unlike BCMRs, will give a personal hearing to any vet who wants one. DRBs accept applications on any discharge issued in the fifteen years before the application, except a bad conduct discharge issued by a general court-martial or a dishonorable discharge.

If the discharge was issued more than fifteen years before the application, the vet must apply to a BCMR. BCMRs also handle applications for upgrades of bad conduct and dishonorable discharges issued by general courts-martial. In addition, they deal with appeals of DRB decisions that did not grant full relief (did not give the vet all he requested).

Army vets should note that the Army BCMR has recently begun to tell veterans they cannot apply to it until they have first had a personal appearance hearing before a DRB. The BCMR has no authority to make this demand, and Vietnam Veterans of America (VVA) intends to challenge the policy. Vets confronting such a demand are invited to contact VVA

Legal Services; 2001 S St., N.W., Suite 710; Washington, DC 20009.

BCMRs also receive applications for corrections of records not related to discharges. See Chapter 14, "Correcting Your Records."

Preparing the Application

If you want to apply for a discharge upgrade, the first step is to request your military personnel records. Unless you must quickly file your application in order to beat the fifteen-year deadline for DRBs, request your records *before* filing your application. Fill out Standard Form (SF) 180, Request Pertaining to Military Records, and send it to the address indicated by the instructions on the form. You can get the form from a VA Regional Office or from your service representative. A sample of this form—filled out for the general purpose of requesting records (and not specifically for discharge review)—may be found in Chapter 13, "Getting Your Records."

In block 1 of the form, write, "COMPLETE SERVICE AND MEDICAL RECORDS." If you believe the military has records in addition to the standard service and medical records, also list these in block 1. Such records may include records of investigations, court-martial transcripts, and hospital records. Where possible, include the names of facilities (for instance, hospitals), and dates (for instance, the dates of a stay in a hospital).

In block 4, write, "To confirm accuracy and completeness of records under the Freedom of Information and Privacy Acts; request fee waiver; discharge review."

Make a copy of the form and mail the original. If you do not receive your records in eight weeks, send another SF 180 (or a photocopy of the first) and mark it "SECOND REQUEST." If you receive records but you believe they are not complete, send a new SF 180 that lists the records you have not received. Attach to the SF 180 a letter in which you explain that you filed an earlier SF 180 and received certain records (specify what you got) but that you believe the military has certain records you have not received.

Unless you are approaching the fifteen-year deadline, *do*

*not file your upgrade application until you have received all
the records available.*

Form to Use

If you are applying to a DRB, use DD Form 293, Application
for the Review of Discharge or Dismissal from the Armed
Forces of the United States. If you are applying to a BCMR,
use DD Form 149, Application for Correction of Military or
Naval Record Under the Provisions of Title 10, U.S. Code,
Sec. 1552. A sample of a completed form of each type is
included at the end of this chapter. Here's some advice on
filling them out:

- First, be sure you have the most current edition of the
  form you must use. At this writing, the most current edi-
  tions are November 1982 for Form 293 and February 1,
  1978, for Form 149.

- Almost always ask for an honorable discharge and a change
  in the reason for discharge to "convenience of the government" or other desirable reason. (Do this in block 7 of
  Form 293 or block 11 of Form 149.)

- Unless you have already prepared a complete "brief" on
  your case—a complete, formal document giving your
  arguments, detailing the reasons for your arguments, and
  including key documents to support your arguments—*do
  not* on the form give your reasons for an upgrade and *do
  not* list supporting documents. (See blocks 11 and 12 of
  Form 293 or blocks 12 and 13 of Form 149.) In each
  block, just write, "To be submitted later," or words to that
  effect. You will have time to submit your reasons and
  documents later, but the sooner you file your application,
  the sooner you will get a decision.

- If you are using Form 149 and it has been more than three
  years since your discharge (or, if you are appealing a DRB
  decision and it has been more than three years since the
  decision), you must give one or more reasons that the
  BCMR should consider your application. (Technically,
  BCMRs can refuse to consider applications for discharges

and DRB decisions older than three years. In practice, however, they generally will accept the vet's reason for not applying earlier and therefore will consider his application.) Common reasons that are usually accepted by BCMRs include:

> "I was not aware that the BCMR could upgrade my discharge."
> "Standards recently have changed."
> "Until now, I have been unable to find a representative (or attorney)."
> "I got my records only recently and discovered the error."

Researching Your Case

In addition to requesting and receiving your complete military records, you and your service representative or lawyer should do other research. This can be done after filing your application for upgrade.

If your rep or attorney has a copy of *MDU* or *SRM* and is experienced in discharge upgrading cases, he or she should know what kind of research must be done and in particular what documents you will need. In addition to your military records, you may need regulations, case decisions, and civilian documents.

It is important to review the military regulations under which you were discharged: you must determine if the military service violated its regulations when it gave you a bad discharge. It is also important to review *current* regulations, because you may want to argue that under the regulations now in force, your conduct would result in a better discharge.

In addition to military regulations, you should become familiar with the regulations governing the panel to which you are applying: a DRB or a BCMR.

Your chances of an upgrade will also be improved if you can find favorable decisions made by DRBs or BCMRs in cases similar to yours. An index to these decisions is available from the Military Review Boards Agency; Attn.: SFBA; Room 520; The Pentagon; Washington, DC 20310.

Civilian documents may also help, especially if one of the reasons you will give for an upgrade is that you have been a good citizen since being discharged. Documents that may be useful include employment records, awards, and newspaper articles about you.

One way to get an idea of which military records and regulations and which civilian documents may help you is to look over the list of "sample contentions" at the end of this chapter. "Contentions" are reasons that support an upgrade. When you find a contention you may want to use, think of records and other documents that support the contention. Your service rep or lawyer should be able to help you find the records, regulations, and documents you need. Finding this evidence is very important. Be sure to reach an understanding with your service rep or lawyer about which of you will be doing this work.

DRB and BCMR Standards and Evidence

As of this writing, many boards tend *not* to upgrade discharges in close cases. This means you should present your case as strongly as possible. In particular, collect as much evidence as possible to support your arguments.

If, after completing your research, you go ahead with the process, you must carefully develop your case in order to counter the military records the board will receive. Military records are often one-sided, giving a strong impression you did something wrong and had no excuses.

In some cases, there is clear evidence that the discharge process violated discharge regulations and as a result harmed your opportunity to get a good discharge. An example is an administrative discharge case in which the military, in violation of regulations, did not provide counsel to a service member.

If clear evidence of a serious violation of a regulation does not exist, a vet will have little chance of getting an upgrade unless he

- Gets extensive assistance from a qualified service rep or lawyer
- Makes a personal appearance at a hearing (if the case is being heard by a DRB)
- Is represented at the hearing by counsel (a service rep or lawyer)
- Submits to the board a well developed brief along with persuasive supporting documents

Although a personal appearance is strongly recommended, sometimes the vet simply cannot travel to a DRB or BCMR to make one. If travel is a problem, check with your service rep or VA Regional Office as to whether a DRB will be traveling to your area. If you cannot appear in person, present a detailed, notarized statement along with your brief.

Probably the most important point to make in this whole chapter is: YOUR APPLICATION MUST NOT BE JUST A PLEA FOR AN UPGRADE SO YOU CAN GET VA BENEFITS. No board will grant your application just so you can get benefits, no matter how badly you need them. You must convince the board that your conduct deserves a better discharge.

You must prove your discharge is either improper (in violation of law or regulation) or inequitable (unfair in light of your conduct in the military or after or both). Boards tend to consider discharges *historically*, trying to decide whether the discharge issued years ago would be issued under today's standards (some of which are more liberal than earlier ones) and trying to decide whether it is fair for the vet to continue to suffer the stigma of a bad discharge years after the conduct that resulted in the discharge.

Among the factors boards consider are whether:

- The vet is a good person but—due to personal problems or limited ability—was unable to perform military duties.
- Mitigating factors (factors that make the vet's conduct seem less bad than it otherwise would) exist.
- The vet's overall service record was good.
- The military engaged in a serious violation of discharge regulations.

The following types of case will usually result in a fairly easy upgrade to a general or honorable discharge. The initials following the type of case indicate the type of discharge that may be upgraded:

- Alcoholism (GD or UD)
- Alcohol-related misconduct (GD or UD)
- Drugs (GD or UD)
- Homosexual tendencies (GD)

- Venereal disease (GD or UD)
- Fraudulent enlistment without intent to defraud (GD or UD)
- Army discharge for personality disorder or character and behavior disorder with no psychiatric diagnosis or where the record contains no general court-martial conviction and only one special court-martial conviction (GD)
- Army discharge for unsuitability despite a clean record (usually before 1966) (GD)
- Bed-wetting (GD)
- Failure to pay debts or support dependents (UD or GD)
- Civilian conduct that occurred while the applicant was in the inactive reserves (UD or GD)
- Serious procedural violations (UD or GD)
- Political associations or beliefs (UD or GD)

The Brief

Submit your brief before any deadline given in any letter from the DRB or BCMR and, in any event, before the DRB or BCMR reviews your case. You need not submit the brief with your application. Consider everything this chapter (and other sources) have explained about facts, regulations, contentions, evidence, and board standards and then, in your brief, clearly and convincingly make your arguments. Attach documents that support the arguments you make. In writing your brief, get help from your service rep or lawyer—or ask your rep or lawyer to write the brief.

If you are applying to a DRB, be sure to follow the instructions on Form 293 on how to submit "issues." "Issues" are the reasons you believe you deserve an upgrade. If you properly submit your list of "issues," the DRB will explain its response to each of them. Because the boards do not like to have to explain their responses, they will not do so unless you follow the instructions *exactly*.

The Hearing

DRBs hear cases in Washington, D.C. As mentioned, DRBs will grant a hearing to any vet who wants one. Sometimes, however, if there are a number of applications pending in a particular area of the country, they will travel to that region. If the vet decides he does not want to appear or cannot appear before the DRB, the DRB will consider his case in Washington without a formal hearing.

BCMRs, on the other hand, only rarely will grant a vet a chance to appear at a hearing. Also, BCMRs generally do not travel from Washington.

Even in a "formal" hearing before a DRB or BCMR, procedures are informal. The vet usually testifies under oath and is questioned by the board. The vet can choose anyone he wants—a service rep, an attorney, or anyone else—to act as his counsel. Counsel presents arguments and asks the vet questions to help the vet to testify effectively. No counsel or anyone else appears at the hearing to represent the government. The board does, however, have most of the vet's military records that relate to the case.

Warning: If you ask for a hearing and then don't show up, you hurt your case very badly. The DRB will go ahead and consider your case without you. *And* it will count its hearing as a personal appearance hearing; as a result, you won't be able to get a personal appearance hearing later. Once a DRB schedules a date and time for a hearing, it doesn't like to be "stood up," and it will hold your absence against you.

If you discover you can't make a hearing (for instance, because of a family emergency or because you can't get off work), be sure to write to the DRB ahead of time to reschedule your hearing. If you can't get word to the DRB two weeks before the hearing, send a telegram or mailgram and withdraw your application. If you can't notify the DRB until after the hearing, at least write to the DRB, explaining why you were unable to attend and asking for another hearing.

A "Records Only Review"

Your case may be a clear winner because it involves a retroactive policy change (a change in military policy that applies to discharges that came before the change) or because a clear error (not just a questionable judgment) was made in the discharge process. In either situation, you will probably want to request a "records only review," also known as a "records review." A records review is a review by a DRB or BCMR without a personal hearing. Such a review is cheaper and quicker than a review that includes a hearing. Check with your service rep or lawyer about whether a records review would be best in your case.

How Long It Takes

If you ask for a records review by a DRB, your case will usually be decided within six months of your application. If you ask for a DRB hearing at a regional location, it will generally occur within a year. If you ask for a DRB hearing in Washington, it will usually take place within six months. It takes from nine months to two years for a BCMR to hear an application. If your case involves a hearing, the decision will generally come one to two months after the hearing occurs.

Reconsideration and Appeal

If you apply for an upgrade and are unhappy with the decision you get (or if some time ago you received a decision with which you are unhappy), you may be able to get the board that made the decision to reconsider your case. In particular, if you had a DRB review before April 1978, you can get another DRB hearing (as long as you apply within fifteen years of discharge).

You may also be able to appeal the decision to the Secretary of the service or to a federal court. (The Vietnam Veterans of America Legal Services specializes in federal court appeals. You may contact VVA Legal Services at 2001 S Street., N.W., Suite 710; Washington, DC 20009.) Also, DRB decisions can be appealed to BCMRs.

If you want to get your decision changed, check with your service representative or attorney. Your chances will be best, of course, if you can present facts or arguments you did not present when your case was first reviewed.

Clemency and Related Programs

Programs of the Nixon, Ford, and Carter administrations have helped certain vets with bad discharges.

In July 1971, Secretary of Defense Melvin Laird (of the Nixon Administration) issued a memorandum relating to veterans who had been discharged for reasons relating to drugs. The memorandum provided that veterans with drug discharges could apply to a DRB or BCMR for an upgrade to at least a general discharge. The memorandum did not directly affect vets discharged after the memorandum was issued.

In September 1974, President Ford began a "clemency" program for vets who had been discharged because they had gone AWOL. Under this program vets could get a clemency discharge. The VA has treated clemency discharges as undesirable discharges.

In March 1977, President Carter announced his "Special Discharge Review Program." Under this program, more than twenty thousand veterans discharged from 1964 to 1973 got upgrades of undesirable and general discharges. Nevertheless, Congress passed a law stating that the VA will not be required to give benefits to veterans who under the program got upgrades of undesirable discharges until these vets also get a DRB review after April 1978 (when the Department of Defense issued new DRB standards).

Special Cases

There are many special cases that make it especially easy or especially hard for certain vets to get upgrades or receive benefits from the VA or another federal agency. Whether you fit the definition of "special case" depends on factors such as whether you were court-martialed, the type of conduct that got you a bad discharge, what kind of discharge you have, when you received your discharge, which board reviewed your discharge (if your discharge has been reviewed), and when the board reviewed it. The case history at the beginning of this chapter, involving a vet who was AWOL for more than 180 days, is one kind of special case. Another is the case of veterans disciplined or discharged due to faulty drug tests conducted in 1982–83 (described near the end of Chapter 14, "Correcting Your Records").

In consulting your service representative or lawyer, be sure to ask if there is anything "special" about your case. Suggest that your rep or attorney check the VVA *Service Representatives Manual* (*SRM*), Chapter 11, pages 11 through 14, and *Military Discharge Upgrading and Introduction to Veterans Adminis-*

tration Law (MDU). The *SRM* pages just noted will refer your
rep or lawyer to the appropriate pages in *MDU*.

ELIGIBILITY FOR BENEFITS
BASED ON CHARACTER OF DISCHARGE

E—Eligible
NE—Not eligible
TBD—To be determined by agency
DV—Eligibility depends on specific disability of veteran

BENEFITS ADMINISTERED BY DoD	HD or GD	UD (DUOTHC)	BCD (SPCM)	DD or BCD (GCM)
1. Payment for accrued leave	E	NE	NE	NE
2. Death gratuity (6 mos. pay)	E	E	E	NE
3. Transportation to home	E	E	E	E
4. Transportation of dependents and household goods to home	E	NE[1]	NE[1]	NE[1]
5. Wearing of military uniform	E	NE	NE	NE
6. Admission to Soldiers' Home	E	NE	NE	NE
7. Burial in Nat'l Cemetery	E	NE	NE	NE
8. Headstone marker	E	NE	NE	NE
BENEFITS ADMINISTERED BY VA[2]				
1. Dependence and indemnity compensation	E	TBD	TBD	NE
2. Compensation for service-connected disability or death	E	TBD	TBD	NE
3. Pension for non-service-connected disability or death	E	TBD	TBD	NE
4. Medal of honor roll pension	E	TBD	TBD	NE
5. Insurance	E	E	E	E
6. Vocational rehabilitation (Disabled Veterans only)	E	TBD	TTBD	NE

7. Educational assistance (including flight training and apprentice training)	E	TBD	TBD	NE
8. War orphans' educational assistance	E	TBD	TBD	NE
9. Home and other loans	E	TBD	TBD	TBD
10. Hospitalization and domiciliary care	E	E or TBD[3]	TBD	NE
11. Medical and dental services	E	TBD	TBD	NE
12. Prosthetic appliances (Disabled Veterans only)	E	TBD	TBD	NE
13. Guide dogs and equipment for blindness (Disabled Veterans only)	E	TBD	TBD	NE
14. Special housing	E	TBD	TBD	NE
15. Automobiles (Disabled veterans only)	E	TBD	TBD	NE
16. Funeral and burial expenses	E	TBD	TBD	NE
17. Burial flag	E	TBD	TBD	NE

BENEFITS ADMINISTERED BY OTHER FEDERAL AGENCIES

1. Preference for farm loans (Dept. of Agriculture)	E	E	E	NE
2. Preference for farm and other rural housing loans (Dept. of Agriculture)	E	E	E	NE
3. Civil service retirement credit (Civil Service Commission)	E	NE	NE	NE
4. Civil service retirement credit (Civil Service Commission)	E	NE	NE	NE
5. Reemployment rights (Dept. of Labor)	E	NE	NE	NE
6. Job counseling and employment placement (Dept. of Labor)	E	E	E	NE
7. Unemployment compensation for ex-servicemen (Dept. of Labor)	TBD	NE	NE	NE

8. Naturalization benefits (Dept. of Justice, Imm. & Naturalization Service)	E	NE	NE	NE
9. Old age and disability insurance (Social Security Administration)	E	TBD	TBD	NE

[1]Dependents overseas may be returned to the United States.
[2]Assumes no statutory bar is applicable.
[3]Treatment of service-connected disabilities permitted.

SAMPLE CONTENTIONS

Here are some arguments that may improve your chances for a discharge upgrade. If these contentions apply to your case, include them in your brief. If there is a hearing in your case, you or your counsel should also make these arguments at the hearing. In both the brief and any hearing, each contention should be accompanied by a detailed explanation.

DRB or BCMR: The following issues are the reasons I believe my discharge should be upgraded to Honorable. If you disagree, please explain in detail why you disagree.

1. Under current standards, I would not receive the type of discharge I did.
2. My conduct and efficiency ratings/behavior and proficiency marks were mostly pretty good.
3. I received awards and decorations.
4. I received letters of commendation.
5. I had combat service.
6. I was wounded in action.
7. My record of promotions showed I was generally a good servicemember.
8. There were other acts of merit.
9. I was so close to finishing my tour that it was unfair to give me a bad discharge.
10. I had a prior Honorable Discharge.
11. I have been a good citizen since discharge.
12. My record of NJPs/Article 15s indicates only isolated or minor offenses.
13. My record of court-martial convictions indicates only isolated or minor offenses. (Sample contentions continue on p. 236.)

Form Approved
OMB NO. 0704-0004

APPLICATION FOR THE REVIEW OF DISCHARGE OR DISMISSAL FROM THE ARMED FORCES OF THE UNITED STATES

DATA REQUIRED BY THE PRIVACY ACT OF 1974

AUTHORITY: 10 U.S.C. 1553, Executive Order 9397, 22 Nov 43 (SSN).

PRINCIPAL PURPOSES: To apply for a change in the type of discharge issued.

ROUTINE USES: Placed in applicant's file. Used in applicant's case in determining the relief sought. To compare facts presented with evidence on record.

DISCLOSURE: Voluntary. If information is not furnished, applicant may not secure benefits from the board.

REQUESTING COPIES OF MILITARY RECORDS. Prior to applying for discharge review, potential applicants or their designated representatives may obtain copies of their military personnel records by submitting a Standard Form (SF) 180, Request Pertaining to Military Records, to the National Personnel Records Center (NPRC), 9700 Page Boulevard, St. Louis, MO 63132.

SEE INSTRUCTIONS BEFORE COMPLETING THIS FORM

1a. NAME OF APPLICANT TO BE REVIEWED (Last, First, MI)	b. SOCIAL SECURITY NO.	c. SERVICE NO. (If different from 1b)
Joe, Gerald I.	310-50-9999	BSS 99.32

2a. ADDRESS FOR ALL FUTURE CORRESPONDENCE (Street, City, State, ZIP Code)	b. TELEPHONE NUMBER (Include area code)	3. BRANCH OF ARMED SERVICE (Check one)
3716 DuPont St. Kenmore, Md. 20899	301-989-6999	☐ ARMY ☒ NAVY ☐ AIR FORCE ☐ MARINE CORPS ☐ COAST GUARD

4. DISCHARGE RECEIVED: (Check one)

☐ HONORABLE
☒ UNDESIRABLE/UNDER OTHER THAN HONORABLE CONDITIONS
☐ GENERAL/UNDER HONORABLE CONDITIONS
☐ BAD CONDUCT (Special court martial only)
☐ OTHER (Explain)

5. DATE OF DISCHARGE (Year, month, day)
1972, Dec. 8

6a. APPEAL FILED IN BEHALF OF INDIVIDUAL TO BE REVIEWED: If the reviewee is deceased or incompetent, then check below the relationship of individual submitting this application. Appropriate evidence must accompany this form.

☐ NEXT OF KIN ☐ SURVIVING SPOUSE ☐ LEGAL REPRESENTATIVE

b. NAME (Last, First, MI)

7. BOARD ACTION REQUESTED

a. ☒ CHANGE DISCHARGE TO HONORABLE   b. ☐ CHANGE DISCHARGE TO GENERAL/UNDER HONORABLE CONDITIONS

c. ☒ CHANGE REASON FOR DISCHARGE TO: _Convenience of the Government_

8. TYPE OF REVIEW REQUESTED *(Check one)*

a. ☒ I and/or *(counsel/representative)* wish to appear at a hearing at no expense to the Government before the Board in the Washington National Capital Region.

b. ☐ I and/or *(counsel/representative)* wish to appear at a hearing at no expense to the Government before a Traveling Panel closest to:

_____
(City, State)

c. ☐ Conduct a RECORD REVIEW of my discharge based on my military personnel file and any additional documentation submitted by me. I and/or *(counsel/representative)* will not appear before the Board.

9. I HAVE ARRANGED TO BE REPRESENTED BY AND AUTHORIZE THE RELEASE OF RECORDS TO:

a. NAME OF COUNSEL/REPRESENTATIVE *(Last, First, MI)*   b. ORGANIZATION

I am making arrangements for Counsel and will

c. ADDRESS *(Street, City, State, ZIP Code)*   d. TELEPHONE *(Include area code)*

supply this information later.

10. ☐ I have read Item 10 of the instructions pertaining to the AVAILABILITY of counsel and elect NOT to be represented by counsel/representative *(leave Item 9 blank)*

DD FORM 293
82 NOV

EDITION OF 1 MAR 77 IS OBSOLETE.

11. SUPPORTING DOCUMENTS: *(Please print name and social security number on each document.)*

a. ☐ Will not be submitted. Please complete review based on available service records.

b. ☐ Will be submitted within 60 days.

c. ☒ Will be submitted within _before my hearing_ days.

d. ☐ Are listed below and are attached to this application: *(Continue on a plain sheet of paper if more space is needed.)*

DOCUMENT 1

DOCUMENT 2

DOCUMENT 3

12. ISSUES. The Board will consider any issue submitted by you prior to closing the case for deliberation. The Board also will review the case to determine whether there are any issues which provide a basis for upgrading your discharge. However, the Board is not required to respond in writing to issues of concern to you unless those issues are listed or incorporated by specific reference below. Read the instructions carefully that pertain to block 12 prior to completing this part of the application. If you need more space, submit additional issues on an attachment.

I expect my counsel to submit issues before my hearing.

ISSUE 1: before my hearing.

ISSUE 2:

ISSUE 3:

ISSUE 4:

a. ☐ Check this block if you have listed additional issues as an attachment to this application.

b. ☐ I previously submitted an application on _____ and am completing this form in order to submit additional issues.
(year, month, day)

I make the foregoing statements as part of my application with full knowledge of the penalties involved for willfully making a false statement. (U.S. Code, Title 18, Section 1001, provides a penalty as follows: A maximum fine of $10,000 or maximum imprisonment of 5 years, or both)

13. DATE (year, month, day)
85-02-13

14. SIGNATURE _Gerald J. ___

UPON COMPLETION, MAIL THIS APPLICATION AS FOLLOWS

ARMY	NAVY & MARINE CORPS	AIR FORCE	COAST GUARD
CO, USARCPAC 9700 Page Blvd St. Louis, MO 63132	NAVAL Discharge Review 801 No. Randolph St. Arlington, VA 22203	AFMPC/MPCDOA1 Randolph AFB, TX 78150	Commandant (G-PE-1) U.S. Coast Guard Headq Washington, DC 20593

Form Approved
Budget Bureau No. 22-R0009

APPLICATION FOR CORRECTION OF MILITARY OR NAVAL RECORD
UNDER THE PROVISIONS OF TITLE 10, U.S. CODE, SEC. 1552
(See instructions on reverse side BEFORE completing application.)

DATA REQUIRED BY THE PRIVACY ACT OF 1974

AUTHORITY: Title 10, U.S. Code 1552, Executive Order 939 - 22 Nov 43 (SSN)

PRINCIPAL PURPOSE: To apply for correction of a military or 1 record.

ROUTINE USES: To docket a case. Reviewed by board members to determine relief sought. To determine qualification to apply to board. To compare facts present with evidence in the record.

DISCLOSURE: Voluntary. If information is not furnished, applicant may not secure benefits from the Board.

BRANCH OF SERVICE

☐ ARMY ☒ NAVY ☐ AIR FORCE ☐ MARINE CORPS ☐ COAST GUARD

1. NAME (Last, first, middle initial) (Please print)	2. PRESENT RATE/GRADE	3. SERVICE NUMBER	4. SOCIAL SECURITY NUMBER
Joe, Gerald I.	N/A	BSS 9932	310-SD-999

5. TYPE OF DISCHARGE (If by court-martial, state type of court.)	6. PRESENT STATUS, IF ANY, WITH RESPECT TO THE ARMED SERVICES (Active duty, retired, Reserve, etc.)	7. DATE OF DISCHARGE OR RELEASE FROM ACTIVE DUTY
undesirable	none	12-08-72

8. ORGANIZATION AT TIME OF ALLEGED ERROR IN RECORD	9. I DESIRE TO APPEAR BEFORE THE BOARD IN WASHINGTON, D.C. (No expense to the Government)
USN ~ USS Intrepid	☒ YES ☐ NO

10. NAME AND ADDRESS OF COUNSEL (If any)

I am making arrangements for counsel and will supply name later.

11. I REQUEST THE FOLLOWING CORRECTION OF ERROR OR INJUSTICE

Upgrade to Honorable. Change reason for discharge to Convenience of the Government and change RE and SPN according ly.

12. I BELIEVE THE RECORD TO BE IN ERROR OR UNJUST IN THE FOLLOWING PARTICULARS:

I expect my counsel to submit particulars before my hearing.

13. IN SUPPORT OF THIS APPLICATION I SUBMIT AS EVIDENCE THE FOLLOWING: *(Veterans Administration records are pertinent to your case, give Regional Office location and Claim Number.)*

To be submitted later

14. a. THE DATE OF THE DISCOVERY OF THE ALLEGED ERROR OR INJUSTICE WAS _1984_ . b. IF MORE THAN THREE YEARS SINCE THE ALLEGED ERROR OR INJUSTICE WAS DISCOVERED, STATE WHY THE BOARD SHOULD FIND IT IN THE INTEREST OF JUSTICE TO CONSIDER THIS APPLICATION

15. APPLICANT MUST SIGN IN THE SPACE PROVIDED. IF THE RECORD IN QUESTION IS THAT OF A PERSON WHO IS DECEASED OR INCOMPETENT, LEGAL PROOF OF DEATH OR INCOMPETENCY MUST ACCOMPANY APPLICATION. IF APPLICATION IS SIGNED BY SPOUSE, WIDOW OR WIDOWER, NEXT OF KIN OR LEGAL REPRESENTATIVE, INDICATE RELATIONSHIP OR STATUS IN APPROPRIATE BOX. ☐ SPOUSE ☐ WIDOW ☐ WIDOWER ☐ NEXT OF KIN ☐ LEGAL REP. ☐ OTHER *(Specify)* ___

16. I MAKE THE FOREGOING STATEMENTS, AS PART OF MY CLAIM, WITH FULL KNOWLEDGE OF THE PENALTIES INVOLVED FOR WILFULLY MAKING A FALSE STATEMENT OR CLAIM *(U.S. Code, Title 18, Sec. 287, 1001, provides a penalty of not more than $10,000 fine or not more than 5 years imprisonment or both.)*

17. COMPLETE ADDRESS, INCLUDING ZIP CODE *(Applicant should forward notification of all changes of address)* 3716 Dupont Street, Kenmore, MD. 20899

18. DATE   Feb. 13, 1985

19. SIGNATURE *(Applicant must sign here.)*   Gerald J. Joe

DOCUMENT NUMBER *(DO NOT WRITE IN THIS SPACE)*

DD FORM 149   EDITION OF 1 APR 69 MAY BE USED
FEB 78

INSTRUCTIONS

1. For detailed information see:

   Air Force Regulation 31-3

   Army Regulations 15-185

   Coast Guard, Code of Federal Regulations
   Title 33, Part 52

   Navy, NAVEXOS P-473, as revised

2. Submit original only of this form.

3. Complete all items. If the question is not applicable, mark—"None".

4. If space is insufficient, use "Remarks" or attach additional sheet if necessary.

5. Various veterans and service organizations furnish counsel without charge. These organizations prefer that arrangements for representation be made through local posts or chapters.

6. List all attachments or inclosures.

7. ITEMS 9 and 10. Personal appearance of you and your witnesses or representation by counsel is not required to insure full and impartial consideration of applications. Appearances and representations are permitted, at no expense to the Government when a hearing is authorized.

8. ITEM 11. State the specific correction of record desired.

9. ITEM 12. In order to justify correction of a military or naval record, it is necessary for you to show to the satisfaction of the Board, or it must otherwise satisfactorily appear, that the alleged entry or omission in the record was in error or unjust. Evidence may include affidavits or signed testimony of witnesses, executed under oath, and a brief of arguments supporting application. All evidence not already included in your record must be submitted by you. The responsibility for securing new evidence rests with you.

10. ITEM 14. 10 U.S.C. 1552b provides that no correction may be made unless request is made within three years after the discovery of the error or injustice, but that the Board may excuse failure to file within three years after discovery if it finds it to be in the interest of justice.

MAIL COMPLETED APPLICATIONS TO APPROPRIATE ADDRESS BELOW

ARMY	NAVY AND MARINE CORPS	COAST GUARD	AIR FORCE
(For Active Duty Personnel) Army Board for Correction of Military Records Department of the Army Washington, D.C. 20310 (For Other than Active Duty Personnel) CO, USARCPAC 9700 Page Blvd. St. Louis, MO. 63132	Board for Correction of Naval Records Department of the Navy Washington, D.C. 20370	U.S. Coast Guard ATTN: Senior Member Board for Correction of Coast Guard Records Washington, D.C. 20591	USAFMPC/DPMDOA1 Randolph AFB, Tex. 78148

REMARKS *(Applicant has exhausted all administrative channels in seeking this correction and has been counseled by a representative of his/her servicing military personnel office. (Applicable only to active duty and reserve personnel.))*

14. My record of convictions by civil authorities while I was in service indicates only minor or isolated offenses.
15. My record of AWOL/UA indicates only minor or isolated offenses.
16. My ability to serve was impaired by my youth and immaturity.
17. My low aptitude scores and level of education impaired my ability to serve.
18. My ability to serve was impaired by my deprived background.
19. My ability to serve was impaired because of marital and family problems.
20. Personal problems impaired my ability to serve.
21. Financial problems impaired my ability to serve.
22. I suffered religious discrimination and that impaired my ability to serve.
23. I faced racial discrimination and that impaired my ability to serve.
24. My use of drugs impaired my ability to serve.
25. My use of alcohol impaired my ability to serve.
26. Medical or physical problems impaired my ability to serve.
27. Psychiatric problems impaired my ability to serve.
28. Matters of conscience impaired my ability to be a "good" servicemember.
29. There was a waiver of moral standards when I enlisted; those pre-service problems impaired my ability to serve.
30. Certain other problems impaired my ability to serve.
31. My ability to serve was impaired because I was not working in the field I was trained for.
32. My ability to serve was impaired because I couldn't speak English very well.
33. The punishment I got was too severe compared with today's standards.
34. The punishment I got at discharge was too harsh—it was much worse than most people got for the same offense.
35. I tried to serve and wanted to, but just couldn't or wasn't able to.
36. My discharge was based on many offenses, but they were mostly only minor offenses.
37. My command abused its authority when it decided to discharge me and decided to give me a bad discharge.
38. When I got back from Vietnam, I just couldn't take state-side duty.
39. I had applied or tried to apply for conscientious objector status, but was unfairly denied or told to forget it.
41. I had applied or tried to apply for a compassionate reassignment but was unfairly denied or told to forget it.
42. My enlistment option was not satisfied or waived.
43. I was being considered for a physical disability discharge and was unfairly denied one.
44. I should have been given a medical discharge because I never was medically qualified to serve.

45. I was enlisted illegally.
46. I was drafted illegally.
47. The urine test for drug abuse was faulty.
48. [other reasons]

16. CLAIMS AND APPEALS

What to Do if the VA Turns You Down

> I have not yet begun to fight.
> —John Paul Jones

This book deals with many different subjects. But in most every area covered by the book, some institution or person makes decisions about whether or not the veteran will get what he wants. In areas such as disability compensation, pensions, and the G.I. Bill, the institution making the decisions is the VA. In areas such as correcting records and upgrading discharges, it's a military board. And there are cases where the decisions are made by another federal agency (such as the Small Business Administration) or by a court (such as in the Agent Orange lawsuit).

And this book tells you how to go about getting the decisions you deserve. It tells you what programs cover you, what form to use to apply, and what to say in the form.

But all may not go as planned. You may deserve a certain kind of decision—for instance, that you have a 50 percent disability and that it is service-connected. You may do everything you're supposed to do to get that kind of decision: you carefully fill out your application, you file it with the VA Regional Office, and you show up for a medical exam. But the decision may go against you. You may get turned down completely for the benefit or service you have requested. Or, even if you are granted something, you may not get all you deserve (you may, for instance, be rated as having a service-connected disability, but get a rating of 20 percent, not the 50 percent rating that would be fair).

Filing an application—or making a request through other means—is called making a *claim*. If the VA or other institution or person decides against you—turns down your claim—what do you do?

ASSESSING YOUR SITUATION

If your claim is turned down completely or in part, the first thing to do is to carefully consider your situation. It is not best to simply get angry and fight to change the decision. For one thing, you may have no reasonable chance of winning, in which case fighting would be a waste of your valuable time. For another, if you *do* have a chance, you must evaluate the many different paths you might take in an attempt to get what you deserve: some of these paths are relatively simple, some relatively complicated; some are well suited to one kind of case, others are well suited to others.

Service Representatives

Over and over, this book recommends that the veteran get help from a service representative (sometimes called a "service officer") who works for a veterans organization such as Vietnam Veterans of America (VVA). Nowhere is this advice more important than in the case of the veteran whose claim has been turned down and who is considering doing something about it.

This chapter will tell you briefly about each of many areas that are important in assessing your situation and in appealing your case. It is helpful for the veteran to know at least a little about these areas. But, generally speaking, it is a bad idea for the veteran to enter these areas without assistance.

An old saying among attorneys is "A lawyer who represents himself has a fool for a client." This saying applies to veterans even more strongly than to lawyers. Both lawyers and veterans

suffer if they represent themselves, because they are not likely
to be very objective: their anger and other passions are likely
to get in the way of good judgment. But lawyers, at least, often
are experts in the areas in which they are thinking of representing themselves. Most veterans are not.

And the areas of veterans claims and appeals are complicated. They involve VA regulations and federal law. They may
involve court cases, pending legislation, and medical research.
It's important to know these complex areas well and it's important to keep up to date: even knowing the law as of last
month may not be enough.

Speaking of lawyers, they can sometimes help the veteran
who is considering appealing a decision. Most of the time,
however, lawyers can't. This is because most veterans cases
involve VA benefits, and federal law for all practical purposes
prohibits lawyers from representing veterans in benefits cases:
the law limits lawyer fees in such cases to $10. (Low-income
vets may qualify for free legal representation from Legal Services or Legal Aid offices.)

So, in most cases, veterans should turn again to service
representatives. Like lawyers, many of them are familiar with
VA regulations and laws. Unlike lawyers, they don't charge
anything.

The first step to take once you have received an unfavorable
decision is to assess your situation. The first step in assessing
your situation is to get advice from your service rep.

RESEARCH

To fully understand what has happened in your case and what
(if anything) you can do about it, you must become familiar
with the laws and regulations under which the VA (or other
institution) made its decision. Depending on your background
and that of your service rep and depending on how much time
each of you has, you may want to do some of the research
yourself. Because most veterans cases involve the VA, this
book emphasizes research relating to VA decisions.

Service Representatives Manual

Research is a complicated process, best handled by experts who have done it before. Still, the veteran can be involved, perhaps in doing some of the research and at least in evaluating his service representative to determine whether the service rep knows what he or she is doing and is doing a good job.

Whether the vet is doing his own research or relying almost entirely on the service representative, one book can help. It is the *Service Representatives Manual* (SRM), first published in 1983 by Vietnam Veterans of America (VVA). It is regularly updated. This manual, containing 640 letter-size pages, includes two chapters important to claims and appeals. One is Chapter 2, "Research," and the other is Chapter 12, "Appeals." A service rep or veteran doing research or handling an appeal should have the *Service Representatives Manual* and should refer to those two chapters. If your service rep does not have this manual or similar resources, you may want to get help from someone else.

Though this chapter will briefly describe some parts of research for VA cases, remember that more detail is available in the manual.

Laws

Federal laws, including those that deal with veterans, must be passed by both houses of Congress and signed by the President. The *United States Code* is a series of volumes that includes all federal laws. The code is divided into parts, each on a separate subject. Each part is called a "title." Title 38 contains all the laws about veterans benefits.

You can find the *United States Code* in any law library and some other libraries. Law libraries are located in law schools, court houses, and bar association offices. More useful than a simple printing of the code itself is the *United States Code, Annotated*, which includes not only the laws, but important notes on them regarding subjects such as court interpretations of the laws. The annotated code is also found in any law library.

Most basic legal references, such as versions of the *United States Code*, are updated at least once a year. In using any such reference, be sure to check the "pocket part," the thin, paperbound volume of updated information that fits in the pocket attached to the inside back cover of a hardbound reference book.

Even the pocket part is not enough to keep the legal researcher up to the minute. It is sometimes also important to know about legislation that has very recently been enacted into law and about legislation that is being considered by Congress. Ask a law librarian for assistance.

Regulations

Certain federal agencies—such as departments, administrations, and commissions—administer certain laws. In administering laws, the agencies issue regulations, also known as "rules." Regulations allow agencies to do what the law intended—or what the agencies *argue* the law intended. For instance, a law may require the Environmental Protection Agency to clean up the air. Under the law, the EPA may issue regulations precisely stating the amount of lead a particular kind of factory can let escape into the air.

Federal regulations are compiled in the *Code of Federal Regulations*. Just as Title 38 of the U.S. Code covers veterans laws, Title 38 of the *Code of Federal Regulations* covers veterans regulations. To keep up to date on regulations, use the *Federal Register*. The *Federal Register* is a daily publication containing, among other things, regulations that have just been proposed or issued by federal agencies, including the VA. Again, a law library will have the volumes and a law librarian can help you use them.

BVA Index

The *BVA Index* is an important reference tool regarding only the VA. It is an index, on microfiche, of decisions by the Board of Veterans Appeals (BVA), the highest authority on appeals within the VA. Most VA Regional Offices have the index. Microfiche copies of the index—and of the text of individual decisions—can be obtained from Appellate Index and Retrieval Service (01C1); BVA; Washington, DC 20420. If you request the index or copies of specified decisions, write a letter saying you are making your request under the Freedom of Information Act.

The VA says it is not required to follow its earlier decisions. Still, by using the *BVA Index*, the veteran can find BVA decisions in cases similar to his own. As a result, he can get a good idea of what the VA and the BVA may do in his case. Previous BVA cases can help the veteran know what to include in his arguments. Specifically, the veteran can bring the cases to the attention of the VA to convince the VA that since benefits were awarded in cases like the veteran's, they should—on the ground of basic fairness—be awarded this time too. To bring the cases to the attention of the VA, the veteran can refer to them in his brief or other form of argument.

Other Resources

In addition to regulations and BVA decisions, the VA issues many other publications that may help a service representative or veteran prepare a case. These publications include manuals, guides, circulars, handbooks, interim issues, information bulletins, technical bulletins, medical bulletins, policy and procedures, operating instructions, statistical reports, and pamphlets. For more information on these publications, check with your service representative, inquire at a VA Regional Office, and see Chapter 2 of the *Service Representatives Manual*.

The VA's General Counsel—its chief lawyer—from time to time issues official opinions on various topics. These opinions are binding on the BVA. The opinions may be read at the District Counsel's office in each VA Regional Office.

Lawsuits against the VA can change VA policies and regulations and can shed light on the meaning of particular policies and rules. The best source of information on recent lawsuits against the VA is the *Veterans Rights Newsletter*, published every two months. This newsletter also updates the *Service Representatives Manual*. To subscribe to the *Veterans Rights Newsletter*, write to Veterans Education Project; P.O. Box 42130; Washington, DC 20015.

APPEALING A DECISION

Many VA decisions should not be appealed. Many decisions are clearly correct and fair. Of those decisions that are not, many cannot be successfully appealed. After assessing your situation—by checking with a service rep, doing some thinking, and perhaps doing some research—you will probably have a good idea of whether your case should be appealed.

If you decide to appeal, you will be embarking on a process that is at least somewhat complicated and that may become *very* complicated. Again, you will probably require assistance. And again, the best available assistance is likely to come from a service representative.

Evaluating Your Representative

Now, however, you will be relying on the service rep more than when you simply got an opinion about whether to appeal the decision. The service rep will no longer be just an informal advisor; he or she will be your representative during the appeal and will have a great impact on whether your appeal will succeed.

Don't just sit back and assume your service rep is doing a good job. First, carefully read your rights as spelled out in the notifications and any other documents the VA has sent you about your claim. Then, keep an eye on your service rep.

Following are some things you should look for in your service representative (or other representative such as a lawyer). Unfortunately, of course, many of your evaluations cannot be made until after your representative has done something on your behalf and perhaps done a poor job. At any rate, here are some factors:

1. Has the rep offered you an opportunity to see all your records and review them with the rep?
2. Has the rep read your VA claims file and is he or she familiar with all parts of your case?
3. Has the rep agreed to meet with you before the day of any hearing to brief you on what to expect and to prepare you to answer questions?

4. Has the rep given you the opportunity far enough before the hearing to ask questions about it?
5. Has the rep discussed with you evidence, such as medical records, that may be useful in presenting in your case?
6. Has the rep discussed with you his or her approach to your case and, specifically, how certain regulations (and perhaps laws) apply to the facts?

The Adverse Decision

After you make your claim, you get a decision from the VA. The first official action that grants or denies a claim for benefits is called an "adjudication" or a "rating decision." Because this chapter is about decisions you may want to appeal, this chapter will deal with adverse decisions: decisions that deny a claim.

The VA must notify you in writing of its decision. You and your service representative should carefully review everything the VA has sent you in order to determine whether your claim has been completely, or only partly, denied. Some claims involve more than one issue, and many decisions provide approval on one or more issues and disapproval on one or more others. An example would be a decision that agrees that a disability is service-connected but provides a disability rating (for instance, 20 percent) lower than what you think is fair (for instance, 50 percent).

If you have filed a claim with the VA (for instance, if you have applied for disability compensation) more than three months ago without receiving any response, you should phone the VA Regional Office (VARO) and check on the status of your claim.

Notice of Disagreement

If you think the VA decision is wrong, the first thing you should do is file a Notice of Disagreement (NOD). You must file it with the VARO that denied your claim. File the NOD as soon as possible. It *must* be filed within a year of the date the VA mailed you notice of its decision (if you do not meet this deadline, you will lose your right to appeal).

The NOD need not be detailed. Still, the more information you provide to explain why you disagree with the decision, the more likely the VARO will be to give you a complete explanation. In most cases, the NOD should say something like this:

> This is my Notice of Disagreement with your decision of June 15, 1985, concerning my claim. I request a Statement of the Case so that an appeal of your adverse decision may be prepared.

You may file your NOD on a blank sheet of paper. In most cases, however, veterans and their representatives use VA Form 21–4138, Statement in Support of Claim. Be sure to include your name and your VA claim number (either a "C" number or your Social Security number).

Statement of the Case

Once you have filed a NOD, the VA is required to issue a Statement of the Case (SOC). The SOC gives the VA's official position on your case. It includes important parts of your claims folder, such as excerpts from the decision of the VA Rating Board (a board of three VA employees with training in areas relating to your claim) and the dates of letters and notices. The SOC will also include a summary of the evidence considered by the Rating Board, the laws and regulations that apply to your case, and the reasons for the VA's decision. In most cases the VA will send the SOC four to six weeks after getting the NOD.

It is important to review your SOC with your service rep. An experienced service representative will be able to assess your chances of a successful appeal. The rep will in most cases also be able to learn from the SOC exactly what is needed for you to succeed in an appeal.

Reconsideration

If, after you have read the SOC, you still think the VA decision is wrong, you may want to appeal it. This chapter sets out the appeals process. But there is another course of action you may take: you may ask for reconsideration by the VARO.

Reconsideration by the VARO may be appropriate if, after reviewing the facts, regulations, laws, and other factors relating to your case, you and your service rep believe the VA made its decision on the basis of incomplete or inaccurate information. Sometimes the Rating Board will tell you what evidence you need to support your claim.

If you want your case reconsidered, write to the VARO, explaining the error you believe was made and enclosing evidence that supports your argument. If, after reconsideration, the VA denies your claim, you are entitled to a Supplemental SOC (SSOC). The SSOC, along with the SOC, then becomes the basis on which to decide whether to appeal. If you have not yet had a VARO hearing, you can request one at this time.

VARO Hearing

VARO hearings are generally conducted by a Rating Board. This will not be the same Rating Board that made the initial decision in your case. You can be assisted by your service representative and can present documents, make arguments, testify, and have others (such as doctors) testify for you. One or more of the three members of the board will ask you questions. They will later decide by majority vote whether to grant the benefit you are claiming. The hearing will be tape-recorded (if you make a request before or at the hearing, you can get a free copy of the transcript).

Besides giving you the opportunity to present arguments and evidence, the hearing gives you the chance to present *yourself*. The board will get a sense of whether you are a truthful, sincere person. Just the fact that you are making a personal appearance may help you, because it is harder for people to turn down people they have met and because the fact that you have taken the trouble to travel to the VARO may make the board believe you sincerely think you are right. Remember that even though you may be frustrated and angry, it will only hurt your case if you make rude or derogatory remarks to board members.

Your service rep should help you prepare for the hearing and should represent you at it. While it is important for you to be present, your representative should make opening and closing statements and should question witnesses.

At many hearings, the tape recorder will be temporarily turned off and board members, your service rep, and you will discuss the case "off the record." Sometimes the off-the-record discussion will not be important. Sometimes, however, the board will give you and your representative a very good idea of what it thinks is the key factual or legal issue in the case. If this happens, your representative should be guided in the rest of his or her presentation by what was said off the record.

After the VARO Hearing

If, after the hearing, the Rating Board decides in your favor, your claim will be granted and your case will be over (unless the board orders a new medical exam or wants to consider evidence it did not have at the hearing). In most cases, however, unless you have submitted new evidence, the board will agree with the original denial of your claim.

If the board decides against you, you can still appeal to the BVA. Whether or not you had a personal hearing at the VARO, you are entitled to one at the BVA.

Filing Your Appeal

If you have exhausted all possibilities at the VARO—or if you have decided to appeal directly to the BVA without asking for reconsideration at the VARO—you must file VA Form 1–9, Appeal to Board of Veterans Appeals. This form will be attached to the SOC you received in response to your NOD.

To keep your case "active," you should generally file your Form 1–9 within sixty days of receiving the SOC. You *must* file it within a year of the date the VA mailed you notice of its original denial of your claim.

Generally, you should have your service rep prepare your appeal form (your Form 1–9). He or she should clearly state the factual issues on which you disagree with the VA and should explain the exact benefits to which you believe you are entitled. He or she should use both factual and legal arguments. And your service rep should fully respond to the SOC: anything not challenged will be taken by the BVA to be true. To be careful, it is wise to state, at the end of the appeal form, "I dispute every item in the Statement of the Case that is not fully consistent with the facts and arguments set forth in this appeal."

Most of the appeal form contains your response to the SOC. Part of it, however, requires you to decide whether you want to have your BVA hearing at the VARO or in Washington, D.C., and whether you want to be present. The BVA travels regularly to the larger VAROs. Smaller ones are visited less frequently. VARO hearings are often booked up long in advance. Check with a VARO or the BVA to see how long it would take to get a hearing scheduled at a nearby VARO. If you choose to appear in person in Washington, it will take about a year before your hearing occurs.

Board of Veterans Appeals (BVA)

The BVA is the final stage of the VA appeal process. The BVA has sixty-five members, appointed by the President. All are full-time VA employees. Each case is heard by a BVA panel of three, usually two lawyers and a doctor. Each panel deals with a specific area, such as neurological problems, PTSD, radiation, or discharges.

If your case involves a specialized legal issue, ask at the hearing that the BVA delay its decision until it has obtained an opinion from the Office of the General Counsel of the VA. If there is a specialized medical issue, ask the BVA to arrange for an independent (non-VA) medical expert to examine you.

If the three BVA panel members unanimously make a decision, that is the end of the appeal process. If one member dissents—disagrees with the other two—the case is referred to the Chairperson of the BVA. If the Chairperson disagrees with the dissent, the majority decision of the BVA panel stands as the final decision. If the Chairperson agrees with the dissent, the case is referred to a panel of at least six members, which makes the final BVA decision.

The final decision can take several forms. The decision may deny the appeal. Or it may return the case to the VARO for further development or for consideration of additional evidence that was presented in the appeal form or at the BVA hearing. Or the BVA may grant the appeal in whole or in part.

Only one of eight appeals to the BVA is immediately successful. One of six is returned to the VARO for further consideration.

Reconsideration of the BVA Denial

BVA decisions are generally the final determination in the VA appeal process. There are three exceptions to this rule:

1. If you lose at the BVA but believe there has been an obvious error of fact or law, you have the right to a rehearing. The BVA Chairperson may grant a full hearing before a panel of six members.
2. There may be a "liberalizing issue." This is a new policy, adopted by Congress or the VA itself because the old policy is believed to be unfair. If a "liberalizing issue" applies to your case, your old claim may be treated as a new one, without any new evidence.
3. If your claim was denied because you were unable to prove a particular fact, you may later find evidence that might have persuaded the BVA to grant your claim. If you present important new evidence, the VA will reopen your file and process your claim from the start, whether or not a final decision has been made.

Like a VARO hearing, a BVA hearing is no place for the inexperienced veteran to represent himself. Again, get the advice and representation of a qualified service representative. If you want to make a personal appearance before the BVA but no panel will be traveling to your area and you can't afford to travel to Washington, a veterans organization may be able to appear in Washington on your behalf.

After the BVA

Generally, if the BVA has decided against you and you don't fall into one of the three categories that qualify you for reconsideration, there is nothing more you can do. In particular, except for disputes regarding insurance and home loans, you cannot successfully appeal to the courts. See the section later in this chapter, "Can You Sue?"

Still, there are always exceptions. Most importantly, there are two situations in which the Administrator of Veterans Affairs—the head of the VA—may review your case.

The Administrator can grant payment equivalent to denied benefits if the benefits were denied "by reason of administrative error on the part of the federal government or any of its employees." This exception to the rule may help some disabled vets who were denied treatment or compensation until they became eligible by getting an upgraded discharge. Still, the law allows only one year of retroactive payments.

The second special situation in which the Administrator can act is one in which an erroneous VA determination has led a veteran to act in a way that resulted in financial loss. If this is the case, the Administrator will grant a payment equal to the loss. In one case, for example, the VA advised a veteran that he was entitled to G.I. Bill benefits. The vet began attending school and then heard from the VA that he was not entitled after all and that he could therefore receive no benefits. The vet asked the Administrator to grant him benefits for the period he had attended school and the Administrator did so.

Avoiding the Normal Appeals Process

Some cases that have been decided by a VARO Rating Board can be appealed directly to the Department of Veterans Benefits in the VA Central Office in Washington. Consideration by the Department of Veterans Benefits is called "administrative review." This process can save a lot of time. Cases where administrative review is appropriate are ones in which one or more of the following is true:

1. The VARO has ignored or misinterpreted the laws and regulations applying to the claim.
2. A formal appeal of the case would probably result in a favorable BVA decision or a BVA decision to return the case to the VARO for further consideration.
3. Time restrictions, such as those caused by a vet's terminal illness, make it impossible for the vet to participate in a lengthy appeal process.

If you or your service representative believes administrative review may be appropriate in your case, the Washington office of a veterans organization such as Vietnam Veterans of America (VVA) may be able to help.

If you lose an administrative review, you can still appeal to the BVA. To preserve your right to do so, be sure you file your Notice of Disagreement and your appeal form before the deadlines noted earlier in this chapter. Note that requesting an administrative review *does not* extend the deadline for filing your NOD and your appeal form.

CAN YOU SUE?

No.

That's the short answer. Only rarely can you successfully sue. You want the long answer? Here it comes.

Anybody can file any lawsuit against anybody else. But the real question is whether you can *successfully* sue. In almost all cases, you cannot successfully sue the VA or the military.

Is this fair? Of course not. VA and military actions and decisions, including VA and military mistakes, can cause severe harm to veterans. If this harm should not have occurred, vets should be able to do something about it, something besides simply appealing *within* the military or *within* the VA. Limiting vets to appealing within the military and the VA is sort of like limiting Chevrolet buyers to appealing within General Motors.

The situation is especially unfair because while vets generally cannot sue the VA, the VA can sue vets. As noted in Chapter 4, "Overpayments," the VA has filed more than 127,000 lawsuits against vets in which the VA has sought the return of alleged overpayments.

But vets are barred by law and by court decision from suing the VA or the military. This may change. In recent years, the Senate has three times passed legislation that would allow vets to sue the VA if they believe the VA has made a wrong decision regarding benefits. But each time, the legislation has not been approved by the Veterans' Affairs Committee of the House of Representatives and therefore has never been the subject of a vote on the floor of the House. If you want to sue the VA, check with your service representative to see if the law has changed since this book was written.

Exceptions to the Rule

Anybody who has been paying attention to this book will know that where there's a rule, there's generally an exception. And there are plenty of exceptions to the rule that you can't successfully sue the VA or the military. But the exceptions are narrow and some are hazy. Here are some situations in which you may be able to sue. In all cases, statutes of limitations apply: you can sue only within a certain period of years after something happened.

The VA used unconstitutional procedures. If the VA used unconstitutional procedures to deny benefits, you can sue the VA to require it to reconsider your case under proper procedures. If you win the suit, you don't necessarily win the benefits: the VA will have to reconsider your case, but it may still decide against you.

The VA used an unlawful regulation. If a VA regulation is inconsistent with the law on which it is based or with the Constitution itself, some courts will allow vets to sue to get the regulation declared unlawful. Again, if you win the suit, you don't necessarily win the benefits.

VA staff were negligent in providing medical services. If a VA doctor or other staff person was not sufficiently careful in providing you with medical services and you were harmed as a result, you can sue the VA for malpractice and you can ask the court for money "damages": payment for the harm caused to you. You *cannot*, however, sue the VA for refusing to provide you with medical services. (For more information on VA medical care, see Chapter 6, "Medical Services.")

You have a bad discharge that should have been upgraded by a Discharge Review Board or a Board for Correction of Military Records. Courts will allow a veteran to sue to get an upgrade, but most courts require the vet to try first at a DRB or a BCMR. If you don't get what you want from one of those boards, you must file your suit within six years of a denial of upgrade. A court will require an upgrade if the board's decision was arbitrary, "capricious," or otherwise unlawful. In upgrade cases, the suit—against the Secretary of the service of which you were a member—must be filed in a United States District

Court. If that court decides against you, you can appeal to a
U.S. Court of Appeals. After that, you can even appeal to the
Supreme Court (which refuses to consider the great majority
of appeals on *any* subject). (For more information on discharge
upgrading, see Chapter 15, "Upgrading Your Discharge.")

*Your records are wrong and a BCMR should have corrected
them.* BCMRs are supposed to change military personnel and
medical records if they are wrong or are unfair to the vet. If a
BCMR denies your application for a correction of records, you
can sue in a U.S. District Court. Again, the suit would be
against the Secretary of your service.

Sometimes the correction of records is a way to get around
the general prohibition of lawsuits by vets. For example, the
VA (and eventually, perhaps the BVA) may deny your claim
for disability compensation because it believes your disability
is not service-connected. The VA may believe the disability is
not service-connected because your military records show no
injury or disease that could have led to the disability. Though
you *can't* sue the VA to make it change its decision on benefits,
you *can* try to get your records changed. And if the BCMR
won't change your records, you can sue the Secretary of your
service. To succeed, you will need strong medical evidence.
(For more information on the correction of records, see Chapter
14, "Correcting Your Records.")

You were illegally discharged. If the military illegally discharged a former service member, he can sue the Secretary of
his service in a U.S. District Court or the U.S. Claims Court
for reinstatement and back pay. This kind of lawsuit cannot be
used by many Vietnam Era Vets, however, because in most
cases it must be filed within six years of discharge.

If you think you fit one of the exceptions just described,
get advice from a lawyer who is experienced in suing the party
you may want to sue. Ask the lawyer to provide an estimate
(preferably in writing) of what he or she thinks your chances
are of succeeding, what you will win if you succeed, and what
his or her fees and expenses will be.

Non-Exceptions to the Rule

The categories just described are the most common exceptions to the general rule that a veteran cannot successfully sue the VA or the military. But other routes have been tried, and have been found to be blocked. If a lawyer or anybody else tells you one of these might work, get a second opinion or just plain don't believe what you're being told:

Suing the military under the Federal Tort Claims Act. Because vets can't sue the VA when it denies them benefits, some vets have tried to sue the military under the Federal Tort Claims Act for injuries they suffered while in the service. Among vets who have sued are those who were exposed to radiation during U.S. nuclear bomb tests and Viet Vets who were exposed to Agent Orange.

Although a civilian can sue the government if he or she is run over by a postal truck, a veteran can't sue the government if he or she was run over during the military by a military truck—or if he or she was exposed to radiation or Agent Orange.

In the 1950 case of *Feres v. United States*, the Supreme Court decided that Congress did not intend for veterans to sue the government under the Federal Tort Claims Act for injuries that occurred during the service. The Court said Congress intended to compensate veterans not through the Tort Claims Act but through the VA disability compensation program. This decision has become known as the "*Feres* doctrine." It has been bitterly opposed by many vets, but Congress has refused to pass a law to change it.

Lawsuits brought by family members of a veteran. Knowing the veteran himself could not sue, members of veterans' families have sometimes sued the military. For instance, children of veterans exposed to Agent Orange have sued the military for the birth defects they believe they suffered as the result of their father's exposure. Some courts have heard these lawsuits; most have thrown them out. In 1985 the Supreme Court probably will clarify whether family members can sue.

Lawsuits focusing on negligence following discharge. Some veterans have sued the military, claiming the military was careless after the veteran was discharged and the veteran as a result was harmed. For instance, vets have argued that the military should have warned the vet that he should have gotten medical care for a particular kind of illness he was likely to get. Most of these lawsuits also have failed.

Suing individual members of the military. A recent Supreme Court decision has closed the door on this kind of suit. The Court said that allowing members of the service to sue each other would disrupt military discipline and undermine military decision-making.

Suing Military Contractors. An attempt to get around the rules against suing the military has been to sue military contractors. Generally, vets have sued military contractors in situations where, if there were no prohibitions against suing the military, both the military and the contractor could be sued.

The best known example of a suit against government contractors is the suit by veterans and their families against the chemical companies that manufactured Agent Orange. See Chapter 7, "Agent Orange." This suit has been settled for $180 million plus interest. One reason it was not settled for a higher amount is that suits by vets against military contractors are not easy to win.

The problem is the "government contractor's defense." This defense generally provides that a government contractor cannot be found to be at fault if its product conformed to contract specifications and its potential dangers were disclosed to the government.

17. WOMEN VETERANS

Problems and Progress

Female ex-service personnel from the Vietnam era (make up) 22 percent of the total number of female veterans.
> —1983 Annual Report of the Veterans Administration

By Jenny Schnaier, VVA national staff

It is significant that in a book about Vietnam Era Veterans there must be a separate section about how women who served their country during the Vietnam Era can obtain the benefits due them. Often in the past, women veterans have been treated in a separate and unequal manner by the Veterans Administration.

As a woman veteran, you should know that all the rights and benefits discussed in the other chapters of this book apply equally to you and to men. Throughout this chapter you will be referred to other chapters that explain in detail how to obtain the benefits due you. It is important for you to make yourself aware of the benefits—and the barriers you face—so you can make full use of the rights you have earned. This chapter also highlights those areas and programs of specific concern to women veterans and the problems that can arise.

BACKGROUND

There are about 1.2 million women veterans in the U.S. today. This figure is from the 1980 Census, in which, for the first time, women were asked if they were veterans. The 1.2 million women represent veterans who served their country during peacetime, World Wars I and II, Korea, and Vietnam.

While this figure looks like a simple statistic, the fact that we now know that women make up 4.1 percent of the veteran population of the U.S. is itself noteworthy. Prior to the 1980 Census, there were no statistics kept nor information gathered on the number of women veterans in the U.S. The federal government does not even know how many women served in Vietnam. It comes as no surprise, then, that the lack of attention and importance given to women when they were in the military was carried through to the Veterans Administration, where, for a long time, women were virtually ignored.

Best estimates are that approximately eight to ten thousand women served in Vietnam, as—among others—nurses, intelligence and security personnel, air traffic controllers, supply and legal personnel, clerks, aerial reconnaissance photographers, and nonmilitary volunteers. During the Vietnam Era, 260,000 women served in the armed forces.

How are these women faring today? Are they making full use of their VA benefits? Are they being treated equally with their male veteran peers? Unfortunately, we are just beginning to learn the answers to these questions. It was not until very recently that the VA began to assess how women veterans were or were not utilizing their benefits. In September 1982, a study by the U.S. General Accounting Office (GAO) found that not only were women veterans receiving unsatisfactory health care in the VA medical system, but, due to privacy problems, many VA facilities could not even accommodate female patients. As a result, women have had to use the fee-basis program for private outpatient health care. This in turn created an inequitable system under which women using the fee program could receive treatment only for service-connected disabilities and emergencies. This effectively prevented women from receiving many kinds of service, while eligible men could receive treatment for nonservice-connected problems for virtually all outpatient needs.

The VA has not been the only system, however, to ignore the contribution of women veterans. The traditional major veterans organizations have done the same thing. Few have sought out women as members, and the Veterans of Foreign Wars (VFW) did not admit women as members until 1978. Vietnam Veterans of America (VVA) is one exception. VVA has always included women veterans as full members, and in 1979 it established a women veterans project. VVA has also established a Special Committee on Women Veterans that aims to address the special issues of women veterans and to seek resolution of those issues.

A new development at the VA is the establishment of its Women's Advisory Committee. In 1983 Congress passed a law setting up this committee to ensure that women receive equal access to programs and benefits to which they are entitled as veterans. In July 1984, the committee issued a report of its findings, which included numerous recommendations for change and development.

In the past there has been much opposition to providing special programs or "outreach" efforts for women veterans. Many who oppose programs for women argue that women veterans are "first and foremost, veterans" and therefore have access to the full range of benefits, information, and assistance provided to all veterans—so why do they need special programs and attention? In fact, the basis of this argument is true—women are legally entitled to the same benefits as men—but data collected in recent years by the VA show that, compared to men, women veterans have applied for fewer benefits due them, such as medical care, hospitalization, and G.I. Bill educational benefits. The Women's Advisory Committee believes this is because women are not aware of the benefits, because they are intimidated by the male-oriented VA system, because VA hospitals don't have the physical accommodations for women, or because—since they make up only two percent of the VA hospital population—it is easy for the VA to overlook women.

GAO REPORT ON WOMEN VETERANS' ACCESS TO BENEFITS

In September 1982, at the request of Senator Daniel K. Inouye, the U.S. General Accounting Office (GAO) completed a study, *Actions Needed to Insure That Female Veterans Have Equal Access to VA Benefits*. The study found that while the VA had made progress toward ensuring that medical care and other benefits are available to females, it had not adequately focused on women's needs. The study examined areas of care for service-connected and other disabilities; psychiatric, gynecological, and readjustment counseling; long-term planning; and outreach. The GAO found inequities in every system with the exception of the Readjustment Counseling Service (the Vet Centers), which had conducted specialized training for its staff on treatment for women veterans. Many of the deficiencies found by the GAO were echoed in the 1984 report of the VA Women's Advisory Committee.

The GAO report noted that VA health care programs have typically been oriented to male health care needs because most veterans are male. It was careful, however, to clarify that:

> the need to plan for and provide medical care that meets the special needs of female veterans is becoming more important in view of the increasing numbers of service connected female veterans coming into the system now, and anticipated in the future.

Due to privacy problems, women often have had limited access to VA programs. Women with service-connected disabilities often could not get care, especially certain kinds of specialized medical care, at a VA facility if it did not have private rooms or separate toilet and shower facilities. Most women, therefore, have had to utilize the fee-basis program. This program provides reimbursements to private health care providers for service-connected disabilities or emergency care only if VA facilities cannot provide the needed services or are geographically inaccessible to the veteran. Veterans with disabilities that are not service-connected are not generally eligible for fee-basis care. Because some VA facilities cannot accommodate women, however, the VA can authorize some fee-basis *inpatient* care for female veterans who do not have service-connected disabilities.

The GAO found that when the VA did authorize fee-basis care there was often no fee-basis treatment program available to women that was similar to VA hospital programs for men. Similarly, some VA hospitals currently have PTSD programs in which an important component of patient care is group therapy with fellow veterans. Few such programs exist for women in or outside VA facilities.

At times, women needing medical care will be accepted into a facility and will be placed in an isolation room (a room, offering privacy, that is normally reserved for critical-care patients). Women must compete with critically ill patients for private space, and their confinement to isolation rooms often keeps women from taking part in programs best suited to their problems.

Perhaps the most blatant form of inadequacy found by the GAO was that full gynecological and obstetrical care was not always provided. In one facility in which the GAO reviewed medical charts, it found that in May and June 1981, pelvic examinations were done for only 27 percent of female patients, breast exams for only 40 percent, and Pap smears for *none*.

The GAO found that because many VA facilities did not offer gynecological services except on an outpatient basis, many VA facilities relied on the fee-basis program to provide gynecological care. Since outpatient care was generally not available on a fee basis for veterans with disabilities that were not service-connected, the result was the denial of gynecological treatment to most female outpatients. Because almost all men's medical needs were treated by the VA, the denial of gynecological care meant women were being treated inequitably.

The GAO found many other deficiencies at the VA, particularly in its planning for the future needs of women \

The GAO did find one area in which staff was trained specifically for working with women veterans. As mentioned, this was the system of Vet Centers. Therefore, this program may be a good place for women veterans to get help. As with all other encounters with the VA, be sure to immediately identify yourself as the veteran (not a spouse), be assertive about your needs, know the pitfalls, and know your benefits and rights.

The GAO went on to say that as long as the VA continued

to organize hospitals to accommodate veterans with and without service-connected disabilities, "it should insure that male and female veterans have equal access to facilities and programs."

It further recommended that the VA increase its staff's awareness of female veterans' unique medical needs and do more to address these needs. The GAO study observed that this was becoming more important because of the increasing number of female veterans and the increasing proportion of them who were expected to have service-connected disabilities. Without a concerted effort by the VA to identify and address female veterans' needs, neither short-term renovation projects nor long-term facility planning will substantially increase women's access to VA medical care.

In response to the GAO findings, Congress passed a law in November 1983. This law contains a provision which requires the Administrator of the VA to take steps to ensure that the agency meets (at its own facilities or through sharing arrangements) the special health care needs of women.

WHAT YOU SHOULD DO

As a woman veteran requesting care, you should always first attempt to use VA facilities. If necessary, request that they be adapted for privacy. According to the new law, the VA is obligated to take care of women veterans who need health care to the same extent it takes care of male veterans. No longer can the VA tell women veterans that it has no facilities to take care of their problems. The VA must either develop the facilities or make arrangements with private facilities.

If you go to the VA for a gynecological exam, be sure you are given a pelvic exam, a breast exam, and a Pap smear. At this writing, the VA by regulation routinely denies hospital care for pregnancy and childbirth, even if the veteran is pregnant when discharged from the military or is unable to pay the costs of hospital care. The only exception is a pregnancy complicated by an illness or injury. The VA considers pregnancy a "physiological condition" and not an illness or injury and therefore believes care for pregnancy is not required by the law that provides for fee-basis care. The courts have thus far upheld the VA's interpretation of the law.

If you need to use the fee-basis program, be sure to apply to use the program *before receiving care*. Except in emergencies, the VA will authorize payments only prior to treatment. If you meet the eligibility requirements for fee-basis (outpatient) or contract hospital (inpatient) care, you should apply for a fee-basis card that authorizes use of non-VA facilities. You can get this card by filling out VA Form 10–7079, Request for Outpatient Medical Service. You may use this card to obtain outpatient medical services from the licensed physician of your choice for the approved disabilities recorded on the card. While your fee-basis card will not contain an expiration date, there are limits placed on the number of visits and the length of treatment.

The VA's Department of Medicine and Surgery does report that, as instructed, all medical facilities currently have made provisions to furnish primary gynecological care. The provisions may be in the form of adding gynecological staff, using doctors who are not gynecologists, setting up once-a-week gynecological clinics, or arranging by contract for care provided by a non-VA facility. A woman who requires inpatient care (hospitalization) for a disability (whether or not service-connected) cannot be turned down for care as long as she meets the general eligibility requirements that all veterans must meet.

The Department also indicates that many facilities have established a women veterans coordinator to help oversee the care given to women and that soon all facilities will be required to establish such a position. If you are turned down for care, discuss your problem with the women veterans coordinator (if one exists) or the Chief of Staff or his or her representative.

For more information on VA health care, see Chapter 6, "Medical Services."

AGENT ORANGE

Another area of concern to all Vietnam Veterans is the adverse health effects of Agent Orange. Many agencies are looking into this subject. As of this writing, no study has included women veterans to determine if they have been affected by the herbicide. To many women, this is a serious omission: according to the VA's Special Assistant for Environmental Sciences, "All U.S. personnel who served in South Vietnam are presumed to have been exposed directly, or indirectly, to Agent Orange." In other words, women veterans serving in Vietnam are presumed to have been exposed to Agent Orange. Women veterans are particularly concerned that serious female reproductive system problems may result from exposure to dioxin (an ingredient of Agent Orange). Therefore, it is critical for women veterans to go to the VA for its Agent Orange exam. Additionally, women veterans—like male veterans—may be eligible for disability compensation or medical care in connection with their exposure to Agent Orange.

Women veterans should lobby and write to both the House and Senate Committees on Veterans' Affairs to demonstrate support for including women in the Agent Orange studies. The VA Women's Advisory Committee has also recommended that a separate study be conducted of the health of women who served in Vietnam and were exposed to Agent Orange and other chemicals. Finally, women who believe they may have suffered harmful effects of Agent Orange should (if they have not already done so) file a claim with the court that is overseeing the settlement of the class action lawsuit by veterans and their families against the manufacturers of the herbicide.

For more information on Agent Orange and the lawsuit, see Chapter 7, "Agent Orange."

MENTAL HEALTH CARE

Another area from which, until very recently, women veterans have been excluded is mental health care. All federal studies designed to examine readjustment problems of Vietnam Veterans—including an extensive 1981 study commissioned by Congress—have excluded women.

Though male Vietnam Veterans and mental health professionals working with them have had to work hard to convince others that PTSD truly exists, women veterans have had an even tougher battle to fight. Before PTSD was first officially recognized by the American Psychiatric Association in the *Diagnostic and Statistical Manual*, Third Edition, in 1980, clinicians and the general public had believed that exposure to combat was the only type of event that led to the development of Post-Traumatic Stress Disorder. Today, however, it is understood that frequent exposure to death and dying *outside* combat can also result in PTSD. Most of the women who served in Vietnam were in medical positions, in which they dealt every day with soldiers who were severely wounded or dying. For many women, such exposure has led to PTSD and other psychological problems. In fact, the only two complete studies on women veterans confirm that many nurses, like many combat veterans, have suffered psychological problems as aftereffects of the war.

Of all the programs designed to help veterans, the Vet Centers appear to have done the most to train their staff and make them aware of the problems and concerns of women veterans. A majority of the centers have received training to help women who were in medical positions. If you are experiencing psychological problems that you believe are related to your Vietnam experience, the Vet Center programs may provide a supportive and enlightened environment. Nevertheless, women report problems when trying to get mental health care at Vet Centers. Be aware of this and try to prepare yourself by doing several things to receive better and more appropriate care than you might otherwise get.

First, be sure to identify yourself immediately as the veteran (not a spouse) requesting services. Be prepared for some opposition or, at best, surprise. If opposition occurs, be assertive. If you are interested in getting involved in a "rap group" for mental health care and a group for women doesn't already exist, see if the Vet Center will locate other women veterans so that a group can be started. Ask if there are any other women veterans you can contact and with whom you can talk, and make your name and phone number available for other women to contact you. If the only groups currently active are all-male, prepare yourself for a session in such a group by talking with your Vet Center counselor about the attitudes of men in the group and the problems that may arise when you join. Also ask the counselor to prepare current group members for your arrival.

Many women report that when they first participate in a group there is uneasiness between them and male group members. Men in the group, however, in most cases eventually come to accept or even welcome the involvement of women. In fact, many women have found that combat veterans, especially ones who have been injured, have a particular respect for and understanding of the experiences of nurses.

If your psychological problems require hospitalization, note that as of this writing there is only one VA hospital psychiatric unit in the country that has set aside bed space for women within the unit (as opposed to elsewhere in the hospital). So be sure to learn about programs that are available to or can be adapted for women. Check with a service representative who works for a veterans organization such as Vietnam Veterans of America (VVA), or check with your nearest VA hospital. If you choose to go to a non-VA facility, be sure to discuss your Vietnam experiences with your psychotherapist, and take it upon yourself to help educate him or her about Vietnam by helping the therapist become familiar with the literature on the war, its aftermath, and PTSD.

Even if you are fairly sure that there are no VA facilities to accommodate your needs, it is important to request care from the VA. The statistics of those who request help and are denied it will at least assist veterans organizations that are working for increased programs and accessibility for women veterans.

You can also get assistance from VVA. This organization can give advice and can provide referrals to local veterans groups. Write to: VVA; 2001 S St., N.W.; Washington, DC 20009. Or call (202) 332-2700.

For more information on PTSD, Vet Centers, and related issues, see Chapter 8, "Psychological Readjustment."

OTHER VETERANS PROGRAMS

Women veterans should also be encouraged to take advantage of other programs available to them, including employment placement and preference, the Job Training Partnership Act, home loan guarantees, G.I. Bill payments for education, and discharge upgrading. All of these issues are discussed elsewhere in the book; therefore only certain aspects will be highlighted here.

Most veterans' G.I. Bill benefits have run out. But if you are still getting benefits and you have a family, be sure to claim both your husband and children as dependents.

HOW TO GET HELP

In all of the areas covered by this chapter, be sure to document all conversations and appointments (by keeping receipts and other documents that are given to you and by keeping your own notes), follow through with a prompt appeal if you feel your claim was improperly denied, and be sure to utilize the proper chains of command within the VA system. See Chapter 16, "Claims and Appeals." If you need additional help with a claim, contact the VVA Legal Services. VVA's Special Committee on Women Veterans is another good place to look for assistance. Both may be reached at the address and phone number given earlier in this chapter for VVA.

The VVA Special Committee is working on building a network of women veterans, with a contact person in each state. These contact people will provide women veterans with information on how to get services, route women to the most appropriate contacts within the VA, and provide information about women veterans. In addition, the Committee works on legislative initiatives, outreach, recruitment, and support for those chapters which specifically provide outreach services to women. One of the committee's early projects was a series of seminars to educate the public about issues relating to women veterans.

HANG IN THERE

The issues surrounding women veterans are still complex and emotional. Women are continuing to fight for their rights and benefits, and progress *has* been made. Today, there are few laws that discriminate against women. But the removal of legal barriers is not always accompanied by the removal of procedural barriers that are supported by those who administer and staff the VA. If you run into obstacles, remember benefits cannot legally be less, nor your requests given less priority, because you are a woman. Be armed with a knowledge of your rights, be prepared for the obstacles in your way, and be assertive about your needs. Women are veterans too, and they are entitled to make full use of the benefits they earned in service to their country.

18. VETERANS IN THE CRIMINAL JUSTICE SYSTEM

PTSD and Other Issues

This chapter is for veterans who since separation have gotten in trouble with the law. It can help those who have been charged with a crime but not yet tried for it, those who have been tried and convicted but not yet sentenced, and even those who have been in prison for years.

Vietnam Era Vets, particularly Viet Vets, who have been charged with or convicted of a crime have special problems and special advantages that to some extent set them apart from others who have been arrested. The biggest difference between vets and nonvets in the criminal justice system is that the vets may suffer from war-related Post-Traumatic Stress Disorder (PTSD). PTSD may make a critical difference in what happens to the vet who has been charged with a crime.

For information on PTSD in general, see Chapter 8, "Psychological Readjustment." Note particularly the discussion of Vet Centers as a source of help for vets with PTSD.

The following discussion of the veteran and the criminal justice system is directed to the vet himself, but the vet should consult with his lawyer about what he learns from this chapter. A veteran who has been charged with a crime is in water too deep and too full of hidden hazards for him to try to swim without the assistance of a lawyer. The lawyer should have a lot of experience in defending people in criminal cases. If the veteran has PTSD and if PTSD may have something to do with his case, the lawyer should also be familiar with this disorder and how it may support arguments on behalf of the veteran who has been charged with or convicted of a crime.

BEFORE TRIAL

Most criminal cases are settled before coming to trial. The prosecuting attorney and the attorney for the defendant (the person charged with the crime) work out a deal, called a plea bargain. Under the plea bargain, the defendant agrees to plead guilty in return for being charged with a lesser offense, being given a shorter sentence than would otherwise be given, being given a different kind of sentence (such as treatment) than would otherwise be imposed, or some combination of these.

PTSD can help the defendant interested in a plea bargain. It can pressure the prosecutor to make a deal, because PTSD may reduce the prosecutor's chances of success if the case goes to trial. It can also present a good reason for sentencing the defendant to a treatment program rather than a normal prison sentence. A defendant's chances of being sentenced to treatment (as a result of a plea bargain or after conviction at trial) are best if he has not injured anyone.

In some cases, the defense lawyer may be able to persuade the prosecutor to simply not prosecute the case. This does not require a plea bargain. Veterans and their attorneys have persuaded prosecutors not to bring charges (or to drop charges), particularly where the alleged crime involved strange behavior, where no one was hurt by the vet's actions, and where the vet recognizes he has a problem and has begun treatment.

Similarly, the prosecutor may agree to argue, along with the defense lawyer, for the court to place the veteran on probation without finding him guilty. Under these circumstances, even the record of probation often can be expunged (erased) after the veteran has completed treatment.

AT TRIAL

For the veteran who has PTSD and has been charged with a crime, a whole new world was created in 1980. In that year, the American Psychiatric Association published its *Diagnostic and Statistical Manual*, Third Edition, better known as *DSM III*. *DSM III* provided the first official recognition of the existence and characteristics of PTSD. Before then, it was difficult to use PTSD in court. Now it isn't.

Most Viet Vets don't have PTSD. And many vets who do have PTSD have committed crimes for reasons having nothing to do with the disorder. But if you have PTSD and your crime is connected to it, your lawyer should use PTSD to help you in court. PTSD may influence the court to find you not guilty, to find you guilty of a lesser crime than the one with which you are charged, or to sentence you to a treatment program (as a condition of probation) rather than to prison.

To use PTSD as a defense, your lawyer must be well prepared. He or she must know what kinds of defense are accepted by the state in which you have been charged (or, if you have been accused of a federal crime, what kinds of defenses are permitted by federal law). He or she must be familiar with how PTSD has been used in previous cases in your state and elsewhere. He or she must know how PTSD occurs, its symptoms, and how it is treated. And your lawyer must know all about your specific case of PTSD: the traumatic event(s) that caused it, the symptoms you have suffered, and how PTSD contributed to events that caused you to be arrested.

Insanity Defense

In most states, a criminal defendant can be found not guilty if it is demonstrated that he or she was insane when the crime was committed. To be insane generally means not to know the nature and consequences of the act committed and not to know it was wrong.

PTSD can be used to prove insanity. The disorder may, for instance, have caused such confusion in the mind of the veteran that when he was firing a gun at an innocent person he may have thought he was back in Vietnam, firing an M-16 at the enemy.

The insanity defense can be used in criminal cases involving both violent and nonviolent crimes. Nevertheless, it is difficult to succeed with an insanity defense, and it is rarely tried except in very serious cases such as murder. An insanity defense or any other defense involving PTSD is most likely to succeed if it is supported by one or more expert witnesses, such as psychiatrists familiar with the disorder.

Other Defenses

The number of other defenses that a criminal lawyer may connect to PTSD is limited only by the lawyer's creativity (and, to some extent, by what PTSD defenses have previously been accepted in the state involved). One is that PTSD has eliminated the *mental state*—such as the intent to kill—necessary to find a defendant guilty. This defense may result in no conviction at all, or at least conviction for a lesser offense than the one with which the veteran is charged.

Another defense that may be supported by PTSD is *self-defense*. For instance, a veteran may believe—though incorrectly—that he is under attack. Some courts may excuse the veteran just as though he were really being attacked.

"*Automatism*" is another defense. Automatism is action without conscious thought. This defense is not often used but may work.

Sentencing

After a veteran has been convicted of a crime, he will be sentenced. If he has PTSD, his lawyer may successfully argue that the sentence should be shorter than normal or should be for treatment rather than typical imprisonment. The judge may approve a shorter sentence out of a sense that "Yeah, he's guilty of the crime, but because of PTSD he's not as bad as a guy without PTSD who committed the same crime." Treatment may be approved if the lawyer can demonstrate that the vet needs it and if the lawyer can arrange for the vet to be accepted into an appropriate treatment program.

In 1982 the California Legislature passed a law that improves the chances of convicted vets getting treatment rather than imprisonment. The law requires judges who are sentencing veterans to consider PTSD and to consider treatment as an alternative sentence. This law, of course, is helpful mostly to veterans who are convicted in California. But the law may influence judges (and legislatures) in other states as well.

AFTER TRIAL

Even the veteran who has been tried, convicted, and sentenced may benefit from arguments based on PTSD and other arguments available to veterans.

Reducing the Sentence

If the judge who sentenced the veteran did not know the vet had PTSD, the vet's lawyer may be able to get the sentence reduced. The lawyer likely would argue that the sentence was based on erroneous information. Most states and the federal courts have strict time limits for filing motions to reduce or correct a sentence.

A sentence may also be reduced by filing a general petition protesting the imprisonment of the prisoner (in state courts this is called a *habeas corpus* petition). This too can argue that the sentence was based on erroneous information, perhaps the information that the defendant was mentally fit for trial. This approach can be used even in old cases, especially because PTSD was not officially recognized until 1980.

The *habeas corpus* approach may also work in cases in which the veteran gets a discharge upgrade after sentencing. The argument here would be that the judge would have imposed a lighter sentence if the defendant had had a better discharge (and therefore seemed like a better person).

Withdrawing a Plea

Sometimes, convicted defendants are permitted to withdraw a guilty plea. A judge will rarely allow this. And if a judge *does* permit it, the veteran may end up not better off but *worse* off.

This is because if the plea is withdrawn, a trial will occur, and, instead of being found not guilty, the vet may be found guilty, often of a more severe offense than the one to which he pleaded guilty after a plea bargain. An attempt to withdraw a plea can be made even years after a conviction.

Seeking a New Trial

A lawyer can make a motion for a new trial based on *newly discovered evidence*. If the veteran and his lawyer were not (and should not have been) aware at trial that the veteran had PTSD or that PTSD was related to the act for which the veteran was convicted, PTSD can be raised as new evidence.

If your lawyer *did* know you had PTSD and that it was connected to the act for which you were convicted, you may be able to get a new trial on the ground that at the original trial you were represented by *incompetent counsel*. This, of course, will require a motion made by a *new* lawyer.

Strict time limits usually apply to motions for a new trial.

Getting Paroled Early

Before releasing a prisoner on parole, parole boards must be convinced the offense was not serious enough to justify continued imprisonment or that the prisoner will not commit another crime or both. PTSD can help prove both these points.

On the other hand, PTSD can work *against* the vet. It may be interpreted by the parole board as evidence that the vet is "violence-prone." To avoid fear on the part of the board that the vet is violent and will commit a violent crime if released, it is important for the veteran to present a post-prison treatment plan as part of the parole request. Vet Centers can sometimes offer a treatment plan.

It is often helpful at parole hearings to have one or more expert witnesses (such as psychiatrists familiar with PTSD) testify or submit written statements on behalf of the veteran.

Appeals

In addition to all the other strategies is the basic alternative of appealing the conviction. Generally, a successful appeal re-

quires the veteran's lawyer to show that the trial judge made
an error of law (not that the judge or jury made the wrong
decision after weighing the facts). Failing to recognize that
PTSD exists or ruling that PTSD cannot be the basis of an
insanity defense might be found to be legal error.

IN PRISON

The vet in prison should spend his time as productively as
possible. This is true whether or not his lawyer is making efforts
to get him released. One reason is that parole boards, when
considering release, review a prisoner's conduct while in prison.

PTSD Programs

Many vets in prison do not have PTSD. Those who do will
benefit from treatment. If you have PTSD and are in prison,
but your prison has no PTSD treatment program, ask your
lawyer or service representative how you might get transferred
to a prison that does have such a program (or how you might
get such a program started at your prison).

Joining a PTSD program may help you reduce your PTSD
symptoms. Progress in such a program may help convince a
parole board that you are ready for release.

Vet Centers

Vet Centers are informal centers for veterans with problems.
While funded by the VA, they operate in storefronts, away
from VA facilities. Many Vet Centers offer services to veterans
in prison. For more information on Vet Centers, see Chapter
8, "Psychological Readjustment."

Veterans Organizations

Some chapters of some veterans organizations, such as Vietnam
Veterans of America (VVA), operate programs for vets in prison.
Check with your service representative.

VA Benefits

Disability compensation: Veterans in prison may apply for VA disability payments. Payments, however, are reduced. Any veteran imprisoned after September 30, 1980, or convicted of a felony committed after October 7, 1980, will not be paid disability compensation in excess of that paid to a vet with a 10 percent disability rating. Still, the money the vet would receive if he were not in prison can be paid to his family. If, for example, a veteran is rated as 100 percent disabled but gets payments at only the 10 percent rate because he is in prison, the difference between the 10 percent rate and the 100 percent rate can be sent to his family—if it needs it. Veterans in prison should encourage their families to apply to a VA Regional Office for an "apportionment"—a division—of the disability compensation. The family must be prepared to explain why it needs the money.

For more information on disability compensation, see Chapter 3, "Compensation."

Educational benefits: Veterans convicted of a felony and confined in a prison are *not* eligible for full educational benefits under the G.I. Bill or other VA programs. The VA will pay only for books, equipment, tuition, and fees not otherwise paid by a government agency (this is because the veteran has no essential living expenses while in prison). Regardless of the reduced VA payments, vets in prison may benefit from joining educational programs offered within the prison or (for certain prisoners) at colleges or other institutions outside the prison.

Thus far, all court challenges by incarcerated vets regarding the restrictions of educational benefits have failed.

HELP FOR LAWYERS

Vets in trouble with the law need lawyers. Lawyers representing vets, especially vets with PTSD, often need help themselves.

Lawyers representing veterans with PTSD will benefit from getting a copy of the excellent article on PTSD in the criminal justice system written by C. Peter Erlinder and published in the March 1984 issue of the *Boston College Law Review*. A copy of the forty-page article may be received by sending a check for $5.00 to: Veterans Education Project; P.O. Box 42130; Washington, DC 20015.

Lawyers representing veterans in criminal cases, whether or not their cases involve PTSD, may also obtain advice from the Vietnam Veterans of America (VVA) Legal Services; 2001 S St., N.W., Suite 710; Washington, DC 20009; (202) 686-2599. The attorneys at the VVA Legal Services can provide other lawyers with copies of briefs that have been used in trials, on appeal, and in parole hearings.

19. WHERE TO GO FOR HELP

Organizations and People

Help! I need somebody
Help! Not just anybody
Help! You know I need someone
Help!

> —*Help!*
> By John Lennon and Paul McCartney

By David F. Addlestone

Up to this point we have listed all your rights and have suggested some practical approaches to getting what you are entitled to, but we've kept cautioning you to get help. The next chapter, "Where to Find Out More," concentrates on written resources. In this chapter, however, we will attempt to describe "people resources" you may be able to find in your area. This is all we could think of; there may be more. Don't be afraid to keep asking, and don't be frustrated by the "referral game," in which social service agencies send people in circles. Frequently the agencies are overburdened and can't help it.

In the first part of this chapter we will describe general resources. Later on we will discuss specific problems, listing the resources most likely to be helpful. Of course, always also refer to the specific chapter in this book that deals with your problem.

ADVOCACY SERVICES

Major Veterans Organizations

The large national veterans organizations—The American Legion, Veterans of Foreign Wars (VFW), Disabled American Veterans (DAV), and AMVETS provide VA benefits representation at every VA Regional Office. The DAV uses its own trained and paid "service officers" exclusively. The others use a combination of national or state-paid service officers or simply use employees of state departments of veterans affairs. All maintain service officers in Washington, D.C., to represent veterans at the Board of Veterans Appeals, the Discharge Review Boards, and the Boards for Correction of Military Records. Very few of these service officers are legally trained; and, because they accept all who request their assistance, they have large caseloads.

Many of these service officers know the system well, have good contacts at the agencies, and work hard for their clients. Others do not. You need to assess your choices and ask questions about your case to determine whether or not the service officer will devote sufficient time to your case. These officers work for *you*, and their organizations are founded on the principle of providing high quality services to veterans. If you are dissatisfied with the quality of their representation, you can change to a new representative by filing a new "power of attorney" (VA Form 23–22) with the VA.

Other, smaller national organizations provide representation at some VA Regional Offices and in Washington, D.C. They include the Paralyzed Veterans of America, Military Order of the Purple Heart, Catholic War Veterans, and Jewish War Veterans. These organizations do not provide representation at traveling Discharge Review Boards.

The VA publishes a *Directory of Veterans Organizations*, which includes the addresses of all the federally chartered veterans organizations—the ones the VA "recognizes" and many others that may or may not provide direct services. To get a copy of this directory, write to: Office of the Administrator; Veterans Service Organization Coordination; Veterans Administration; Washington DC 20420.

Vietnam Veterans Organizations

The largest Vietnam Veterans service organization is run by
the Vietnam Veterans of America Legal Services (VVALS).
VVALS is the in-house law firm of VVA. Its lawyers represent
veterans and supervise volunteer lawyers and law students who
represent veterans in Washington, bring lawsuits to advance
Vietnam Veterans issues, and publish or help publish materials
(such as this book) to assist Vietnam Veterans. VVALS trains
and provides support to VVA service representatives. These
service representatives either have legal training, were trained
at VVALS' service school, or work for a state or county agency
and have been recommended by a VVA chapter. To handle a
VA Regional Office case they must have been accredited by
VVALS and approved by the VA. A program of continuing
education keeps them current. At this writing, the VVA service
representative program is growing rapidly but does not provide
representation at all VA Regional Offices. Some VVA chapters
have unaccredited chapter service representatives who can help
with case development. For referral to a VVA chapter, write
to: VVA; 2001 S St., N.W.; Washington, DC 20009; or call
(202) 332-2700. All VVA chapters have a copy of the VVA
Service Representatives Manual. Contact VVALS at 2001 S
Street, N.W., Suite 710; Washington, DC 20009; (202) 686-
2599; for referral to a service rep in your area or to determine
what services VVALS can provide in your case. Frequently,
VVALS can steer you to local representation or can handle the
case in Washington.

VVALS limits its representation to Vietnam Era Veterans
and their families and will decline representation if it feels it
cannot add anything to a veteran's case. VVALS tries to concentrate on the hard cases where the services of legally trained
counsel might make a difference.

There are several other Vietnam Era Veterans organizations
which provide representation in some regions but apparently
none has claims representatives of its own in Washington. A
number of excellent local organizations provide a wide range
of advocacy services for Vietnam Era Veterans. Some of these
are:

Swords to Plowshares
2069A Mission St.
San Francisco, CA 94110
(415) 552-8804

Seattle Veterans Action Center
2024 E. Union St.
Seattle, WA 98122
(206) 625-4656

Veterans Outreach Center, Inc.
459 South Avenue
Rochester, NY 14620
(716) 546-1081

Veterans Multi-Service Center
5031 Grandy
Detroit, MI 48211
(313) 267-6585

Vets House
114 North Carroll St.
3d floor
Madison, WI 53703
(608) 255-8387

San Jose G.I. Forum
1680 E. Santa Clara St.
San Jose, CA 95116
(408) 258-0663

Nam Vets Association
P.O. Box 954
Hyannis, MA 02601
(617) 778-1590

American Red Cross

The Red Cross is getting out of veterans *benefits* work in 1985. In the past it had maintained offices in many VA Regional Offices and had provided benefits counseling and representation. However, Red Cross chapters across the country are still available to provide help and sometimes representation in discharge upgrading and correction of records problems. The Red Cross also maintains a Discharge Review Service at the Pentagon to provide representation in Washington.

Red Cross chapters are a good source for referrals to other local social service agencies and veterans advocates. Sometimes it is necessary to check Red Cross records to prove a family crisis occurred while you were in service.

State Veterans Agencies

Almost every state and territory has a veterans agency (generally called the Department, Division, or Bureau of Veterans Affairs). Most of these provide claims representation at the VA Regional Offices in the state. Few provide any representation at traveling Discharge Review Boards. The employees of these agencies represent the veteran on behalf of the agency or sometimes on behalf of a veterans organization that has accredited the agency. Many of these agencies are run by officials given their positions as political plums or are controlled by a large veterans organization. In some states, Vietnam Veterans have gained control.

The quality of the representation provided by these state agencies varies from the terrible to excellent. VVALS has accredited some state agencies to act for it in some VA Regional Offices where local VVA chapters can watch them work and where a state employee is responsible to oversee VVA cases and forward them to VVALS for appeals. These VVA State Service Representatives will be involved in VVALS' continuing education program.

County Veterans Services

On a community level veterans services are provided through counties in thirty-seven states. In a minority of states, the state government funds and supervises local service offices.

County service offices ordinarily provide assistance in (1) filing claims with the Veterans Administration, (2) gaining admission to a VA hospital, (3) applying for any state veterans benefits or services (*e.g.*, State Civil Service veterans preference), and (4) obtaining military records.

To locate a county veterans service representative, consult the local telephone directory under listings for the name of your county. If there is no listing under that heading, consult the listings for the name of your state.

As with state agencies, the quality of the services of these agencies varies. VVA Legal Services has accredited a few.

VA Benefits Counselors

These are VA employees housed in the Veterans Service Division of a VA Regional Office. They also visit VA hospitals. They provide initial intake services at the regional office but they do not normally represent veterans. Do not be confused and think you are being given advice by an advocate working for *you* unless in the unusual case the benefits counselor agrees to act as your representative.

If you appear to be eligible for benefits, a benefits counselor will review for you the types of benefits to which you may be entitled. Ideally, he or she will give you sound advice as to the conditions of entitlement for each benefit, discuss any changes in your plans or activities that might affect your entitlement to particular benefits, and explain the type of proof, if any, that you will have to give the VA before benefits you desire will be granted.

If there is a question as to your eligibility, this official should not do anything more then tell you that you might not be eligible, tell you the conditions for eligibility, and inform you of the procedures for determining eligibility. It is not the benefits counselor's job to send you away. At the very least, he or she should offer to assist you in filling out forms necessary for an official (and *written*) determination of eligibility. And this person should advise you of your right to have assistance from counsel in completing these forms before you submit them.

Some VA benefits counselors (also known as "contact representatives") may give you the impression that they make the decisions. They don't. If they tell you otherwise and turn down your claim, demand that they tell you how to appeal their "decision." Or ask to speak to their superior. On the other hand, some are very knowledgeable and helpful. If you like the contact representative to whom you are sent, make a note of that person's name. The VA permits these contact representatives to act as counsel at hearings, and some of them prepare for hearings very carefully. So consider asking your contact representative to be your counsel at any hearings that may occur at the regional office.

Lawyers in Private Practice

It's hard to find a lawyer for most veterans cases because of the federal statute making it a criminal offense for a lawyer to accept more than $10 in a VA benefits case. This limit does not apply to VA claims involving overpayments, Discharge Review Board and Board for Correction of Military Records cases, or non-VA-related veterans legal issues. However, because of the statute and the prominence of the traditional veterans organizations in the VA claims area, few attorneys are familiar with veterans law. There are some exceptions besides VVA Legal Services.

Selecting a Lawyer

This is a hard one. There are great ones and awful ones; cheap ones and expensive ones. When selecting a lawyer ask around. Reputation is often important. VVALS or a VVA chapter may be able to make a referral. Just because you have an initial discussion, that doesn't mean you are stuck with that lawyer. The only money, if any, you will owe is an initial consultation fee. Size the lawyer up and see if he or she is really interested in investing the time in your case. You usually do not need a brilliant lawyer—just one with common sense who will work hard.

Legal Aid and Legal Services

The federally funded Legal Services Corporation (LSC) maintains law offices for low-income people that provide free services in almost every county in the country. Many of these are listed in the telephone directory under "Legal Aid" or "Legal Services." Any bar association, court house, or lawyer can direct you to the nearest LSC-funded office. Additionally, some city and county bar associations maintain their own legal aid societies.

Most LSC offices are highly experienced in handling claims involving government agencies (such as the VA) but they may be reluctant to handle veterans cases because of the free counsel available from veterans organizations. All Legal Services have access to written materials on veterans law and the support services of the National Veterans Legal Services Project, an LSC-funded law firm in Washington, D.C., that provides free advice on veterans cases to LSC-funded offices and other lawyers providing services to low-income veterans.

Legal Services are routinely overloaded with work, and they may decline to represent you. You can appeal this decision within the LSC-funded office. LSC-funded offices also usually have a large network of referrals who may be able to help you with a variety of problems—from your veterans benefits problem to housing, medical and family difficulties—for a low fee or no fee.

Bar Associations

Lawyers in all areas join together in "bar associations" to do what lawyers do. In some places the associations do things for the public good. They might maintain a lawyer referral service listing specialties, or they might encourage multiple attorneys to share the work on worthy cases for no pay ("*pro bono* work"). Beware: although a lawyer may claim to be a specialist in a certain area of the law, that usually means very little.

Judge Advocates

If you are retired from the military because of medical reasons or longevity, you may be eligible for free legal assistance from the Judge Advocate's office at a nearby military installation. The legal assistance provided to active-duty people and retirees is limited in scope but it may be a resource worth investigating.

Public Defenders

Public Defenders are employed by the state or city to defend persons charged with crimes who are unable to hire their own attorney. Some are very good and some are awful. Often they can be of assistance with referrals or problems of incarcerated people.

CIVIL RIGHTS ORGANIZATIONS

Many organizations that are involved in the advancement of the rights of certain groups or civil liberties issues in general maintain referral lists of lawyers who are sympathetic to the plight of those in need of help. Some of these organizations maintain offices in larger cities. Examples are the American Civil Liberties Union, the National Association for the Advancement of Colored People, the Urban League, and Common Cause.

GENERAL SERVICES

Community Based Organizations

During the 1960s and 1970s many local citizens groups were formed, often with the encouragement of government agencies. Some still exist. Some are organized around constituent issues such as housing, health, economic issues, and even veterans. This type of organization can provide counseling, referral, and a variety of other services.

Unions

Many unions provide social services, counseling, and legal representation for their members. Some even have veterans representatives.

Employment Assistance

If you are looking for a job or want to train for a job, you should contact the nearest state employment security agency. Check your telephone directory under the name of your state. These agencies use a variety of names, such as "Job Service" and "Employment Security." When you visit a state employment service office be sure to ask to see the Veterans Employment Representative. He or she will know the services and programs for which you are eligible. If you have a service-connected disability and need training, you should contact the nearest VA Regional Office and ask about vocational rehabilitation.

Agent Orange Commissions

Twenty-one states have established Agent Orange Commissions. These commissions often involve local people concerned about the effects on the environment of toxic substances. These commissions should also be able to provide veterans with referrals for needed services.

Vet Centers

These VA-funded storefront counseling offices for Vietnam Era Veterans, in addition to providing readjustment counseling, often provide guidance in a variety of areas. They should be particularly good at community referrals and acting as "point man" to help with a VA hospital problem. See the listings in Appendix A near the end of this book.

Miscellaneous Agencies

Other institutions that may be able to provide useful information are religious organizations, the United Way, the Black United Fund, local social service agencies, and especially the public library. While many such institutions in your area may be unfamiliar with veterans problems, it won't hurt to try them.

SPECIFIC PROBLEM AREAS

VA Benefits/VA Overpayment Claims

See "Advocacy Services," earlier in this chapter.

Discharge Review/Records Correction

Legal Aid or Legal Services; Vietnam Veterans of America Legal Services; other veterans organizations. VVA Legal Services maintains a referral list.

Agent Orange

VVA Legal Services referral list; VVA chapters; VVA regular publications; state Agent Orange Commissions; for birth defects and genetic counseling contact the March of Dimes.

Readjustment Psychological Counseling

Vet Centers, community mental health organizations, VA Medical Center Mental Health Services, Disabled American Veterans, VVA chapters. Spouse and child abuse programs may also be included. VVA Legal Services referral list.

Medical Help

If no VA Medical Center is available, check the physician referral service of the local medical society. For birth defects, contact the March of Dimes. If the case involves potential medical malpractice by a VA medical facility, consult an attorney as soon as possible. In most states there is a two-year deadline ("statute of limitations") on lawsuits that begins from the time the malpractice should have been detected.

Incarcerated Veterans

Vet Centers; *Veterans Rights Newsletter* (VRN) and other Veterans Education Project (VEP) materials are in many prison libraries.

Housing and Foreclosure

Legal Aid; veterans organizations; VVA chapter; community housing organizations.

Education

VA benefits counselors; college or other school veterans affairs office (may be combined with another office, such as financial aid or admissions).

Employment

State employment security agency; if you have problems with a federal contractor and veterans hiring, contact Office of Federal Contract Compliance; listings at public library; unions; county employment agencies.

Women Vets

VVA Women Veterans Project; Vet Centers; also:

Women Veterans Information Network
P.O. Box 2894
Oakland, CA 94609

Gay and Lesbian Veterans

World War II Project
Box 42332
San Francisco CA 94101

Gay and Lesbian Advocates and Defenders
100 Boylston St.
Suite 900
Boston, MA 02117

Military Law Task Force
National Lawyers Guild
1168 Union St.

Suite 202
San Diego, CA 92101
(619) 234-1884

The Gay Veterans Association
263A W. 19th St.
New York, NY 10011

AWOLS

Persons still AWOL from service may have received discharges
while they were gone or charges may still be pending. Some
attorneys specialize in these cases. For referrals, contact:

CCCO Western Region
1251 Second Ave.
San Francisco, CA 94122
(415) 566-0500

MCMC
421 South Wabash Ave.
#200
Chicago, IL 60605
(312) 363-4672

CCCO
2208 South St.
Philadelphia, PA 19146
(215) 545-4626

SOS GI Assistance
PO Box 6586
Washington, DC 20009
(202) 745-0072

20. WHERE TO FIND OUT MORE

Publications

By Keith D. Snyder

This chapter could be subtitled "Checking It Out." If you ever get the feeling that you're getting a bureaucratic runaround, research the problem, check it out. If you ever get the feeling that the "No" from a VA employee is not correct, research the problem, check it out. Pin down the VA employee; make him or her tell you the exact basis for the "No." Don't take "Oh, Title 38 says so" as an answer: get the number of the section of Title 38. Then check *that* out.

For information on laws and regulations that cover veterans issues—and on how to find those laws and regulations—see Chapter 16, "Claims and Appeals."

You may be pleasantly surprised to discover the VA employee was mistaken. Or you may find that you were told the truth and can save yourself the time, effort, and irritation of appealing a denial.

Many, perhaps most, times the answer you're given is right. But most VA employees, like most other bureaucrats, don't like to have to explain their answers, and many may really not know what the real reason for their answer is.

Besides not liking to explain what the section number or

regulation is that is the reason for their answer, VA employees have a poor reputation for helping vets find the appropriate regulations or other materials the VA uses to decide cases.

Because of the difficulty of getting a straight answer and of getting a copy of the pertinent regulations, vets should work with an experienced or legally trained service representative like those found through Vietnam Veterans of America (VVA). However, because many vets want to "go it alone"—or want to be certain their representative is fully and correctly pursuing their case—this chapter is designed to explain some of the resources you can consult to "check out" what a VA employee has said or done. *Among the most basic resources are the laws and regulations described in Chapter 16.*

Also explained here are several "unofficial" sources of information about veterans issues.

If you do decide to go it alone—work on your case without the help of a service representative—it can be very important to know ahead of time what kind of information the VA is looking for when you apply for a particular benefit. Sometimes only a DD 214 has to be consulted to prove the periods of service. Many other times the VA will be looking for very particular kinds of information. Particularly in disability claims, where if certain symptoms are present a higher rating can be granted, it can be critical for a vet to know ahead of time what the VA is looking for.

VA doctors are supposed to follow the directions in the 1985 *VA Physicians Guide to Disability Evaluation Examinations*. No one suggests you learn what the symptoms of a given condition are and list them on an application when they are not really present. However, especially in PTSD claims, you should know that the VA doctor who examines you will be asking what you may consider very sensitive questions: How well do you get along with your family? Was there a specific incident in Vietnam that you still have nightmares about? The vet who has no idea that these kinds of questions are going to be asked may find himself unwilling, or even unable, to answer them fully.

Knowing what the VA is supposed to ask is also important in case the pertinent questions are *not* asked. In that case you should seek an exam by another doctor—one who is more thorough. Because important questions often are not asked, it is all the more irritating that the VA doesn't make its regulations and policies readily available. Instead, the VA seems to take the attitude that if the vet knows what the VA is looking for in evaluating a claim, the vet will lie.

HOW TO GET VA PUBLICATIONS

The VA doesn't make it easy for a vet to review its publications. The vet has a few options to consider before trying the nearest VA office:

1. Try the nearest veterans service organization; many VVA chapters maintain libraries of VA publications that are available to vets.
2. Try the nearest Legal Aid or Legal Services office; even if you are not eligible for free legal representation, these offices may let you use their libraries.
3. Try the public library; some may have VA publications or be willing to order them.

If none of the above are available, visit the nearest VA Regional Office. According to VA regulations, VAROs maintain public reading facilities in which vets can review and photocopy VA publications. Ask for the reading room. If the person you ask doesn't know what that is, ask to use the library in the Adjudication Service or in the District Counsel's office. If you have tried all these offices and gotten nowhere, go home and write two letters: one to the VARO Freedom of Information Act Office, the other to the VVA Legal Services.

As explained later in this chapter, there are certain "magical" phrases to include in letters to the FOIA Office. The letter to the VVA Legal Services doesn't need to include any magical language; just tell VVA what your experience was when you visited the VARO and tried to review VA publications. Include the date of your visit, the name of the VARO, which offices and which VA employees you spoke to, and what you were told. VVA is working on the problem of getting access to important VA publications and would like to compile a list of vets' experiences with each VARO.

How to Write a FOIA Letter

The Freedom of Information Act is a law that grants the public access to government records. Access can be limited in certain cases and sometimes an agency can legitimately charge a fee for searching for and copying records. In dealing with the VA, there should be no charge for searching for any of the publications noted in this chapter. Avoiding a charge for copying materials is another question, however. To avoid charges for copying, the person requesting copies must be very careful in wording a letter; even then the VA may demand money.

CAUTION: Before making a "shotgun" request for a lot of VA publications, figure out what you need. Start by reviewing an index; two indexes are available.

One, the *VA Publications Index*, is incomplete and hard to use and is not kept as up-to-date as the law requires. VVA Legal Services is working on this problem. (The index is available at VA Regional Offices.) The Board of Veterans Appeals (BVA) has put together a much better index and keeps it more current. This index, called the *VADEX*, includes references not just to VA regulations but also to many VA internal publications that frequently are more important than the regulations. This is because VA employees often get their information from manuals rather than from the regulations on which the manuals are based. The *VADEX* also indexes opinions by the VA's General Counsel, its chief legal officer. These opinions often spell out how the VA is to interpret its regulations. Unfortunately, the *VADEX* is found only at the VA Central Office in Washington. The VVA Legal Services has a copy and plans to make it available to VVA chapters throughout the country. Vets can buy a copy from a private contractor, but the price is $25.

Address your Freedom of Information Act request to:

Freedom of Information Act Office
VA Regional Office
(fill in address)

The first sentence of a FOIA letter should be:

"This is a request under the Freedom of Information Act as amended, 5 U.S.C. 552."

The following paragraphs may or may not be appropriate. Which ones you select depend on whether you have already tried to obtain the publications at the regional office and whether you are writing as an individual or on behalf of an organization.

"I am writing to request a copy of the following VA publications:
[insert list of publications, giving publication number and title]
On [insert date] I visited your regional office and attempted to review these publications but access to them was denied by [insert name]. I now request that you either mail copies of the above publications to me or that you state the location of a reading room at which I can review these materials and copy portions that I need.

As provided in the Freedom of Information Act, I request that you waive any fees associated with complying with this request because (1) the information is required in order to obtain benefits to which I believe I am entitled and (2) providing these materials is in the public interest because furnishing the information can be considered as primarily benefiting the general public. Furnishing these materials will benefit the public because I intend to donate them to the public library or otherwise make them available to the general public after I have used them. If you decide to charge a fee, I request permission to review the records which I have requested and to select those which I want copied.

As provided in the Freedom of Information Act, I will expect to receive a reply within ten working days of your receipt of this request.

                    Sincerely,
                    [insert full name and address]

Make a copy of your letter for safekeeping; send the original to the VA Regional Office via certified mail, return receipt requested, so you will know when it was received. If you get no answer within ten days, you can legally assume your request has been denied and you can then appeal to the Administrator of the VA (VA Central Office; Attn. FOIA Appeal; Washington, DC 20420). Send the Administrator a copy of your letter to the VARO and explain that you are appealing the denial of access. The Administrator has twenty business days to answer your appeal. If you still get no answer, you can consider going to court to request a federal judge to order the VA to respond. The VVA Legal Services is available to help in preparing an appeal letter or helping you decide if going to court is a good idea.

NON-VA PUBLICATIONS

The National Library of Medicine is a good source of lists of other publications to consult. In the past, the library has prepared bibliographies on Agent Orange and Post-Traumatic Stress Disorder (PTSD). To find out what is available, send a note and a gummed, self-addressed mailing label to: Literature Search Program, Reference Section; NLM; 8600 Rockville Pike; Bethesda, MD 20209.

The Government Printing Office offers a list of its publications. Write: Superintendent of Documents; GPO; Washington, DC 20402.

Nongovernment Publications

Many veterans organizations publish newsletters or magazines. These newsletters vary widely in content, viewpoint and quality. Some of the magazines published by the larger vets organizations are very slick looking but consist mostly of advertisements and editorials on foreign policy, dates of reunions, and miscellaneous "lightweight" articles. If you are looking for a broad range of veterans information, get a copy of the *VA Directory of Veterans Organizations* (available from Office of the Administrator; Veterans Service Organization Coordination; Veterans Administration; Washington, DC 20420) and write to the organizations listed to get a copy of their publications.

If you are looking for a "hardcore" publication that will keep you posted on new laws, new lawsuits, changes in VA policies, and new strategies for dealing with stubborn VA officials, there is one. One veterans organization is committed to arming veterans and vets' advocates with tools they can use to assert their rights. This is Vietnam Veterans of America (VVA). In conjunction with the Veterans Education Project, the VVA Legal Services publishes the *Veterans Rights Newsletter*. A free sample copy can be obtained by writing to: VVA Legal Services; Attn. *VRN*; 2001 S St., N.W., Suite 710; Washington, DC 20009. Some of the articles published in the *Veterans Rights Newsletter* also appear in VVA's general membership newsletter, the *VVA Veteran*, which is sent each month to all VVA members.

Some organizations that the VA doesn't list in its directory publish newsletters that are good sources of information. Some of these include:

On Watch
Military Law Task Force
1168 Union
Suite 202
San Diego, CA 92101

Objector
CCCO-Western Region
1251 Second Ave.
San Francisco, CA 94122

Other organizations that the VA doesn't list publish materials that some vets will find helpful. For example, the Midwest Committee for Military Counseling (421 South Wabash; Chicago, IL 60605) published *Fighting Back: Help for Lesbian and Gay Draft, Military and Vets Cases*. The Veterans Education Project (PO Box 42130, Washington DC 20015) publishes a series of "self-help guides" and packets on a wide range of topics. For example, VEP offers a "Stress Disorder Packet" that includes copies of internal VA guidelines used in processing PTSD disability claims. The packet includes a list of 250 mental health professionals around the country who specialize in treating PTSD; lists of Board of Veterans Appeals decisions in which

PTSD claims were allowed; a pre-sentencing report and transcript of expert testimony presented in a criminal case involving a Vietnam Vet. Other VEP packets include materials on Agent Orange and overpayments.

Prices and availability of newsletters and books from nongovernment sources change frequently. Contact the organizations listed for their current publications and prices.

In April 1974, long before the American public embraced Vietnam Veterans, *Penthouse* became the first major magazine to begin regularly publishing articles for and about Viet Vets. Its early articles have evolved into "The Vietnam Veterans Adviser," a monthly column written by William R. Corson. The column provides vets with timely and useful information and advice. To suggest topics, vets may write to Dr. William R. Corson; Washington Office; *Penthouse*; 1707 H St., N.W., Suite 807; Washington, DC 20006.

This chapter also has not listed the hundreds of books published over the past five years about the Vietnam experience. The best source of what is currently available is the nearest public library. Librarians are peculiarly suited to compiling lists of books. They do it for free and are pleased to do it.

Although published bibliographies have a tendency to go out of date quickly, two from 1983 lay a good foundation:

Vietnam War Bibliography, compiled by Christopher L. Sugnet and John T. Hickey (Lexington, Mass.: Lexington Books, 1983).

Vietnam War Literature: A Literary Bibliography, compiled by Eddie Yeghiayan (University of California, Irvine, 1983).

APPENDICES

APPENDIX A

VET CENTERS

IMPORTANT NOTES: Vet Centers often change their locations within cities. Also, for some Vet Centers (especially those expected to open by late 1985), addresses or phone numbers or both were not available in time for publication. If the center nearest you has moved, first try the phone number listed here (the center may have kept the same number). If the center has moved and changed its number, or if you need the number of a center whose number is not listed here, ask Directory Assistance to check its listings under "V" for "Vet Center" or "Veterans Center" and under the Veterans Administration heading in the listings under "United States." If Directory Assistance can't help, call the nearest Vet Center for which you have a correct number, or call the nearest VA Medical Center. (Unlike Directory Assistance, the Vet Center or Medical Center should be able to give you not just a phone number but also an address.) Some Vet Centers listed here may not yet be open.

ALABAMA, BIRMINGHAM

2145 Highland Avenue
Suite 250
Birmingham, AL 35205
(205) 933-0500

ALABAMA, MOBILE

110 Marine Street
Mobile, AL 36604
(205) 694-4194

ALASKA, ANCHORAGE

4201 Tudor Centre Drive
Suite 115
Anchorage, AK 99508
(907) 277-1501

ALASKA, FAIRBANKS

515 7th Avenue
Room 230
Fairbanks, AK 99701
(907) 456-4238

ALASKA, KENAI

905 Cook Street
P.O. Box 1883
Kenai, AK 99611
(907) 283-5205

ALASKA, WASILLA

P.O. Box 870954
Wasilla, AK 99687
(907) 376-4318

ARIZONA, PHOENIX

807 North 3rd Street
Phoenix, AZ 85004
(602) 261-4769

ARIZONA, PRESCOTT

Expected to open by late
1985

ARIZONA, TUCSON

727 North Swan
Tucson, AZ 85711
(602) 323-3271

ARKANSAS, LITTLE ROCK

1311 West 2nd Street
Little Rock, AR 72201
(501) 378-6395

CALIFORNIA, ANAHEIM

859 South Harbor Blvd
Anaheim, CA 92805
(714) 776-0161

CALIFORNIA, CONCORD

1899 Clayton Road
Suite 140
Concord, CA 94520
(415) 680-4529

CALIFORNIA, ESCONDIDO

157 East Valley Parkway
Suite 10
Escondido, CA 92025
(619)747-7305

CALIFORNIA, EUREKA

Expected to open by late
1985

CALIFORNIA, FRESNO

1340 Van Ness Avenue
Fresno, CA 93721
(209) 487-5660

CALIFORNIA, LOS ANGELES

251 West 85th Place
Los Angeles, CA 90003
(213) 753-1391

2000 Westwood Blvd
Los Angeles, CA 90025
(213) 475-9509

CALIFORNIA, MONTEBELLO

709 West Beverly Blvd
Montebello, CA 90640
(213) 728-9984

CALIFORNIA, NORTHRIDGE

18924 Roscoe Boulevard
Northridge, CA 91335
(213) 993-8862

CALIFORNIA, OAKLAND

616 16th Street
Oakland, CA 94612
(415) 763-3904

CALIFORNIA, RIVERSIDE

4954 Arlington Avenue
Riverside, CA 92504
(714) 359-8967

CALIFORNIA, SACRAMENTO

Expected to open by late
1985

CALIFORNIA, SAN BERNARDINO COUNTY

Expected to open by late
1985

CALIFORNIA, SAN DIEGO

2900 6th Avenue
San Diego, CA 92103
(619) 294-2040

CALIFORNIA, SAN DIEGO COUNTY

Expected to open by late
1985

CALIFORNIA, SAN FRANCISCO

1708 Waller Street
San Francisco, CA 94117

(415) 386-6726
(415) 386-6727

2989 Mission Street
San Francisco, CA 94110
(415) 824-5111
(415) 824-2141

CALIFORNIA, SAN JOSE

967 West Heddings
San Jose, CA 95126
(408)249-1643

CALIFORNIA, SANTA BARBARA

Expected to open by late
1985

COLORADO, BOULDER

207 Canyon Boulevard
Suite 201A
Boulder, CO 80303

COLORADO, COLORADO SPRINGS

875 West Moreno Avenue
Colorado Springs, CO 80905
(303) 633-2902

COLORADO, DENVER

1820 Gilpin Street
Denver, CO 80218
(303) 861-9281
(303) 861-7521

CONNECTICUT, HARTFORD

370 Market Street
Hartford, CT 06510
(203) 244-3543
(203) 244-3544

CONNECTICUT, NEW HAVEN

562 Whalley Avenue
New Haven, CT 06510
(203) 773-2235
(203) 773-2246

CONNECTICUT, NORWICH

Expected to open by late
1985

DELAWARE, WILMINGTON

1411 N. Van Buren Street
Wilmington, DE 19806
(302) 571-8277

DISTRICT OF COLUMBIA, WASHINGTON

737½ 8th Street, S.E.
Washington, DC 20003
(202) 745-8400
(202) 745-8401

FLORIDA, FT. LAUDERDALE

400 N.E. Prospect Road
Ft. Lauderdale, FL 33334
(305) 563-2992
(305) 563-2993

FLORIDA, JACKSONVILLE

255 Liberty Street
Jacksonville, FL 32202
(904) 791-3621

FLORIDA, MIAMI

412 N.E. 39th Street
Miami, FL 33137
(305) 573-8830
(305) 573-8831

FLORIDA, ORLANDO

5001 S. Orange Avenue
Suite A
Orlando, FL 32809
(305) 420-6151
(305) 420-6152

FLORIDA, PALM BEACH COUNTY

(Temporary address and
phone)
c/o Vet Center
400 N.E. Prospect Road
Ft. Lauderdale, FL 33334
(305) 563-2992
(305) 563-2993

FLORIDA, PENSACOLA

(Temporary address)
P.O. Box 12803
Pensacola, FL
(904) 432-2788

FLORIDA, SARASOTA

(Temporary address and
phone)
c/o Vet Center
235 31st Street, North
St. Petersburg, FL 33713
(813) 327-3355

FLORIDA, ST. PETERSBURG

235 31st Street, North
St. Petersburg, FL 33713
(813) 327-3355

FLORIDA, TALLAHASSEE

3423 Thresher Drive
Tallahassee, FL 32312
(904) 488-8703

FLORIDA, TAMPA

1507 W. Sligh Avenue
Tampa, FL 33604
(813) 228-2621

GEORGIA, ATLANTA

65 11th Street, N.E.
Atlanta, GA 30309
(404) 881-7264

GEORGIA, SAVANNAH

Expected to open by late
1985

HAWAII, HONOLULU

1370 Kapiolani Blvd
Suite 201
Honolulu, HI 96814
(808) 546-3743
(808) 546-3723

IDAHO, BOISE

103 West State Street
Boise, ID 83702
(208) 342-2612

IDAHO, POCATELLO

1975 South Fifth
Pocatello, ID 83201
(208) 232-0316

ILLINOIS, CHICAGO

547 West Roosevelt Road
Chicago, IL 60607
(312) 829-4400
(312) 829-4401

ILLINOIS, CHICAGO HEIGHTS

1600 Halsted Street
Chicago Heights, IL 60411
(312) 754-0340

ILLINOIS, MOLINE–ROCK ISLAND

Expected to open by late
1985

ILLINOIS, NORTH CHICAGO

Expected to open by late
1985

ILLINOIS, OAK PARK

155 South Oak Park Avenue
Oak Park, IL 60302
(312) 383-3225
(312) 383-3226

ILLINOIS, PEORIA

605 N.E. Monroe
Peoria, IL 61603
(309) 671-7300

ILLINOIS, SPRINGFIELD

Expected to open by late
1985

INDIANA, EVANSVILLE

101 N. Kentucky Avenue
Evansville, IN 47711
(812) 425-0311

INDIANA, FORT WAYNE

528 West Berry Street
Fort Wayne, IN 46802
(219) 423-9456
(219) 423-9457

INDIANA, GARY

4144 Broadway
Gary, IN 46409
(219) 887-0048

INDIANA, INDIANAPOLIS

(Temporary address and
phone)
811 Massachusetts Avenue
Indianapolis, IN 46204
(317) 269-2838

IOWA, DES MOINES

3619 6th Avenue
Des Moines, IA 50313
(515) 284-6119
(515) 284-6120

IOWA, SIOUX CITY

706 Jackson
Sioux City, IA 51101
(712) 233-3200

KANSAS, WICHITA

310 South Laura
Wichita, KS 67211
(316) 265-3260

KENTUCKY, LEXINGTON

249 West Short Street
Lexington, KY 40507
(606) 231-8387

KENTUCKY, LOUISVILLE

736 South 1st Street
Louisville, KY 40202
(502) 589-1981

LOUISIANA, NEW ORLEANS

1529 N. Claiborne Avenue
New Orleans, LA 70116
(504) 943-8386

LOUISIANA, SHREVEPORT

(Temporary address)
c/o Psychology (116B)
VA Medical Center
510 East Stones
Shreveport, LA 71130

MAINE, BANGOR

96 Harlow Street
Bangor, ME 04401
(207) 947-3391
(207) 947-3392

MAINE, PORTLAND

175 Lancaster Street
Room 213
Portland, ME 04101
(207) 780-3584
(207) 780-3585

MARYLAND, BALTIMORE

1420 W. Patapsco Avenue
Patapsco Plaza
Baltimore, MD 21230
(301) 355-8592

1153 Mondawmin
Concourse
Baltimore, MD 21215
(301) 728-8924

MARYLAND, ELKTON

7 Elkton Commercial Plaza
Elkton, MD 21921
(301) 398-0171

MARYLAND, SILVER SPRING

8121 Georgia Avenue
Suite 500
Silver Spring, MD 20910
(202) 745-8210
(202) 745-8396

MASSACHUSETTS, AVON

810 West Main Street
Avon, MA 02322
(617) 580-2730

MASSACHUSETTS, BOSTON

480 Tremont Street
Boston, MA 02116
(617) 451-0171
(617) 451-0172

MASSACHUSETTS, BRIGHTON

71 Washington Street
Brighton, MA 02135
(617) 782-1032
(617) 782-1013

MASSACHUSETTS, BROCKTON

15 Bolton Place
Brockton, MA 02401
(617) 580-2730
(617) 580-2731

MASSACHUSETTS, LOWELL

Expected to open by late
1985

MASSACHUSETTS, NEW BEDFORD

Expected to open by late
1985

MASSACHUSETTS, SPRINGFIELD

1985 Main Street
Northgate Plaza
Springfield, MA 01103
(413) 737-5167

MASSACHUSETTS, WORCESTER

Expected to open by late
1985

MICHIGAN, DETROIT

18411 West Seven Mile
Road
Detroit, MI 48219
(313) 535-3333
(313) 535-3334

MICHIGAN, GRAND RAPIDS

1940 Eastern Avenue S.E.
Grand Rapids, MI 49507
(616) 243-0385

MICHIGAN, LINCOLN PARK

1766 Fort Street
Lincoln Park, MI 48146
(313) 381-1370

MICHIGAN, OAK PARK

20802 Greenfield Road
Oak Park, MI 48237
(313) 967-0040

MICHIGAN, SOUTHGATE

14405 North Line
Southgate, MI 48195
(313) 282-9852
(313) 282-9853

MINNESOTA, DULUTH

405 E. Superior Street
Duluth, MN 55802
(218) 722-8654

MINNESOTA, ST. PAUL

2480 University Avenue
St. Paul, MN 55114
(612) 644-4022
(612) 644-5601

MISSISSIPPI, BILOXI

(Temporary address)
c/o Psychology (116B)
VA Medical Center
Biloxi, MS 39431

MISSISSIPPI, JACKSON

158 E. Pascagoula Street
Jackson, MS 39201
(601) 353-4912

MISSOURI, KANSAS CITY

3600 Broadway
Suite 19
Kansas City, MO 64111
(816) 753-1866
(816) 753-2075

MISSOURI, ST. LOUIS

2345 Pine Street
St. Louis, MO 63103
(314) 231-1260

MISSOURI, SPRINGFIELD

Expected to open by late
1985

MONTANA, BILLINGS

415 North 33rd Street
Billings, MT 59101
(406) 657-6071

MONTANA, MISSOULA

929 Southwest Higgins
Avenue
Missoula, MT 59803
(406) 721-4918

NEBRASKA, LINCOLN

920 L Street
Lincoln, NE 68508
(402) 476-9736
(402) 476-6713

NEBRASKA, OMAHA

5123 Leavenworth Street
Omaha, NE 68106
(402) 553-2068

NEVADA, LAS VEGAS

214 South 8th Street
Las Vegas, NV 89101
(702) 388-6368

NEVADA, RENO

341 South Arlington Street
Reno, NV 89501
(702) 323-1294

NEW HAMPSHIRE, MANCHESTER

14 Pearl Street
Manchester, NH 03104
(603) 668-7060
(603) 668-7061

NEW JERSEY, JERSEY CITY

626 Newark Avenue
Jersey City, NJ 07306
(201) 656-6986

NEW JERSEY, NEWARK

75 Halsey Street
Newark, NJ 07102
(201) 622-6940

NEW JERSEY, PLEASANTVILLE

Expected to open by late
1985

NEW JERSEY, TRENTON

318 East State Street
Trenton, NJ 08608
(609) 989-2260
(609) 989-2261

NEW MEXICO, ALBUQUERQUE

4603 4th Street, N.W.
Albuquerque, NM 87107
(505) 345-8366
(505) 345-8876

NEW MEXICO, GALLUP

211 West Mesa
Gallup, NM 87301
(505) 722-3821
(505) 722-3822

NEW MEXICO, SANTA FE

Expected to open by late
1985

NEW YORK, ALBANY

875 Central Avenue

West Mall Office Plaza
Albany, NY 12208
(518) 438-2508

NEW YORK, BABYLON

116 West Main Street
Babylon, NY 11702
(516) 661-3930

NEW YORK, BRONX

226 East Fordham Road
Rooms 216/217
Bronx, NY 10458
(212) 367-3500
(212) 367-3501

NEW YORK, BROOKLYN

165 Cadman Plaza, East
Brooklyn, NY 11201
(718) 330-2825
(718) 330-2816

NEW YORK, BUFFALO

351 Linwood
Buffalo, NY 14209
(716) 882-0505

NEW YORK, JAMAICA HILLS

148-43 Hillside Avenue
Jamaica Hills, NY 11435
(718) 658-6767
(718) 658-6768

NEW YORK, MANHATTAN

166 West 75th Street
Manhattan, NY 10023
(212) 944-2917
(212) 944-2930

NEW YORK, ROCHESTER

(Temporary address and
phone)
Federal Bldg.
100 State Street
Rochester, NY 14614
(716) 263-5716

NEW YORK, SYRACUSE

800 Irving Avenue
Room 915A
Syracuse, NY 13210
(315) 476-7461

NEW YORK, WHITE PLAINS

200 Hamilton Avenue
White Plains Mall
White Plains, NY 10601
(914) 684-0570

NORTH CAROLINA, CHARLOTTE

1523 Elizabeth Avenue
Charlotte, NC 28204
(704) 333-6107
(704) 333-6108

NORTH CAROLINA, FAYETTEVILLE

4 Market Square,
Fayetteville, NC 28301
(919) 323-4908

NORTH CAROLINA, GREENVILLE

Expected to open by late
1985

NORTH CAROLINA, GREENSBORO

Expected to open by late
1985

NORTH DAKOTA, FARGO

1322 Gateway Drive
Fargo, ND 58103
(701) 237-0942

NORTH DAKOTA, MINOT

108 Burdick Expressway
Minot, ND 58701
(701) 852-0177

OHIO, CINCINNATI

31 East 12th Street
4th Floor
Cincinnati, OH 45202
(513) 241-9420
(513) 241-9421

OHIO, CLEVELAND

10605 Carnegie Avenue
Cleveland, OH 44106
(216) 791-9224
(216) 294-7495

11511 Lorain Avenue
Cleveland, OH 44111
(216) 671-8530
(216) 671-8531

OHIO, CLEVELAND HEIGHTS

2134 Lee Road
Cleveland Heights, OH
44118
(216) 932-8471

OHIO, COLUMBUS

1751 Cleveland Avenue

Columbus, OH 43211
(614) 291-2227

OHIO, DAYTON

438 Wayne Avenue
Dayton, OH 45410
(513) 461-9150
(513) 461-9151

OKLAHOMA, OKLAHOMA CITY

4111 North Lincoln,
Suite #10
Oklahoma City, OK 73105
(405) 521-9308

OKLAHOMA, TULSA

1605 South Boulder
Tulsa, OK 74119
(918) 581-7105

OREGON, EUGENE

1966 Garden Avenue
Eugene, OR 97403
(503) 687-6918

OREGON, GRANTS PASS

Expected to open by late
1985

OREGON, PORTLAND

2450 S.E. Belmont
Portland, OR 97214
(503) 231-1586

OREGON, SALEM–CORVALLIS

Expected to open by late
1985

PENNSYLVANIA, ERIE

Expected to open by late
1985

PENNSYLVANIA, HARRISBURG

127 State Street
Harrisburg, PA 17101
(717) 782-3954

PENNSYLVANIA, MONROEVILLE

4328 Old William Penn
Highway
Monroeville, PA 15146
(412) 372-8627
(412) 372-8628

PENNSYLVANIA, PHILADELPHIA

1107 Arch Street
Philadelphia, PA 19107
(215) 627-0238

5601 North Broad Street
Room 202
Philadelphia, PA 19141
(215) 924-4670

PENNSYLVANIA, PITTSBURGH

954 Penn Avenue
Pittsburgh, PA 15222
(412) 765-1193

PENNSYLVANIA, SCRANTON

Expected to open by late
1985

PENNSYLVANIA,
WILKES-BARRE

(Temporary address and
phone)
c/o Psychology Department
1111 East End Blvd.
Wilkes-Barre, PA 18711
(717) 824-3521

PUERTO RICO, ARECIBO

Expected to open by late
1985

PUERTO RICO, PONCE

Expected to open by late
1985

PUERTO RICO, RIO
PIEDRAS

Suite LC-8A/9 Medical
Center Plaza
La Riviera
Rio Piedras, PR 00921
(809) 783-8269

PUERTO RICO, ST.
CROIX

St. Croix, PR 00921

PUERTO RICO, ST.
THOMAS

Havensight Mall (116V)
St. Thomas, PR 00802
(809) 774-6674

RHODE ISLAND,
PAWTUCKET

172 Pine Street
Pawtucket, RI 02860
(401) 728-9501
(401) 728-9502

SOUTH CAROLINA,
GREENVILLE

904 Pendleton Street
Greenville, SC 29601
(803) 271-2711

SOUTH CAROLINA, NO.
CHARLESTON

3366 Rivers Avenue
No. Charleston, SC 29405
(803) 747-8387

SOUTH CAROLINA,
COLUMBIA

1313 Elmwood Ave.
Columbia, SC 29201
(803) 765-9944

SOUTH DAKOTA, RAPID
CITY

610 Kansas City Street
Rapid City, SD 57701
(605) 348-0077

SOUTH DAKOTA, SIOUX
FALLS

100 West 6th Street
Suite 101
Sioux Falls, SD 57102
(605) 332-0856

TENNESSEE,
CHATTANOOGA

Expected to open by late
1985

TENNESSEE, JOHNSON
CITY

Expected to open by late
1985

TENNESSEE, KNOXVILLE

1515 E. Magnolia Avenue
Suite 201
Knoxville, TN 37917
(615) 971-5866

TENNESSEE, MEMPHIS

1 North 3rd Street
Memphis, TN 38103
(901) 521-3506

TEXAS, AMARILLO

Expected to open by late
1985

TEXAS, AUSTIN

3401 Manor Rd.
Suite 102
Austin, TX 78723
(512) 476-0607

TEXAS, CORPUS CHRISTI

3134 Reid St.
Corpus Christi, TX 78202
(512) 993-9160

TEXAS, DALLAS

5415 Maple Plaza
Suite 114
Dallas, TX 75235
(214) 634-7024

TEXAS, EL PASO

2121 Wyoming Street
El Paso, TX 79903
(915) 542-2851
(915) 542-2852

TEXAS, FORT WORTH

Seminary South Office
Building
Suite 10
Fort Worth, TX 76115
(817) 921-3733

TEXAS, HOUSTON

4905A San Jacinto
Houston, TX 77004
(713) 522-5354
(713) 522-5376

TEXAS, HOUSTON

Second center expected to
open by late 1985

TEXAS, LAREDO

717 Corpus Christi
Laredo, TX 78040
(512) 723-4680

TEXAS, LUBBOCK

Expected to open by late
1985

TEXAS, MIDLAND

Expected to open by late
1985

TEXAS, SAN ANTONIO

107 Lexington Avenue
San Antonio, TX 78205
(512) 229-4025

1916 Fredericksburg Road
San Antonio, TX 78201
(512) 229-4120

UTAH, PROVO

Expected to open by late
1985

UTAH, SALT LAKE CITY

216 East 5th Street South
Salt Lake City, UT 84111
(801) 584-1294

VERMONT, WHITE RIVER JUNCTION

Building #2,
Gilman Office Complex
White River Junction, VT 05001
(802) 295-2908

VERMONT, WILLISTON

RFD #2, Tafts Corners
Williston, VT 05495
(802) 878-3371

VIRGIN ISLANDS, ST. THOMAS

Havensight Mall
St. Thomas, VI 00802
(809) 774-6674

VIRGINIA, FAIRFAX COUNTY

Expected to open by late
1985

VIRGINIA, NORFOLK

7450½ Tidewater Drive
Norfolk, VA 23505
(804) 587-1338

VIRGINIA, RICHMOND

Gresham Court Box 83
1030 West Franklin Street
Richmond, VA 23220
(804) 353-8958

VIRGINIA, ROANOKE

Expected to open by late
1985

WASHINGTON, SEATTLE

1322 East Pike Street
Seattle, WA 98122
(206) 442-2706

WASHINGTON, SPOKANE

North 1611 Division
Spokane, WA 99207
(509) 326-6970
(509) 326-6979

WASHINGTON, TACOMA

4801 Pacific Avenue
Tacoma, WA 98408
(206) 473-0731
(206) 473-0732

WEST VIRGINIA, CHARLESTON

Expected to open by late
1985

WEST VIRGINIA, HUNTINGTON

1014 6th Avenue
Huntington, WV 25701
(304) 523-8387

WEST VIRGINIA, MARTINSBURG

Expected to open by late
1985

WEST VIRGINIA, MORGANTOWN

1191 Pineview Drive
Morgantown, WV 26505

(304) 291-4001
(304) 291-4002

WISCONSIN, MADISON

147 South Butler Street
Madison WI 53703
(608) 264-5343

WISCONSIN, MILWAUKEE

3400 Wisconsin
Milwaukee, WI 53208
(414) 344-5504

WYOMING, CASPER

641 East Second Street
Casper, WY 82601
(307) 235-8010

WYOMING, CHEYENNE

3130 Henderson Drive
Cheyenne, WY 82001
(307) 778-2660

APPENDIX B

VET CENTER REGIONAL MANAGERS

REGION I

John Parsons, Ph.D.
Acting Regional Manager
Vet Center (10B/RC113)
172 Pine Street
Pawtucket, RI 02860
(401) 728-9501

REGION II

Husher L. Harris, M.A.
Regional Manager
Operation Outreach
(10B/RC2)
500 Virginia Avenue,
Suite 204
Baltimore, MD 21204
(301) 821-7860/7861

REGION III

Joseph Gelsomino, Ph.D.
Regional Manager

Operation Outreach
(10B/RC3)
VA Medical Center
Bay Pines, FL 33504
(813) 398-6661, Ext. 4466

REGION IV

Michael R. Jackson
Regional Manager
Operation Outreach
(10B/RC4)
Hines VA Medical Center
Building 16, Room 110
Hines, IL 60141
(312) 343-5131

REGION V

Thomas Scarano, Ph.D.
Regional Manager
Vet Center (10B/RC504)
1820 Gilpin Street
Denver, CO 80218
(303) 861-9281

REGION VI

Shad Meshad
Regional Manager
Operation Outreach
(691/10B/RC6)
VA Medical Center
11301 Wilshire Boulevard
Los Angeles, CA 90073

VET CENTER NATIONAL DIRECTOR

Director
Readjustment Counseling
Service (11RC)
Veterans Administration
810 Vermont Ave., N.W.
Washington, DC 20420

APPENDIX C

SPECIALIZED VAMC (VA HOSPITAL) INPATIENT AND OUTPATIENT PTSD PROGRAMS

FACILITY	CONTACT PERSON OR PROGRAM CHIEF	# OF BEDS
1. Menlo Park, California	(415) 493-5000	90
2. North Hampton, Massachusetts	(413) 584-4040	19
3. Bay Pines, Florida	(813) 391-9644	20
4. Coatesville, Pennsylvania	(215) 384-7711	13
5. Tomah, Wisconsin	(608) 372-3971	10
6. Topeka, Kansas	(913) 272-3111	24
7. North Chicago, Illinois	(312) 688-1900	25
8. Augusta, Georgia	(404) 724-5116	25
9. Montrose, New York	(914) 737-4400	26
10. Cleveland, Ohio	(216) 526-3030	

11. Lyons, New Jersey   (201) 647-0180   20
12. Tacoma, Washington
13. Phoenix, Arizona

APPENDIX D

VIETNAM VETERANS OF AMERICA (VVA)

History, Membership Application

Vietnam Veterans of America (VVA) is the only major national organization of Vietnam Era Veterans. Three of the coauthors of this book work for VVA in its Legal Services office. This book is officially supported and endorsed by VVA and is copyrighted in the name of the Vietnam Veterans of America Foundation.

Following are a brief history of VVA as well as a membership application for veterans and others who may want to join or otherwise support the organization.

VIETNAM VETERANS OF AMERICA PAST, PRESENT AND FUTURE

By Ken Berez, VVA national staff

Why is there a need for another veterans organization, when so many already exist? A brief history of the Vietnam Veterans movement answers the question.

By the late 1970s, the more established veterans groups, for their own private reasons, failed to make a priority of the issues and concerns of special importance to Vietnam Veterans. As a result, a vacuum was created within the nation's legislative and public agenda. In January, 1978, a small group of Vietnam Veteran activists came to Washington seeking allies to rally around the cause of creating an advocacy organization devoted exclusively to the needs of the Vietnam Veteran. VVA, initially known as the Council of Vietnam Veterans, began work.

Council members believed that if the nation's attention was focused on the specific needs of Vietnam Vets, surely a grateful nation would quickly take remedial steps. However, despite persuasive arguments before the Congress which were amplified by highly supportive editorials printed in many leading American newspapers, we failed to win even a single legislative victory to bring new and needed programs into creation to help Vietnam Vets and their families.

It soon became apparent that arguments couched simply in terms of morality, equity, and justice were not enough. The United States Congress would respond to the legitimate needs of Vietnam Veterans only if the organization professing to represent them had political strength. In this case, strength translated into numbers meant membership. By the summer of 1979, the Council of Vietnam Veterans was transformed into Vietnam Veterans of America, a membership service organization made up of and devoted to Vietnam Veterans.

Hindered by the lack of substantial funding for development, the growth of our membership was at first slow. The big breakthrough came when the American hostages were returned from Iran in January 1981. It was as though our country went through an emotional catharsis that put the issues of the Vietnam Era on the table for public discussion. The question was asked, why parades for the hostages but not for Vietnam Vets? Many veterans complained about such a lack of recognition and appreciation for past national service. Now Vietnam Era Vets wanted action in the form of programs that would place the latest generation of veterans on the same footing as veterans from previous wars.

Membership grew steadily, and for the first time, VVA secured significant unsolicited contributions. The combination of the public's willingness to talk about the Vietnam War and the basic issues that it raised, and the veterans coming forward, was augmented by the nation's dedication of the Vietnam War Memorial in November of 1982. The week-long activities rekindled a sense of brotherhood among the veterans and a feeling that we had shared an experience that was too significant to ignore.

Today, Vietnam Veterans of America has a national membership of more than twenty thousand. Its chapters (170 in 1985) are located in thirty-six states, the District of Columbia, and Puerto Rico. VVA places great emphasis on coordinating its national activities and programs with the work of its local chapters, and VVA is organized to help ensure that victories gained at the national level are implemented locally. Extended locally, pressure and supervision minimize the dilution of programs passed in Washington; and grass roots support, quickly and easily mobilized, acts as a catalyst for further change to better the condition of the Vietnam Veteran.

VVA is governed by a national board of directors and by national officers—twenty-three men and women democratically elected by 210 VVA delegates sent by their respective chapters to the VVA biannual convention. VVA's essential purpose is to promote the educational, economic, health, cultural and emotional readjustment of the Vietnam Era Veteran to civilian life. This is done by promoting legislation and public awareness programs to eliminate discrimination suffered by Vietnam Vets. Since August 1981, VVA has been recognized by the Veterans Administration as a veterans service organization representing veterans with claims before the VA. The VVA Legal Services, as explained in detail in this book, adds a tremendous amount of credibility to our representation of veterans.

Legislative victories have included the establishment of the Vet Center system and its extension until 1988; passage of Public Law 97-306, which provides for increased job training and job placement assistance for unemployed Vietnam Vets; and, most recently, the first laws compensating veterans for Agent Orange poisoning. All were passed in large measure as a result of VVA's legislative lobbying efforts. The Vietnam Veterans in Congress (VVIC), formed in 1978 through the efforts of VVA and now having a membership of thirty-four, helped to guide through Congress these and other legislative measures.

VVA helps to provide greater public awareness of the outstanding issues surrounding Vietnam Veterans by disseminating written information on a continual basis. The *VVA Veteran*, a monthly newsletter, is mailed to all VVA members and friends of VVA. In addition, self-help guides on issues ranging from Agent Orange to Post-Traumatic Stress Disorder (PTSD) to discharge upgrading are published and made available to anyone interested.

With revenues being generated strictly by private fund-raising efforts, a public willingness to accept and support us, and a veteran constituency ready to make its mark, VVA is now in an excellent position to call upon the shared experiences of our generation to build a more and more significant organization to serve the needs of its members.

VVA has taken on a substantial task. We have had many successes and some failures. VVA is learning to be a new kind of veterans service organization, independent of the cozy relationship that some other veterans organizations have had with the primary agency responsible for veterans programs, the Veterans Administration. VVA is concerned with the broader implications of our experiences as American citizens who happen to be Vietnam Veterans.

MEMBERSHIP APPLICATION
VIETNAM VETERANS OF AMERICA

Membership in Vietnam Veterans of America, Inc., is open to Vietnam Era Veterans
Associate Membership is open to the Public at Large

2001 S Street, NW
Suite 700
Washington, DC 20009-1125
(202) 332-2700

Name _____ Phone _____

Address _____

City _____ State _____ Zip _____

$20.00 Annual Dues Enclosed _____ (This entitles me to a membership card and the monthly publication *VVA Veteran*)

Return this form to
● Vietnam Veterans of America ●
2001 S Street, NW
Suite 700
Washington, DC 20009-1125

_____ I am a Vietnam Era Veteran (served anytime from Aug. 5, 1964, to May 7, 1975) and would like to be a Member.

_____ I am not a Vietnam Era Veteran, but would like to be an Associate Member.

_____ I am an incarcerated Vietnam Era Veteran and cannot afford the dues but want to be a member (no dues required while incarcerated).

I want to give more. Enclosed is my check for
_____ $20 _____ $50 _____ $
(all contributions are tax deductible)

_____ Send information on Life Membership.

_____ Send information on Product Sales (lapel pin, bumper sticker, etc.).

_____ Send information on publications that report up-to-date changes in veterans advocacy issues discussed in this book.

_____ Send me the address of the nearest VVA chapter.

_____ Send me information on how to start a VVA chapter in my area.

ABOUT THE AUTHORS

Except as noted here and in the text, Craig Kubey wrote this book. David Addlestone, Richard O'Dell, Keith Snyder, and Barton Stichman provided the research on which this book is based. This included extensive original research for this book, careful verification of what Kubey wrote, and providing access to publications they previously authored. Chief among these publications are two detailed manuals: the VVA *Service Representatives Manual* (by Snyder, O'Dell, and Addlestone) and *Military Discharge Upgrading and Introduction to Veterans Administration Law* (by Addlestone, Snyder, Stichman, John Kosloske, Lewis Milford, and the National Veterans Law Center of the Washington College of Law). Addlestone also wrote Chapter 19, "Where to Go for Help." Snyder wrote Chapter 20, "Where to Find Out More." Stichman drafted the section on litigation in Chapter 16, "Claims and Appeals."

Craig Kubey is a writer living in California. He studied at the University of California campuses at Berkeley, Santa Cruz (where he received an A.B. in psychology), and Davis (where he got his law degree). He is a member of the bars of California and the District of Columbia. Kubey has worked for the Center on Administration of Criminal Justice at Davis, for former Congressman Robert Drinan, and three times for Ralph Nader. Nader, Kubey, and others established the Equal Justice Foundation, a Washington public interest group. Kubey is the author of two 1982 national bestsellers, *The Winners' Book of Video Games* and *Scoring Big at Pac-Man*. He is working on books on a variety of subjects.

David F. Addlestone, an attorney, is Director of the Vietnam Veterans of America Legal Services. He was an Air Force Judge Advocate and a public defender and spent a year in Vietnam (1970–71) with a public interest law firm representing U.S. service members in courts-martial. Since then he has devoted his practice to military and veterans law and has co-authored numerous books and articles in these areas.

Richard E. O'Dell, Administrative Services Manager of the Virginia Division of War Veterans Claims, is a Vietnam combat veteran. He is also a member of the VVA National Board of Directors and serves on VVA's Advocacy Committee. O'Dell is State Service Representative in Virginia for Vietnam Veterans of America. In addition, O'Dell serves as an Assistant State Service Officer for The American Legion and Veterans of Foreign Wars. For twelve years he has worked on veterans issues throughout the South.

Keith D. Snyder is Editor of the *Veterans Rights Newsletter* and numerous other publications oriented toward helping veterans understand their rights. He has a long-standing interest in "translating" the jargon of lawsuits and legislation into information usable by nonlawyers. He served four years (1969–72) as a hospital corpsman in the U.S. Navy. He is also the proud father of an active four-year-old son, Max, and resides in Kensington, Maryland.

Barton F. Stichman is an attorney who during the past ten years has specialized in litigation on behalf of veterans. He is currently Litigation Director of Vietnam Veterans of America. He has written extensively on military and veterans law.

Addlestone, Snyder, and Stichman are on the staff of the VVA Legal Services.